Practical Research Methods for Librarians and Information Professionals

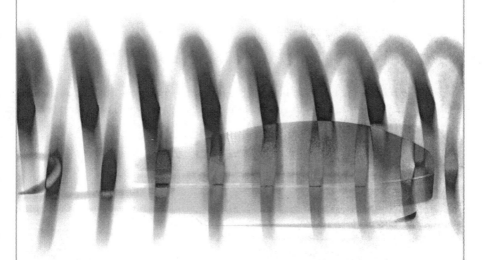

Susan E. Beck and Kate Manuel

Neal-Schuman Publishers, Inc.

New York   London

Published by Neal-Schuman Publishers, Inc.
100 William St., Suite 2004
New York, NY 10038

Copyright © 2008 Neal-Schuman Publishers, Inc.

Printed and bound in the United States of America.

The paper used in this publication meets the minimum requirements of American National Standard for Information Sciences - Permanence of Paper for Printed Library Materials, ANSI Z39.48-1992.

Library of Congress Cataloging-in-Publication Data

Beck, Susan E.
    Practical research methods for librarians and information professionals / Susan E. Beck,
Kate Manuel.
        p. cm.
    Includes bibliographical references and index.
    ISBN 978-1-55570-591-6 (alk. paper)
    1. Library science—Research—Methodology. 2. Information science—Research—
Methodology. I. Manuel, Kate. II. Title.
    Z669.7.B43 2008
    020.72—dc22
                                                                    2008024093

Contents

List of Figures

Preface

In today's results-based environment, research provides concrete evidence that successful library managers use to justify budgets, services, and programs. Thoughtful studies can evaluate and enhance almost every aspect of our professional lives.

Despite the many benefits, some librarians consider research daunting or time-consuming. Others may consider formal studies the exclusive domain of academicians. Based on our professional experience, we believe that investigative projects can and should be performed by librarians in all settings and at all levels, and that the process can be both enlightening and enjoyable.

In *Practical Research Methods for Librarians and Information Professionals*, we show how the process can be used by practicing librarians. In Chapter 2, we present the seven basic steps of research. In the subsequent chapters, we examine the nine methodologies most commonly used in librarianship. The information on each methodology is organized using these same common steps. This approach helps readers see the underlying similarities among different methodologies.

The exemplary studies highlighted in this text were chosen because they successfully illustrate specific points regarding a particular methodology. Many of these studies date from the past five years and so they address some of the technological possibilities of newer forms of computer-assisted research or data processing. By using actual studies rather than hypothetical scenarios, we show how research is successfully conducted in the real world, even under less than perfect conditions. Since we focus on the needs of practitioners, the studies that we profile are written mainly by practicing professionals, not academicians. Librarians undertaking a research project while working a non-academic full-time job face unique challenges. Moreover, their investigations often differ from those conducted by academic researchers both in topic and in surrounding conditions.

While *Practical Research Methods for Librarians and Information Professionals* provides an introduction to the skills that library school students and other beginner researchers will need in their careers, even those who have conducted several studies can use it to investigate new methodologies and their applications.

Since the projects highlighted throughout the text come from academic, public, school, and special libraries, librarians from all work settings are likely to find material relevant to their needs and interests.

ORGANIZATION

Practical Research Methods for Librarians and Information Professionals describes nine major approaches commonly used within librarianship and other fields:

1. Content analysis
2. Interviews
3. Focus groups
4. Observation
5. Usability testing
6. Experimental studies
7. Bibliometrics
8. Action research
9. Classroom research

Chapter 1, "The Benefits of Research," introduces the most compelling reasons for undertaking a study and explains a few assumptions that frame the subsequent chapters. Chapter 2, "The Research Process," outlines the seven fundamental steps:

1. Finding a topic, or potential applications.
2. Formulating questions, or moving from a general topical area of interest to specific hypotheses.
3. Defining research populations, or deciding whom or what to study.
4. Selecting a research design and measurement instrument(s), or determining how to gather relevant data about the research population(s).
5. Gathering data or other evidence to answer the question(s).
6. Interpreting evidence.
7. Telling others about what you did and found out.

Chapters 3 through 9 focus on the specifics of the methodologies. Each chapter includes numerous examples drawn from the literature of librarianship to illustrate the methodology.

Chapter 10, "Avoiding Common Pitfalls in Research," is a troubleshooting guide for complications and problems. Finally, Chapter 11, "Synergies in Research," concentrates on strategies for maximizing job and research productivity by using job assignments as the basis for investigative projects.

We believe research, in addition to being a source of vital knowledge, should be a personally rewarding experience. We hope this book will guide you in developing successful projects based on your own needs and interests. Above all,

Practical Research Methods for Librarians and Information Professionals seeks to present research as a worthy pursuit for all librarians.

Vietnamese novelist Bao Ninh once eloquently said that to write is to "think on paper." Thought of in that way, much professional writing could be described as "thinking on paper" about research-derived quantitative or qualitative data. If you are willing to think—to ask the difficult questions about the topic at hand and to pursue the answers—you can conduct a successful study.

Acknowledgments

No book is the sole creation of its authors, and our work is no exception. Many individuals and groups have helped shape this volume. The Texas Library Association Reference Round Table deserves a big thank you for giving us the opportunity to present ways practitioner librarians can conduct research projects at their 2004 conference in San Antonio. That presentation kick-started us to think seriously about writing a book on research methodologies, aimed at an atypical audience: regular, working librarians. We relied heavily on the expertise of Jivonna Stewart and Deanna Litke, of the InterLibrary Loan unit at New Mexico State University Library, for their timely provision of the hundreds of research articles that we analyzed to create this book. We are indebted to them for both their cheerful service and their true belief in saving the time of the reader. We also wish to thank New Mexico State University Library for allowing Susan to take a half-year sabbatical to concentrate on the book. Finally, we realize that we would not have been able to undertake such a large writing project without the moral support and strength of our two husbands, Jim Scanlon and Nicholas Perry. Both Jim and Nick, along with our respective dogs, Guinness and Gaspode, are all very happy to say farewell to the book project.

Chapter 1

The Benefits of Research

Research: investigation or experimentation aimed at the discovery and interpretation of facts, revision of accepted theories or laws in the light of
new facts, or practical application of such new or revised theories or laws.
(*Merriam-Webster's Collegiate Dictionary*, 2003)

WHY RESEARCH MATTERS

To a busy librarian, research can seem like the straw that broke the camel's
back. Most librarians already have jobs with more responsibilities than they
can comfortably handle. Increasingly, librarians find themselves needing to develop or maintain knowledge and skills in two or more of the following areas:
acquisitions, cataloging, collection management, events programming, grant
writing, instruction, interlibrary loan and document delivery, systems and automation, management and personnel, outreach and publicity, preservation and
archiving, and reference. One study found that more than one-third of adver-
tised positions in 1998 were for blended positions, or jobs fusing together duties
once associated with several separate positions. This number is up 18 percent
from 1983, when only 14 percent of jobs were blended (Lynch and Smith
2001). With so much to do, librarians can be tempted to view research as a
burden or a luxury not possible in their own professional situations.

Research can also be scary, especially for those who lack prior training in research methodologies but are now being told to "publish" so as not to "perish."
Most Master's level library and information science programs offer, at best, a
single research methods course (Liebscher 1998), and in only 38 percent of
these programs is a research methods course required (O'Connor and Park
2002). Small wonder, then, that studies show only 42 percent of practicing librarians "occasionally or frequently do research related to their job or to the Library and Information Science profession" (Powell, Baker and Mika 2002, 70).
Even fewer of them, in all probability, publish the results of their research. There
is no reason to suspect that librarianship differs from other academic fields

where, overall, "some 85 percent of publications [are authored by] some 15 percent of those who could potentially write them" (Frongia 1995, 221). Unfortunately, this gap between the number of potential authors and the number of people who actually publish means that valuable ideas, perspectives, and viewpoints are being lost.

Research does not have to be a burden, a luxury, or a terrifying prospect. Research lies at the foundation of professional knowledge and practice within librarianship. It is how librarianship, as a profession, knows what it knows. Research also yields persuasive quantitative and qualitative data. Numbers, telling quotations, and other forms of "proof" matter in convincing fellow librarians and other people of libraries' contributions to the greater good. Finally, research can help improve both the professional opportunities of individual librarians and the position of librarianship within society. Historically, production and sharing of research findings have been ways in which people and professions have improved their status.

Personal Benefits

Consider the hypothetical situation of Tracy Thompson, a reference librarian at a medium-sized public library in a working-class suburb. Currently, the library's reference desk is staffed only until 5:00 p.m. on Fridays, although the building is open to the public until 7:00 p.m. Because she often works late in her office on Fridays, Tracy knows that a number of people visit the library between 5:00 p.m. and 7:00 p.m. Some of them even stop Tracy to ask her questions, convincing her that the library should staff the reference desk until 7:00 p.m. on Fridays to better serve the community. Tracy shares her thoughts at a reference staff meeting. Some of her colleagues agree with her ideas, while others object that the reference desk was once staffed until 7:00 p.m.—but no one ever asked questions then. The head of reference is, of course, worried about the personnel and budgetary implications of additional staffing hours. Tracy continues to campaign for staffing the reference desk from 5:00 p.m. to 7:00 p.m. on Fridays, while others continue to oppose her efforts. The debate soon takes on an adversarial tone, with different sides arguing what they take to be the self-evident "truths" of the situation. Nothing is resolved, and some coworkers develop hurt feelings that later taint all of their interactions with each other.

Similar scenarios happen all the time in libraries. This example could have had a very different outcome had Tracy, or someone else at her library, conducted research on this issue. Gate counts of the number of people entering the library building could have been kept. With these counts, the total number of people entering the library between 5:00 p.m. and 7:00 p.m. on Fridays could have been compared to the numbers entering at other times of the week. These totals could also have been compared to the proportion of all library users asking reference questions at other times of the week. Those visiting the library between 5:00 p.m. and 7:00 p.m. on Fridays could have been surveyed, interviewed, or involved in focus groups in order to investigate their reasons for visiting the library at that time. Other libraries' service hours and usage statistics could have been obtained and used as benchmarks. Any of these options—and others not even mentioned here—could have made a difference in this common scenario.

<h2>HEURISTIC BENEFITS</h2>

Research leads to knowledge for the researcher in several important ways. First, the researcher gains in-depth knowledge of the subject matter being researched. This knowledge, in turn, should and often does lead to changes in practice. These changes in practice do not necessarily affect the library as a whole nor, perhaps, even the unit or department in which the researcher works. These changes in practice can be personal on-the-job changes that affect only the individual researcher. They could also affect the researcher at some later point in his or her career. In the above example of the study to expand library hours, Tracy and her coworkers would have come to know more about the temporal patterns of patrons' use of the library. The library would have had one response if a survey revealed that 80 percent of those using the library between 5:00 p.m. and 7:00 p.m. on Fridays were there to check out videos. It would undoubtedly have had a different response if a survey revealed that 60 percent of Friday evening users worked a split shift at a local factory Sunday through Thursday and could not get to the library to ask their reference questions until Friday nights.

The act of researching also teaches the researcher valuable lessons about how to conduct research. If Tracy and her coworkers had conducted a survey of their users, they would have learned more about survey question construction, random sampling, conducting interviews, and running focus group sessions. Had they been novice researchers, their learning would have been most profound. They would have had to learn about sampling populations, survey instrument design, response rates, and many other topics. Despite their best intentions, they would probably have made many mistakes, which is not a bad thing. Many people learn best from their own mistakes. It is more important for first-time researchers to master the techniques of research than to conduct a publishable study. Even if they were experienced researchers, Tracy and her coworkers could still have learned more about conducting research from their investigation of library service hours. For example, they might have decided to implement their first Web-based survey and experienced a response rate different from their prior print surveys, prompting them to research the effects of different survey media on respondents. This expanding knowledge of research methodologies is valuable in its own right, and can also enable librarians to better assist users who are trying to locate and evaluate research studies in other fields.

Finally, increased knowledge of research methodologies helps highlight how people know what they know. Tracy starts off basing her knowledge directly on her personal experiences, without taking time to reflect on the possible meaning and significance of those experiences. She knows that several people have stopped her in the library between 5:00 p.m. and 7:00 p.m. on Fridays to ask her questions, and she concludes that the library should provide reference service during those hours. She has not yet begun to ask questions of her experiences, as a researcher would:

- How many, out of all the people in the building on Friday evenings, have actually asked her questions?
- Are the people asking the questions representative of the people who are not asking questions?
- Even if the phenomenon she has observed is "real," do the costs of providing reference service on Friday nights outweigh the benefits?

Tracy would learn a good deal about her own assumptions if she were to conduct a survey that showed, for example, that 80 percent of those using the library between 5:00 p.m. and 7:00 p.m. on Fridays were there to check out videos for viewing by their family over the weekend. She would learn, among other things, that the anecdotal evidence furnished by her interactions with a few, perhaps atypical, people is not a sufficient basis for implementing significant changes in a library's services.

PERSUASIVE BENEFITS

The knowledge gained from conducting research is persuasive in a variety of ways. Consider Tracy's situation. She would be better able to persuade her coworkers and library administrators with data from surveys, interviews, focus groups, or benchmarking than with her own views on how things are and what should be done. Suppose that Tracy had learned that 80 percent of Friday evening library users were there to check out videos and that 52 percent of them were frustrated because the videos they wanted were already checked out by the time they got to the library. With this data, Tracy could make a case to library administrators for implementing a hold system for videos, or for expanding the video collection. The data presented through research makes a case for informed change.

Research also helps by creating a persuasive ethos for the researcher. Once a librarian has conducted one or more research studies that are more or less successful, that librarian gains a higher degree of respect from his or her peers that he or she might not have received prior to conducting the research studies. An experienced librarian-researcher gains respect and attains a higher persuasion factor not only from peers but also from supervisors and administrators.

ADVANCEMENT BENEFITS

Knowledge gained from research can also lead to career advancement. Tracy could use her findings and the resulting programs as the basis for making presentations, writing publications, becoming an authority on this topic, or consulting on library hours and services. The career benefits of research are obvious for academic librarians, whose research plays an important part in the promotion and tenure process. But they are not the only librarians who can use research to bolster their careers. A number of school library media specialists, public librarians, and corporate librarians have built professional reputations, as well as supplemental writing careers, upon their research. Barbara Stripling, Carol Leita, and Mary Ellen Bates can serve as examples of non-academic librarians pursuing research. Advancement is not necessarily being promoted to a job with a larger paycheck and a more impressive title. We encourage readers to consider advancement in the sense of intellectual growth as well as in the advancement of one's public persona as a researcher. Quality research leads the librarian-researcher to be much more connected with and more accessible to library professionals worldwide.

Professional Benefits

HEURISTIC BENEFITS

Knowledge in library science, like knowledge in all other disciplines, results from an "incremental process," a "development-by-accumulation," whereby "items have been added, singly or in combination, to the ever growing stockpile that constitutes [disciplinary] technique and knowledge" (Kuhn 1970, 1–2). In other words, one researcher discovers something and another researcher builds on it. (Kuhn himself finds this view of "normal science" too linear and simplistic to account for "scientific revolutions" with their "factual and theoretical novelty" leading to changes in worldview. However, if no prior facts and theories have emerged from prior research efforts, no revolutionary departure from them is possible.)

Consider Constance Mellon's pioneering qualitative theory of library anxiety, which stated that students' fears about using the library seriously impede their ability to function effectively in that setting. Later, researchers built upon that theory by validating instruments for measuring library anxiety (Bostick 1992), by correlating library anxiety with learning style preferences (Jiao and Onwuegbuzie 1999), and in other ways. Tracy's hypothetical findings about the use of her public library on Friday evenings could form a similar basis for professional knowledge if, for example, they were combined with Jamal's findings about the use of the academic library at his large public university and with Veronica's findings about the use of the library at her private, liberal arts college. Librarianship could then begin to develop some general theories about the relationships between time of day, library type, and library use that could guide practitioners everywhere in planning for library services.

Every research project has a potential role to play in the development of disciplinary knowledge. Not every research project plays such a role, since not all research projects are suitable for sharing with a wide audience. However, smaller or "not so good" studies still play an important role in shaping the researcher. Everybody needs the opportunity to fail and to learn from that failure.

PERSUASIVE BENEFITS

The persuasive benefits of individuals' research for the profession are also significant. Consider, for example, research conducted by the American Library Association that found that the 16,000 public libraries in the United States outnumber McDonald's franchises. Numerous writers have drawn upon this finding in attempting to describe the benefits of libraries to a public bedazzled by the Internet. Arthur Plotnick (2003) draws upon this statistic in attempting to persuade his readers that the answer to the question "Who loves you like the library?" is "no one." Former American Library Association (ALA) president Nancy Kranich (2001) refers to this same statistic in answering "very" to the question of "How relevant are libraries in the Digital Age?" Many other librarians have used this same public library/McDonald's franchises statistic in presentations, library newsletters, and elsewhere, making it a clear example of how one research project can generate findings of use throughout the profession. Because the ALA found and presented this data, other researchers in need of compelling evidence of libraries' continuing significance in an electronic world did not need to "reinvent the wheel" by conducting their own research. They could instead build on the research done by others.

ADVANCEMENT BENEFITS

Finally, research allows professions to advance themselves and their causes within society. Without delving too much into the history and sociology of professions in the United States, it is safe to say that the possession and promulgation of quantitative and qualitative data is key to a profession's standing. As Mary Biggs (1991, 75) notes, "without [research], there can be no articulation of practical procedures that are sufficiently consistent, efficient, specialized, and mystified to win society's recognition that they add up to a 'profession.'" Writers on "discipline envy" within academe have similarly noted a hierarchy of disciplines based on the amount and types of data they generate and possess. This hierarchy is characterized by the valuation of the "'dry' sciences over 'wet' sciences, quantitative . . . over qualitative . . . numbers over narration . . . theorists in general over practitioners" (Garber 2001, 66). At times, it seems as if everyone's discipline wants to emulate the "dry" sciences (e.g., mathematics, physics) because they generate large quantities of data (much of it numerical) and articulate

Figure 1-1: The Benefits of Research

	Personal	Professional
Heuristic benefits	• Answer questions about effective ways to provide library resources and services to users • Understand better how one thinks and learns	• Data and knowledge gained from individual research projects can be "cumulative," leading to a bigger picture view of phenomena
Persuasive benefits	• Argue more effectively for proposed programs and solutions • Data persuasive to decision makers	• Argue more effectively for proposed programs and solutions • Data persuasive to decision makers
Advancement benefits	• Promotion, tenure, and salary increases may be tied to research activities • Develop speaking, writing, or consulting career based on research activities	• Data and knowledge gained from research projects key to profession's social standing

universal laws. For example, cliometrics, or the study of history using economic models and advanced mathematical methods of data processing, has been described as historians' attempt to be more like a "dry" science (Sykes 1988). Current accountability mandates reflect this view in their focus on concrete "proof" of a return, in the form of benefits or outcomes realized, on investments of money, resources, or time ("How Can Colleges Prove They're Doing Their Jobs," 2004). It is no longer enough to say that one represents an institution that "is good," or that "does good" for society; rather, one must be able to demonstrate concretely the professions' contributions to those outside the profession.

The heuristic, persuasive, and advancement benefits of research to both individual librarians and the library profession are shown in Figure 1-1.

USING THIS BOOK

This book is intended to provide busy librarians with a guide to various research methodologies. Although our book is titled research methods and not methodologies, we recognize that there are differences between the two terms. The terms "methodology" and "method" are used interchangeably throughout the text because within the library and information science literature the two terms appear to have such similar meanings that they are often indistinguishable. However, we firmly believe there is a difference between the two terms, and throughout the book we are profiling a "methodology" instead of a "method." We take our definition of methodology from W. James Potter, professor of communication at the University of California, Santa Barbara, who, in his 1996 book, *An Analysis of Thinking and Research about Qualitative Methods*, wrote: "Methodologies are perspectives on research; they set out a vision for what research is and how it should be conducted. They are the connection between axioms and methods." Research methods, in contrast, are

> tools—techniques of data gathering, techniques of analysis, and techniques of writing. Because it is a tool, a particular method can often be used by many different methodologies (both qualitative and quantitative). Therefore, methodologies are at a more abstract (or general) level than are methods. Methodology is like a strategy—or plan—for achieving some goal; methods are the tactics that can be used to service the goals of the methodology. (Potter 1996, 50)

Content analysis is an example of a research methodology, while a survey is an example of a research method. Content analysis focuses on the analysis of texts or messages of any kind through word counts, thematic analysis, or referential analysis. Different approaches to conducting content analysis are possible. A survey, in contrast, is a type of instrument used to gather data from people. Surveys can, in fact, be used in support of different methodologies.

Our book is intended to give a big picture view. *Practical Research Methods for Librarians and Information Professionals* does not focus on tips and techniques for specific methodologies. We do not believe, for example, that teaching how to conduct an analysis of variance (ANOVA) teaches how to conduct a research study. Instead, we provide a broad overview of nine different methods.

Consider this difference as similar to reading a book on interpersonal communication in a foreign culture against reading a foreign language dictionary. Which would be most helpful in learning to cope and communicate in a foreign country? The dictionary or the cultural overview? Our work is similar to the interpersonal communication work. We provide, in broad brushstrokes, the important elements of each of the methodologies profiled, but we do not tell the researcher exactly what to do in a specific situation.

Thinking about Research

Before we transition to the research process and individual methodologies, however, you-the-reader need to know a bit more about how we-the-authors think about research and about the common dichotomy drawn between quantitative and qualitative methodologies. Myriad authors—both outside of and within the library profession—have written introductions to research, attempting both to define what constitutes research and to show how research should be done. Research can be tricky to define, as evidenced by the fact that nearly all of these authors have provided their own definitions. We find that the dictionary definition of research as "investigation or experimentation aimed at the discovery and inter-pretation of facts, revision of accepted theories or laws in the light of new facts, or practical application of such new or revised theories or laws" (*Merriam-Webster's Collegiate Dictionary* 2003) more than suffices for our purposes. We especially like the *Merriam-Webster's Collegiate Dictionary* definition because of its use of the word "discovery" in defining research. For us, "discovery" gets at the heart of what research is all about by suggesting the spirit of adventure and exploration that researchers should have. Researchers are curious. They constantly want to learn more. They believe that there are new things out there waiting to be found. They are willing to try new things and fail. They persevere despite obstacles.

In our experience, two beliefs commonly get in the way of this spirit of ad-venture and exploration—and stifle the development of would-be researchers. First is the belief that the "truth" about particular phenomena (for instance, why students cite Web pages) is obvious to everyone and does not need further ex-ploration. The fictitious Tracy Thompson, introduced earlier in this chapter, is an exemplar of this belief. If a researcher thinks the answers to all of the ques-tions are obvious, then there really does not seem to be much point to research. Why bother to research why students cite Web pages if everyone "knows" that they do it because they are lazy, ignorant of superior library resources, or im-properly guided by their professors? Effective researchers need to be able to question first impressions about the causes of phenomena, and even to question whether the phenomena they have noted really exist. Perhaps students do not cite a disproportionately large number of Web pages, given their topics. A will-ingness to question anything and everything helps make a good researcher. Some questions will lead nowhere. Others, though, could transform our under-standing of the researched phenomena.

A recent study by Oberholzer and Strumpf (2004) on the effects of file sharing on record sales provides a good example of the willingness to question and transform findings. For years, the prevailing view has been that file sharing on peer-to-peer networks like Napster caused declining record sales. Most people presume that file sharing causes diminished record sales because they "know" young adults are frequently sharing music files, and it makes sense to conclude that young adults would purchase less music because of this sharing. In addition, a number of researchers have found that file sharing causes diminished record sales based on survey data and focus groups, which asked young adults how frequently they shared files and how file sharing had impacted their music purchases. Oberholzer and Strumpf, however, were willing to question both the file-sharing-causes-diminished-record-sales conclusion and the survey and focus group methodologies by which prior researchers had demonstrated a causal relation-ship between file sharing and record sales. They gathered server logs showing file-sharing activities and then compared the song/album titles being shared with record sales data. Their research showed that "downloads have an effect on sales which is statistically indistinguishable from zero" (2004, i), representing a substantial challenge to the traditional notion that file sharing is primarily responsible for recent declines in music sales. (Who is right? We will revisit that question momentarily.)

The second belief that commonly stifles the development of would-be researchers is that one must have perfection in all aspects of the data gathering and interpreting situation before research can or should occur. This belief may lead to thoughts such as, if there is a possibility that respondents might lie in interviews, do not bother conducting the interviews. If a single respondent might complete two survey forms for his/her own innocent or malicious reasons, do not do the survey. If several possible explanations for patterns of periodical use exist, one cannot learn anything from that data. Whether they are looking for reasons for their research projects to fail in order to avoid the work of such projects, or whether they truly believe everyone else but them really attains perfection in data gathering and interpretation, those who seek perfection tend not to do much research. Perfection is never going to exist! This is not to say that perfection in data gathering and interpretation is not a goal toward which conscientious researchers should strive. All researchers should strive toward this goal, just as they should all seek the "truth" of the phenomena they are studying. However, researchers must remain constantly aware that perfection and truth are points that they get ever closer to without ever actually arriving at. Just as no one is ever going to capture the absolute truth that accounts for every occurrence of a social science phenomenon, no one is going to conduct the perfect study. Not even the physical sciences get to absolute, eternal truths by perfectly implemented methodologies. At first, gravity seemed a better explanation for why objects with mass tended to accelerate toward each other than the Aristotelian explanation that all things "try to move toward their proper location." Then, Einstein introduced the notion of general relativity, which modeled gravity as a curvature within space-time that changes as mass moves. Now, physicists are researching quantum gravity, which seeks to reconcile quantum mechanics with general relativity. Applying this to the preceding example about file sharing, in all likelihood both Oberholzer and Strumpf and their predecessors are "right" and have captured important aspects of the truth about the relationship between file sharing and music sales by their different methodologies. Research is a journey, not a destination. There is always more that can be learned both about the methodologies and techniques and about the topics of particular research projects.

Quantitative, Qualitative, and Other Methodologies

We would also like to dispel some of the angst that can surround discussions of quantitative and qualitative methodologies. Some researchers get very preoccupied by the meanings of these terms and by the supposed superiority of one sort of methodology over another (usually quantitative over qualitative). Indeed, we were once taken to task by a colleague who believed our qualitative study to be flawed because we had interviewed "only" forty-some faculty members. In our conversation, we learned the individual had only been exposed to, or involved in, quantitative methodologies, in which bigger is often (but far from always) better when it comes to sample size. This individual had no familiarity with qualitative methods, but sought to judge a qualitative study in terms of quantitative methods. (This is not to say that there were no grounds for critiquing this study, just that criticism based on a sample size of forty in an interviewing project was not one of those grounds.) Thus, we would like to review the meanings of quantitative and qualitative and dispel the myth that one is inherently "superior."

At their most basic level, quantitative methodologies involve "the measurement of quantity or amount" relating to a researched phenomenon, while qualitative methodologies involve the measurement of "quality or kind" relating to a researched phenomenon (*Merriam-Webster's Collegiate Dictionary* 2003). A quantitative approach seeks a number—seeks to know how many—in relation to the research question(s). A qualitative approach seeks data that helps to explain "how human beings understand, experience, interpret, and produce" that part of the "social world" relating to the research question(s) (Sandelowski 2004, 893). A quantitative approach might seek to measure how many people in various patron categories (undergraduate student, graduate student, faculty member, and so forth) use particular databases at an academic library at particular time periods. A qualitative approach, in contrast, might seek to understand why patrons pick a database, or how they feel about the experience of using it.

While some have argued that quantitative and qualitative are "distinctive and largely irreconcilable epistemologies," or ways of understanding the world (Bryman 2004, 895), others view them as different approaches to data collection and analysis. With the latter view, multistrategy research—or research combining quantitative and qualitative approaches—becomes possible. We take the latter view, in large part because much research is, in fact, multistrategy research. A simple dichotomy between numbers/quantitative and no numbers/qualitative is too artificial. Numbers can factor into qualitative research, as when a content analysis reports finding examples of seven uses of a particular theme in a passage of text. Similarly, classroom research often combines quantitative and qualitative approaches to document the nature of programs, methods, techniques, and other processes of interaction in classrooms in association with their outcomes in learners' behaviors and attitudes (cf. Chaudron 2001). For example, in tracking the effectiveness of a particular approach to teaching writing, a classroom research project might draw upon quantitative data about students' SAT scores and grade point averages, as well as upon qualitative data such as the themes expressed in student journal entries about the composition process.

Neither quantitative nor qualitative methodologies are superior in any absolute sense. Rather, different sorts of methodologies work better for different things. Using a qualitative methodology, such as interviewing or focus groups, to study citation patterns would not be a good strategy, since people are unlikely to remember the dates and types of sources they cited in even their most recent writings. Conversely, using a quantitative methodology such as bibliometrics to understand *why* people cite the sources they do is not a good strategy, since one cannot infer why someone cited a source from the mere existence of a citation to that source.

Publishing

Finally, this book is not intended as a comprehensive guide for librarians on getting published. There are already a number of resources in existence that do this and do it well. Still, the resources shown in Figure 1-2 offer a selective list of resources that librarians can draw upon for help with everything from formatting and submitting manuscripts to working with editors, handling copyright forms, and dealing with rejection.

More fundamentally, though, this book takes the view that researchers who have done good, original work have no difficulties in getting published, provided that they can explain that work and its significance to others in coherent prose. Good research is that which correctly applies an appropriate research methodology to a problem of significance, while original research is that which contributes to changes—additions or corrections—in the body of knowledge on a topic.

Figure 1-2: Guides to the Publication Process

Alley, Brian, and Jennifer S. Cargill. 1986. *Librarian in Search of a Publisher: How to Get Published.* Phoenix, AZ: Oryx Press.

Crawford, Walt. 2003. *First Have Something to Say: Writing for the Library Profession.* Chicago: American Library Association.

Gordon, Rachel Singer. 2004. *The Librarian's Guide to Writing for Publication.* Lanham, MD: Scarecrow Press.

Johnson, Richard David. 1985. *Writing the Journal Article and Getting It Published.* Chicago: Association of College and Research Libraries.

Nancekivell, Sharon. 2004. "Writing a Publishable Journal Article: A Perspective from the Other Side of the Desk." *Science Next Wave.* Available: http://nextwave.sciencemag.org/cgi/content/full/2004/04/14/2.

Sellen, Betty-Carol. 1986. *Librarian/Author: A Practical Guide on How to Get Published.* New York: Neal-Schuman.

REFERENCES

Biggs, Mary. 1991. "The Role of Research in the Development of a Profession or a Discipline." In *Library and Information Science Research: Perspectives and Strategies for Improvement*, 72–84. Norwood, NJ: Ablex.

Bostick, Sharon. 1992. "The Development and Validation of the Library Anxiety Scale." Ph.D. dissertation, Wayne State University.

Bryman, Alan. 2004. "Quantitative and Qualitative Research, Debate About." In *The Sage Encyclopedia of Social Research Methods*, 895–896, edited by Michael Lewis-Beck, Alan Bryman, and Tim Futing Liao. Thousand Oaks, CA: Sage.

Chaudron, Craig. 2001. "Progress in Language Classroom Research: Evidence from *The Modern Language Journal* 1916–2000." *The Modern Language Journal* 85 (1): 57–76.

Edwards, Derek. 2004. "Discourse Analysis." In *The Sage Encyclopedia of Social Science Research Methods*, 265–268, edited by Michael Lewis-Beck, Alan Bryman, and Tim Futing Liao. Thousand Oaks, CA: Sage.

Frongia, Terri. 1995. "Active Mentorship in Scholarly Publishing: Why, What, Who, How." In *The Politics and Processes of Scholarship*, 217–230. Westport, CT: Greenwood Press.

Garber, Marjorie. 2001. *Academic Instincts*. Princeton, NJ: Princeton University Press.

"How Can Colleges Prove They're Doing Their Jobs?" 2004. *The Chronicle of Higher Education*, September 3. Available: http://chronicle.com/weekly/v51/i02/02b00601.htm (accessed May 17, 2007).

Jiao, Qun G., and Anthony J. Onwuegbuzie. 1999. "Identifying Library Anxiety through Students' Learning-Modality Preferences." *Library Quarterly* 69 (2): 202–216.

Kranich, Nancy. 2001. "How Relevant Are Libraries in the Digital Age?" *The Hindu*, April 15. Available: http://hindu.com/thehindu/2001/04/15/stories/1315046h.htm (accessed May 17, 2007).

Kuhn, Thomas. 1970. *The Structure of Scientific Revolutions*. Chicago: University of Chicago Press.

Lewis-Beck, Michael, Alan Bryman, and Tim Futing Liao. 2004. *The Sage Encyclopedia of Social Science Research Methods*. Thousand Oaks, CA: Sage.

Liebscher, Peter. 1998. "Quantity with Quality? Teaching Quantitative and Qualitative Methods in an LIS Master's Program." *Library Trends* 46 (4): 668–680.

Lynch, Beverly P., and Kimberley Robles Smith. 2001. "The Changing Nature of Work in Academic Libraries." *College & Research Libraries* 62 (5): 407–420.

Mellon, Constance. 1986. "Library Anxiety in College Students: A Grounded Theory and Its Development." *College & Research Libraries* 47 (2): 160–165.

Merriam-Webster's Collegiate Dictionary. 2003. 11th ed. Springfield, MA: Merriam-Webster.

Ninh, Bao. 1995. *The Sorrow of War: A Novel of North Vietnam*. New York: Pantheon.

Oberholzer, Felix, and Koleman Strumpf. 2004. "The Effect of File Sharing on Record Sales: An Empirical Analysis." Available: http://unc.edu/~cigar/papers/ FileSharing_March2004.pdf (accessed May 17, 2007).

O'Connor, Dan, and Soyeon Park. 2002. "Research Methods as Essential Knowledge." *American Libraries* 33 (1): 50.

Plotnick, Arthur. 2003. "Who Loves You Like the Library?" *The Writer Magazine*, November. Available: http://writermag.com/wrt/default.aspx?c=a&id=1178 (accessed May 17, 2007).

Potter, W. James. 1996. *An Analysis of Thinking and Research about Qualitative Methods*. Mahwah, NJ: Lawrence Erlbaum.

Powell, Ronald R., Lynda Baker, and Joseph Mika. 2002. "Library and Information Science Practitioners and Research." *Library and Information Science Research* 24 (1): 49–72.

Sandelowski, Margarete. 2004. "Qualitative Research." In *The Sage Encyclopedia of Social Science Research Methods*, 893–894, edited by Michael Lewis-Beck, Alan Bryman, and Tim Futing Liao. Thousand Oaks, CA: Sage.

Sykes, Charles. 1988. *ProfScam: Professors and the Demise of Higher Education*. New York: St. Martin's Press.

Chapter 2

The Research Process

In every discipline, the process of research follows the same basic steps or stages. Known in many fields as the scientific method (see Figure 2-1), the research process begins with a topic of interest to the researcher and, more often than not, requires that a problem be solved. While defining this problem, the researcher generates a series of questions and also formulates hypotheses, or "educated guesses," as to what the research findings will be. Hypotheses both provide a logical means to locate the data and serve as a way of resolving the research problem. Next, the researcher decides how, as well as who and what, to study. These two stages involve defining the population to be studied and then crafting a research design that results in yet another stage, that of collecting measurable data. Each of these stages has the shared goal of resolving the research problem. Once the data are collected, they are carefully analyzed and the hypotheses are tested. Finally, the researcher writes up the findings, telling the research story and offering conclusions.

At this point, it is important to note that the research process is neither linear in nature nor rigid in procedure. In fact, the process of research is both iterative and cyclical. The researcher asks questions, formulates a plan to answer those questions, gathers data in a methodical fashion and, possibly, in the process of data analysis and interpretation, arrives at a new set of questions to be asked. At each stage of the process, the researcher might also reposition and refine the research plan. Thus, at any point in the research process, a researcher can revisit any of the prior steps: difficulties in proposing a hypothesis, for example, might lead a researcher to realize she has not identified or defined the problem narrowly enough, while difficulties in designing data gathering mechanisms might lead her to reshape the hypothesis. The stages of the research process outlined below and shown in Figure 2-2 form the structure of each of the following chapters. These research steps or stages are the same ones that everyone learned in high school or, at the latest, as undergraduates. They are also the same steps that many librarians present in instructional sessions focused on teaching the basic research process to students.

Figure 2-1: The Scientific Method

1. Identify and define the problem.
   a. Conduct literature review.
   b. Gather preliminary data.
2. Propose a hypothesis as a means of explaining the problem.
3. Gather data relevant to the hypothesis.
4. Process and interpret data in order to empirically test the hypothesis.
5. Ascertain whether the interpretation resolves the problem.

Figure 2-2: Non-linear Diagram of the Scientific Method

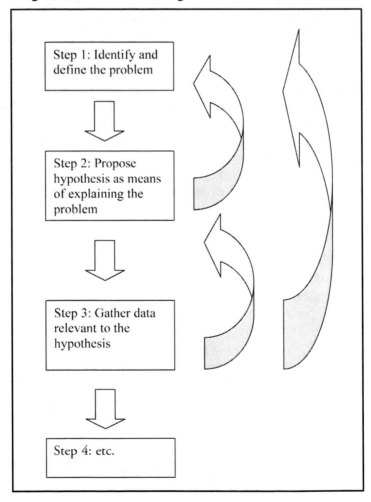

Keep in mind that this chapter is designed only to review the basic outlines of each step of the research process. Subsequent chapters, which are organized in terms of the steps of this research process, will provide more details on, for example, formulating research questions or defining populations. (In other words, do not look for extensive discussion of sampling here. Rather, look under the research methodology within which you would be employing sampling.)

FINDING A TOPIC

Finding a topic is all about you, the researcher: your job and its responsibilities, how you get things done, how you view research, your preferred approach to research, and how you see yourself doing research. Finding a research topic is not only about what topic you want to research, but also relies upon a good fit between you, the research topic, and the method. The table in Figure 2-3 briefly sketches out each methodology profiled in this book by its research focus and the researcher characteristics. Although we discuss these topics in the following

Figure 2-3: Comparison of Methodologies According to Research Focus and Researcher Characteristics

Methodology	Research focus	Researcher characteristics
Action research	Workplace problem that is locally focused and solvable Practical problem (e.g., shelf configurations, workflows) Involves multiple stakeholders and their perspectives Goal is improvement of services or processes	Practical and consensus building Reflective and emotionally detached Ability to manage a variety of information sources Views the research process as co-participatory
Bibliometrics	Recorded information sources and their countable characteristics (e.g., number of citations or authors) Could be institution specific (e.g., sources cited in dissertations written by students from one's institution) but often isn't (e.g., all chemists)	Ability to see the "countableness" of things and their significance Willingness to invest in learning about the laws of bibliometrics Willingness to conceptualize a problem broadly
Classroom research	An existing teaching component that yields multiple data sets. Teaching component can be online or face to face, library users or staff Goal is improvement of methods, materials, etc. Uses small research questions	Practical Ability to manage a variety of information sources Views teaching as a process of continuous improvement

(Cont'd.)

Figure 2-3: Comparison of Methodologies According to Research Focus and Researcher Characteristics *(Continued)*

Methodology	Research focus	Researcher characteristics
Content analysis	Recorded information sources that can be categorized Could be institution specific but isn't always Uses small research questions Is inductive and seeks different understanding of the information sources Uses linguistic data	Ability to categorize and recognize possible categories Ability to disregard aspects of the sources that are not relevant Desire to work with texts and a sophisticated conception of texts
Experimental	Anything that has comparable categories (e.g., male/female, before/after) Must have a formal hypothesis Could be locally focused but need not be Uses numerical data (almost always)	Analytical and rigidly self-controlled (i.e., resists taking short cuts) Unafraid and appreciative of numbers Ability to visualize problems broadly but construct a research study narrowly Likes testing things
Focus groups	Opinions and feelings of a user group are the central concern Exploratory and focused on gaining a broader understanding of users' perceptions Typically concerned with solving a local problem	Problem solver and "tinkerer" Appreciates others' viewpoints Comfortable with multiple perceptions and ability to problem solve from them Can deal with a variety of people
Interviews	Exploratory and inductive Focused on how people see and understand their world Phenomenon under investigation is not universal but is small group based	People-oriented Likes to listen to others Ability to manage chunks of texts Ability to see themes in the text and note their relationships Realizes knowledge gained from the study may not be directly or immediately applied
Observation	Explores observable human behavior Inductive Concentrates on a local problem or can be broader and more theoretical Uses small research questions	Realizes knowledge gained from the study may not be directly or immediately applied Ability to disregard aspects of behaviors that are not relevant Patient and willing to watch people do things for long periods of time without involving oneself Ability to deal with complex and incongruent data

(Cont'd.)

**Figure 2-3: Comparison of Methodologies According to Research
Focus and Researcher Characteristics** *(Continued)*

Methodology	Research focus	Researcher characteristics
Usability testing	Product improvement Exploratory Uses small, contained questions that could be sequential or cumulative Locally based problem that is solvable Typically focused on computerized systems or resources	Problem solver and a "tinkerer" Ability to break large problems into manageable parts Accepts totally new ways of solving the problem Ability to watch people use a product badly and improperly without intervening

N.B. These methodologies reflect those profiled in this book and do not represent all possible research methodologies.

chapters, the chart helps researchers to look at these methodologies in a different, more personal way. We encourage you to consult the chart in Figure 2-3 as a way of determining whether a specific methodology is right for you.

Some argue that the first step in any type of research project is a question (Powell and Connaway 2004). However, the first step is much more basic. Finding a topic to focus on is always the first step. Finding a topic that is interesting and exciting to the researcher is essential both to the success of the project and to the mental health of the researcher. Take, for example, the hypothetical case of Bradley Blackwood, Digital Reference Librarian, just finishing up his second year at Sarah Bellum Memorial Library at State University. Brad knows that his tenure clock is ticking and that his third-year review is rapidly approaching. He has yet to publish anything of significance. As he searches for a research topic, he vacillates between two possible projects. Should he expand on a research paper he wrote in library school that studied self-citedness among library school faculty in relation to the perceived reputation of the faculty members' institutions? He received an A on the paper and his professor praised his research design. It would not be too difficult to update the study since he has done the bulk of the work already; however, Brad has grown increasingly bored with the topic of self-citednesss among library faculty.

On the other hand, Brad is interested in studying the similarities and differences in user and librarian communication styles in chat and face-to-face reference transactions. Last year, Brad played a leading role in implementing a chat reference service, and he is responsible for scheduling and maintaining the service within his department. Several of his coworkers have complained about the superficiality of conducting a reference interview online. They have concerns that chat reference favors the technology over the needs of the user. They also worry that the technology gets in the way of establishing a helpful yet effective conversation style with users. Brad is not convinced that chat reference should be eliminated because of these concerns. However, as the chat reference coordinator, he wonders how technology changes the reference interview. In his role of coordinator, Brad has kept all transaction logs since the service's inception, so he has a data set upon which he can draw. In fact, Brad has already pulled several days worth of chat reference data, read it several times looking for similarities in question negotiation styles between librarian and users, and made some preliminary notes as to patterns. He has also been keeping up with the research literature in library journals on chat reference, noting areas other librarians are researching.

Which project should Brad choose? Self-citedness of library school faculty in relation to perceived institutional reputation, or differences between librarian-user communication styles in chat and face-to-face reference transactions? Obviously, Brad should follow his passion, chose the topic that motivates him, and not opt for the other just because it covers known territory and would be easy to update.

For new researchers, however, even this fundamental advice about following your interests in selecting a research topic may seem hard to implement. What about those times when you feel that you need to do research due to professional pressures, but you really do not have any strong feelings about potential topics? How do you identify potential topics about which you might eventually come to have strong feelings? When you are just getting started as a researcher, it is helpful to remember that research is, in one sense, like a cocktail party conversation. You cannot join in the conversation unless you are at the party where the conversation is taking place. Similarly, you will have a hard time joining the scholarly conversation that underlies research unless you are where that conversation takes place. That conversation takes place at conferences, in library literature, in electronic discussion groups, in blogs, and in informal conversation with colleagues. The more you participate in all of these activities, the more likely you are to find that research topics simply come to you: someone else's comments trigger an idea about how you could do a similar study in a different setting, or about how you would go about gathering data to back up your disagreement with something someone else has said. Moreover, as you join in the scholarly conversation, you will start to realize that the world of research does not consist of one big conversation that involves all partygoers/researchers. Rather, there are many smaller conversations with smaller numbers of researchers. This realization should lead you to another good source of potential research topics. Join in—if only by listening—on the conversation of a neighboring group and bring its insights back to your own conversational group. Many researchers have done this, for example, by conducting studies applying the insights of Total Quality Management (TQM) to library management or findings about generational differences to library instruction.

One good way to find out which topics you do care about is to sit down with a sheet of paper, or a blank Word document, and start typing in a stream-of-consciousness fashion about what you think is most important to librarianship now. If you find yourself going on, for example, about how people think everything is on Google when it really is not, you might find a research topic that compares the currency or comprehensiveness or accuracy of search engine content with that in print or in library databases.

Be attuned to your own interests, and do not discard the topics that you care about simply because they seem to have already been done, or are "out of vogue" in the library literature. Methodological or topical trendiness is a poor substitute for a methodology or a topic to which you are committed. You are the best guide to which topics interest you, and you should not pick a topic simply to please your boss, your coworkers, a journal editor, a potential grant-funding agency, or anyone else. You are the one who is going to have to work intensively with the topic over a long period of time, so it is best to have something you genuinely care about. Once you have "your" topic, there are always slants you can put on that topic to make it fit potential publication or presentation venues. Thus, you might revisit a topic that already seems "done" in order to show that something has changed, or that we do not really know all that we thought we knew about this topic.

Finally, in choosing a topic, researchers need to think carefully about any ethical concerns that could arise. The Brad Blackwood scenario raises a very important ethical situation. Brad's hypothetical research study involved chat reference transactions and, as chat reference coordinator, he had already collected a year's worth of data. Unfortunately, he will not be able to use this data set in his research. Why not? There is nothing wrong with the data itself, but Brad has not obtained informed consent from his colleagues who have contributed to all those chat reference logs. Users asking reference questions have also contributed, and he has not obtained informed consent from them, either. He cannot go back now and get consent from the librarians and from the users after the fact because his subjects were not informed about the study from its inception. The primary rule in any study involving human subjects is "first, do no harm." All research studies that deal with human subjects dictate quite strongly that researchers must inform subjects about the study and that they must obtain their consent to participate in the study. Not only do they need to be told about the purpose of the study but they also need to be informed regarding how the data will be used and that the researcher has found no risks in the study that might harm the participants. We should interpret the term "harm" quite broadly here. Certainly there would be no physical "harm" in reprinting verbatim an electronic reference transaction that occurred in chat reference. Neither the user nor the librarian was in imminent danger of losing life or limb. However, harm could be caused by publishing transactions that allow Brad's coworkers to be identified by their well-known speech habits or regular use of certain figures of speech or words. Although these chat reference transactions may well illustrate a specific point, they might also shame or humiliate Brad's coworkers. This public shaming, although inadvertent, is certainly harmful. In Brad's case, he will have to discard the last year's worth of transaction logs and begin collecting anew. Before he does this, though, he will also need to submit his research study proposal to his university's institutional review board for approval. Then, if the study is approved, he needs to explain the study to his colleagues, answer any questions they might have, and obtain their consent, in writing, to participate in the study. He also needs to insert a consent form at the chat reference gateway on his library's web site to obtain users' consent.

FORMULATING QUESTIONS

The other classic piece of advice regarding choosing a topic also holds true: find a manageable and executable focus for your topic. In searching for a focus, researchers begin to ask questions about what they wish to learn and know more about. Professors Wayne C. Booth, Gregory G. Colomb, and Joseph M. Williams in their book *The Craft of Research* note that "A research problem is motivated . . . by incomplete knowledge or flawed understanding. You solve it not by changing the world but by understanding it better" (2003, 59). Thus, one way to begin formulating questions is to create a document with two columns, one listing what you know about your proposed research topic (from your own experience and from others' research) and the other listing what you do not know about this topic (from your own experience and from others' research). Listing what you do not know is not as impossible as it sounds. You generally start to see what you do not know as you list what you do know.

For example, suppose Brad Blackwood were to embark on a study of the differences in communication styles between chat and face-to-face reference transactions. From his own experiences and prior research, he already knows the following about the face-to-face and chat reference transactions:

- Reference transactions are typically multipart: introduction, question clarification, advising in the form of instruction/demonstration, and conclusion.
- Studies have found that reference transactions are successful only 55 percent of the time (Herndon and McClure 1986).
- Most people do not ask questions about their real topic; instead, they ask reference librarians for assistance on broader topics.
- Many users feel guilty about asking the reference librarian for help, believing that they should know how to find the information on their own.

Knowing this, Brad is better able to see the gaps in the existing knowledge, which helps him to formulate his question. To begin with, Brad could ask himself, what is meant by the term, "communication styles"? Are there different communication levels and how do these relate to the reference interview? What constitutes the different parts of a typical reference transaction? How do these different parts relate to communication styles? What is the measurement of a successful versus an unsuccessful transaction? Should Brad narrow his focus and look at a specific type of communication interchange within a reference transaction? And, if so, what might that specific type of communication interchange be?

Brad might decide to focus on similarities and differences in the reference staff's clarification-negotiation strategies (questions such as: "So what you are saying you want is X?" "Could you tell me what project this information is needed for?" and "What is it that you *really* want, anyway?") in face-to-face and chat reference. Alternatively, Brad might want to focus on differences in the politeness and formality levels found in chat and face-to-face reference transactions. These questions lead Brad to examine the literature of communication styles and the reference interview all the more deeply, helping him to refine and shape his research project.

An approach to question formulation focused on what is already known and what is not known also helps researchers with convenience samples, like Brad. Brad has massive amounts of transaction log data to sort through, but this stack will not help him much until he decides what he wants to focus on. Sometimes researchers can begin their research from a convenience sample (i.e., using data that is readily available), by accumulating many examples of something and then circling back in the research cycle to find a topic that goes with these samples. There is nothing inherently wrong with such an approach, provided that researchers recognize that the study is limited by not having a random sample. However, it is best to figure out as early as possible what, specifically, one is studying. Researchers usually do this by carefully and thoughtfully formulating their research question.

DEFINING THE POPULATION

As researchers define the problem to be solved, they also begin simultaneously to define the research design, the method that will be employed in that design, and the population to be studied. At this point, it is important to note that researchers do not "choose" their populations in the sense of cherry picking from a list of topics, a list of research questions, and a list of populations. Instead, their research question defines the population. This is an important distinction and it is one that novice researchers might do in reverse, putting the cart before the horse. In the Brad Blackwood scenario, if he wanted to focus on users' politeness levels in chat reference, his population could consist of the library users in the chat reference transaction. On the other hand, if he were interested in politeness levels demonstrated by both librarians and users, his population would consist of both groups. Finally, if Brad were researching differences between face-to-face and chat reference politeness levels, his population would be made up of both chat reference transactions and those conducted face to face. Each of these categories would give Brad answers to his research question, but would do so in different ways depending on his exact research question. All populations in a research study flow from the research problem itself.

It is also important to note that populations can be both people and things. Populations can include:

- periodical publications in a specific subject area (e.g., in studies examining publication patterns)
- Web sites (e.g., in testing the usability of library Web sites)
- library holdings (e.g., in assessing library collections)
- library users (e.g., in analyzing user group preferences)
- librarians (e.g., in studying librarians' personality types and job preferences)

All populations have certain characteristics that define them as a group. Most, but not all, research studies are performed on a population sample rather than on an entire population, due to the impracticalities and expense of studying an entire population. Imagine trying to study the collection strengths of all libraries regardless of type, or examining reading preferences of all library users worldwide. Both are insurmountable tasks, and neither would yield much meaningful data, as these two studies are far too large in scope.

In limited circumstances, librarians are able to study an entire population, but only if it includes a manageable number of subjects and it is feasible to undertake such a study. Classroom research is one such methodology in which population sampling is not necessary. We will discuss this in detail in Chapter 9.

When looking at a sample of a larger population, as most research studies do, the researcher must ensure that the sample is representative of the population as a whole in order to make generalizations about that group. There are many tests as to the "representativeness" of a population sample. This work does not examine the details of this process nor does it attempt to explain all facets of population sampling. Other works wholly focused on population sampling, or an aspect thereof, provide a more comprehensive and detailed examination of the rationale, procedures, and methods involved. Readers interested in exploring sampling in further detail are encouraged to consult the works listed in Figure 2-4.

SELECTING A RESEARCH DESIGN

At this point in the research process, the researcher has decided on a topic, formulated research questions, and, based on the research question, has a population in mind. The next step is to think about designing the study so that it fits the research question. The whole purpose of a well-developed research design is to be able to test the hypotheses, eliminating any alternative explanations of

Figure 2-4: Suggested Works on Population Sampling

Cochran, William G. 1977. *Sampling Techniques.* New York: Wiley.

Fink, Arlene. 2003. *How to Sample in Surveys.* Thousand Oaks, CA: Sage.

Kish, Leslie. 1997. *Survey Sampling.* New York: Wiley.

Levy, Paul S., and Stanley Lemeshow. 1991. *Sampling of Populations: Methods and Applications.* New York: Wiley.

Powell, Ronald R., and Lynn Silipagni Connaway. 2004. "Survey Research and Sampling." In *Basic Research Methods for Librarians.* 4th ed., 57–87. Greenwich, CT: Libraries Unlimted.

Stuart, Alan. 1984. *The Ideas of Sampling.* London: Griffin.

the results. In essence, the research design is the framework, the plan of attack, the strategy, and the tactics of carrying out a research project. Once the problem has been well formulated, the research design must be crafted to provide a structure for the detailed steps in the study. The research design is fairly specific, consisting of a series of guidelines for systematic gathering of data. In charting the research design, researchers need to address four very important questions that work together in shaping the entire research project (Leedy 1989).

1. What are the data needed?
2. Where are the data located?
3. How will the data be secured?
4. How will the data be interpreted?

Let's examine Brad Blackwood's research project in light of the four questions above. He already knows what data he needs; the transaction logs will furnish his data. Brad already has access to all of the transaction logs, answering the question of the data's location. He now needs to consider in his research design how the data will be secured so that the privacy of both the user and the librarian are protected. ("Securing data" can also mean ensuring against loss or corruption of data.) He also needs to consider how both parties' identities will be masked so as to avoid potential researcher bias. One of these problems is already solved for Brad in that the interactive reference chat system does not record participants' identities. However, Brad must also control for possible bias in correlating the chat reference system's time and date stamp with librarians' work schedules. In considering the final question, that of determining how the data will be interpreted, Brad is well positioned. He has already read a great deal on the phases of reference interview, noting both terminologies for different types of reference interactions and the characteristic roles of librarians and users. Suppose Brad takes as his hypothesis that the clarification-negotiation strategies in chat reference will not be as developed as those found in face-to-face encounters. In his research design, Brad will need to determine to what degree the data supports his hypothesis.

Selecting a research design is arguably the most important step in the research process. It is often the step in which the would-be researcher discovers that as interesting as a topic/question might be, there is no realistic way to study it. Suppose, for example, that you are passionate about the topic of misshelved books. You are very bothered when the catalog record says the book is "on the shelf" but a visit to the stacks fails to find the book. You wonder whether misshelvings are due to poor shelving practices by library workers, or improper reshelving by library users. You decide upon a research question of gauging the impact of misshelved books on library service and a population of the misshelved books themselves. However, once you start to sketch out your research design you discover a problem: misshelved books are by definition an impossible population to study since the characteristic that makes them of interest to you (that they are misshelved) prevents you from being able to find the items comprising the population. While book shelvers and shelf readers may happen upon misplaced books from time to time, there is no systematic way to know in advance which books are misshelved.

With most topics, though, there are myriad research designs that could be used to identify, locate, and interpret the necessary data. In the broadest sense, you could think of the different research methodologies that this book introduces as encompassing different research designs. These research methodologies are also much more than "mere" research designs, as will become apparent as you read more. These methodologies also entail different ways of identifying topics, formulating research questions, defining populations, gathering data, interpreting evidence, and telling the story of your research project. However, for now, it is enough to think of different methodologies as different ways of identifying, locating, and interpreting data in relation to a research question.

You could take a single research topic—such as children's picture books—and select research designs using each of these different methodologies as is shown in Figure 2-5. There are occasionally times when your topic constrains your choice of research design; you cannot, for example, study photosynthesis by having plants complete a questionnaire. However, in the vast majority of cases, an almost infinite number of research designs are possible for a given research question and population. Your task as the researcher is not to pick the "correct" research design but rather to apply your design correctly to your research question and population.

In the case of Tracy's study of library usage on Friday evenings, discussed in Chapter 1, a well-developed survey instrument will accurately measure why people use the library at that particular time. Tracy would be missing a vital component in her research if she prepared a questionnaire that asked participants why they used the library during certain periods of time but only offered

Figure 2-5: Comparison of Methodologies According to Questions and Data Gathering Methods

Methodology	Research question	Data gathering methods
Action Research	How well is the childrens picture book collection meeting the needs of the library's community?	Identify stakeholders (parents, children, librarians) Work with stakeholders to identifiy relevant sources of data and ways to gather it Gather data using a variety of methods (e.g., observation, interviews, surveys)
Bibliometrics	Do biologists cite to Dr. Seuss books differently than physicists?	Identify which biology and physics journals to examine Search citation database (cited reference books and journal title search) Create frequency counts
Classroom Research	Did the reference staff training on helping users find children's books work?	Identify multiple sources of relevant data and ways to gather it Gather data using a variety of methods (e.g., pre- and post-instruction, in-house use and circulation statistics, staff interviews, and pre- and post-observation
Content Analysis	How do children's picture books portray librarians and libraries?	Define picture books that include libraries or librarians Define categories that depict libraries or librarians Construct a codebook to guide the coding of data
Experimental	Do different shelving methods (display or spine front) change usage?	Set up comparison groups (representative and random) Identify and/or create instruments to measure differences Identify potential sources of bias with the measurement instrument or process and work to minimize these Measure differences
Focus Groups	How has reading children's picture books in the library shaped library users' view of the library?	Select focus group members Create questions to elicit desired data Identify recording method to capture group members' responses Conduct focus group and record responses

(Cont'd.)

Figure 2-5: Comparison of Methodologies According to Questions and Data Gathering Methods *(Continued)*

Methodology	Research question	Data gathering methods
Interviews	How does a parent's history of reading as a child shape how they encourage library use in their children?	Identify interview participants Create questions to elicit desired data Identify recording method to capture group members' responses Conduct interviews and record responses
Observation	When alone in the children's room, how do young children (age 6 or younger) interact with picture books?	Identify initial set of behaviors to observe Establish observation schedule Identify locations to observe behavior Set up schedule for observation Observe behaviors
Usability Testing	What is the most effective design for electronic, read-aloud picture books?	Identify specific features of the electronic read-aloud picture books to test Develop steps to test features Identify subjects to test read-aloud picture book Run test

selections of "to check out materials," "to read materials in the library," "to surf the Internet," "to search for jobs," "to check my e-mail," and "to do my homework." Without a fill-in-the-blank or open-ended comment option, she might miss other reasons, such as that the most important reason for Friday evening library use is that this is the only time during the week most people can get to the library. Regarding the overall purpose of survey instruments, Arlene Fink, author of *The Survey Instrument*, explains that "[r]esearchers use surveys to find out about people by asking questions about feelings, motivations, plans, beliefs, and personal backgrounds," further noting that if "the questions on the survey instrument don't work towards those purposes, the survey is flawed" (1995, 41). Thus, if Tracy has decided to use surveys as a data collection method to address her question of Friday evening library use, she either needs to revise her survey to include fill-in-the-blank options for her questions, or she should rethink her data collection instrument and methods, looking at methods that allow for more open-ended responses.

One more example of a mismatch between the research method and its corresponding research question can be found in the hypothetical case in which Megan O'Flynn, head of reference, wishes to ascertain the basic reference knowledge and skill competencies of the staff serving at the reference desk. Instead of employing an instrument such as a criterion-based test that measures skill with and knowledge of reference sources and strategies, Megan has her staff self-assess their skills because she feels her staff might be put off by an exam. The survey instrument Megan uses poses twenty reference questions, but does not require an answer for any of the questions. In its place, the survey asks respondents to self-rate their ability to answer correctly a particular question on a scale of 1 to 5. When Megan views the results of her survey, she is surprised to find that the members of her reference staff believe they are much more skilled than they are, having rated themselves relatively high in all areas, but especially high in the areas of law, business, and medicine. What Megan finds surprising is that none of her staff have had any training, formal or informal, in those three subject areas, nor have they shown much interest in learning about legal, medical, or business reference. Megan's survey did not measure competencies in reference skills; it measured something else entirely, perhaps comfort levels with reference questions.

GATHERING DATA

Selecting a research design and gathering data go hand in hand. One shapes and informs the other. A well-thought-out research design is one that is clear, thorough, and logical in its procedure. Such a well-thought-out research design dictates the how, when, where, and the why of data collection. When the research design is not well-thought-out (e.g., the Megan O'Flynn example described above) or when a well-thought-out design is not implemented as designed (e.g., the Stephanie Stolta example that follows), then the research project falls apart like the proverbial house of cards.

In looking at data collection techniques, let us examine a data collection disaster. Stephanie Stolta is interested in studying non-users of the library's new online tutorial introducing the research process. Stephanie realizes that many first year students are using the tutorial as an assignment for their introductory composition class; however, after spending over nine months designing and constructing the tutorial, Stephanie is disappointed that her creative work is not getting the amount of use that she had hoped for. Stephanie is the library liaison to the College of Business, she is on good terms with the business faculty, and, because she is taking graduate courses in business as an undeclared student, she has access to the 180-plus graduate students in the MBA program. With that in mind, Stephanie decides to survey this particular population to find out why the MBA students are not using the online library research tutorial. She constructs a Web-based survey form, sends out an e-mail announcement to the MBA student electronic discussion list asking for participation, and then waits for the responses to come pouring in. Several weeks later, Stephanie notes her response rate is only 3 percent, too low to be statistically significant. Over the next two months, Stephanie mounts a determined public relations campaign, sending out two more e-mail requests and a mass mailing asking the MBA students to take her survey. Her response rate then soars to 78 percent and Stephanie is very happy indeed. Unfortunately, the library server crashes, and Stephanie loses almost half her data. She had neglected to download the survey data on a daily basis, waiting several weeks at a time before downloading.

Let us now examine some of the problems in this data collection disaster. Among other shortcomings, Stephanie's survey form has no mechanism to collect demographic data and, thus, cannot safeguard against multiple submissions. Her high response rate might be due to multiple submissions from the same individuals, but because of a flawed survey design, she has no way of knowing whether her survey results contain multiple submissions or not. Moreover, the online tutorial's intended audience does not match the survey's subjects. Seeing that the tutorial is introductory in its purpose, with the beginning academic library user as its intended audience, it is not surprising that the MBA students chose not to use it. Stephanie also neglected to ensure protection of her data set and lost half of it. Because Stephanie was neither careful nor clear-thinking in her data collection—much less her research design—she is forced to abandon her entire research project. There were multiple problems in this unfortunate project. First off, Stephanie did not have a well-thought-out research design to guide her throughout the process. Secondly, she did not properly implement the research design she chose, and, finally, she was careless in protecting the data that she did collect. All of these missteps (and the astute reader will note many more that we haven't mentioned due to lack of space) resulted in a waste of time, even though this disaster could have been avoided with a little clear-headed thinking and with, perhaps, a consultation or two with colleagues.

Also of critical importance is the testing of the data collection instrument for both reliability and validity. Arlene Fink, in her succinct way, defines both of these important terms: "A reliable survey instrument is consistent; a valid one is accurate. For example, an instrument is reliable if each time you use it (and assuming no intervention), you get the same information. . . . Valid survey instruments serve the purpose they were intended to and provide correct information" (1995, 41). Both reliability and validity must be verified before applying the treatment or collecting data. Regarding validity, let us look at an item from a typical library instruction evaluation form (see Figure 2-6). In this case, a single survey item asks not one but two questions.

Figure 2-6: Problematic Evaluation Instrument

The librarian spoke loudly and clearly.
- ☐ Yes
- ☐ No
- ☐ Don't know

Because of its duality, the question could potentially confound users. Take, for example, the presentation of Boris, a visiting librarian from Murmansk, who was more than audible in his delivery, but whose accent was so pronounced that it rendered his presentation almost incomprehensible. In the case of Boris' presentation, the assessment item in Figure 2-6 might well produce unforeseen and unwanted results, where respondents are perplexed as to how best to answer the question. Some might check the "yes" box because Boris spoke loudly; others would check the "no" box because they couldn't understand a word Boris said; still others, completely in the dark after carefully considering the question, check "don't know" because even though they heard his voice, they certainly didn't understand his words. Overall, the validity of this assessment item is questionable at best as it doesn't measure what it is designed to measure.

INTERPRETING THE EVIDENCE

Many novice researchers make the assumption that the analysis phase of the research process is all about statistics. It isn't. In the interpretation and analysis phase, the researcher seeks a big picture view of the data in order to see how it relates to the research problem. Data analysis is, in fact, the most thoughtful stage of the research process, because this is where researchers consider all of the possibilities implied by the data. They also need to examine, to the greatest extent possible, what the data do not show. Thus, this second to last step in the research process is critically important. It ought not be rushed or undervalued.

Some researchers might believe that once all the facts and figures are presented, their research work is done. Not at all. To describe what one has done in a research project without analyzing what the results mean does not resolve the research problem. In any type of data analysis, librarians need to ask very hard questions. Not only should librarian-researchers avoid making hasty assumptions, but they also ought to try to view the data from as many angles as possible. When finding unexpected results, librarians need to step back and try viewing the data through new or different eyes. Researchers should ask themselves the following questions as they interpret and analyze the data.

- Can I really know x from my data?
- Can I make the assumption that x really causes y?
- Might there be another, equally valid explanation that remains to be explored?
- If so, how might I explore that?
- Do the data and the research design support my findings?
- Have I thoroughly explored the negative findings?
- If I have not, am I giving these negative findings short shrift?
- Have I looked at all aspects or subgroups of the study?

- If I didn't find what I expected to find, have I ignored that and continued to analyze data until I found something more interesting?
- Can I completely support my generalizations with the data I have?

It is clear that honesty, healthy skepticism, an avoidance of prejudice, and a willingness to abandon preconceived opinions are essential characteristics for researchers when undertaking data analysis.

Obviously, simply gathering data and presenting it is not enough. In a case like Brad's above, collecting a healthy stack of chat reference transcriptions and regurgitating these verbatim, reporting that the librarian said this and the user said that, would leave the reader saying "so what?" The bored reader abandons the chat reference study and then moves on to a more interesting and informative one. Certainly no one wants that to happen to their research article, especially if it has not even made it into publication and is still in the peer review stage. In order to avoid this unfortunate scenario—as well as ensure the addition of something of value to the profession—researchers owe it to themselves to ask difficult questions. If they do not, their readers will ask them at a later date. To ensure that your analysis is done well, you might consider running your data by coworkers or friends who can give an honest assessment; reading in other fields to see what a different paradigmatic approach to the data would say; or presenting the project at a juried conference to gather informed feedback. All of these help researchers to finely tune their data analysis to help shape and polish the research study.

TELLING THE STORY

In describing a research project and its findings, researchers need to remember that there are several different potential audiences and environments for their research story:

- coworkers attending a staff presentation or reading an internal report on the research project
- conference goers attending their poster session or presentation
- other professionals reading their published article

In the last case, researchers should note that there are various levels of formality and hierarchy in the published professional literature. Library journals vary greatly. Some journals focus by subject or job assignment (e.g., *Cataloging and Classification Quarterly, Behavioral Sciences Librarian*); some concentrate on a specific library type (e.g., *School Library Quarterly, Journal of Academic Librarianship*), and others are more restrictive in the articles they accept (e.g., *JASIST, Scientometrics*). Some projects are not appropriate for all of these different spheres. Just because a project was well received by staff at the annual in-service training and the poster session garnered much interest at the regional library conference does not assure that researchers will be published in the next issue of *JASIST*. Also, some research projects find their natural path to publication, but not all do—and that fact should not be considered a tragedy. Moreover, some projects do make it to the publication stage but may not appear in the "most so-phisticated" journals of the profession. It is important that researchers recognize the audience for their research study.

In addition to understanding the audience, researchers should consider how to tell the story. One structures the story of one's research differently for a staff presentation than for a poster session and still differently for a peer-reviewed journal publication. That said, it should be mentioned that all research reports possess a similar structure regardless of the type of methodology employed. They begin with a literature review, then state the research question (often in the form of a hypothesis), describe the research methods and materials, present the research findings, and finally conclude with suggestions for future research. General outlines for the research report are found in so many sources that this work does not need to reproduce them in any detail. However, it is especially important for librarians who would publish to follow generally accepted guide-lines as far as citation style, page layout, and writing conventions when writing up a research report. The publication guides shown in Figure 1-2 will provide guidance in this area as well.

Most importantly, the research report should be infused with some zing that indicates the librarian's own excitement and interest. If the project were dull, lifeless, and uninteresting, the librarian would never have undertaken it in the first place. Thus, in writing up the study, it is important to share the excitement of discovering the research problem, how a hypothesis was determined, the methods employed to solve the problem, the populations that were studied, and the analysis that was employed in studying the problem. All of these need to be involving and appealing to both the writer and the reader.

REFERENCES

Booth, Wayne C., Gregory G. Colomb, and Joseph M. Williams. 2003. *The Craft of Re-search*. 2nd ed. Chicago: University of Chicago Press.

Fink, Arlene. 1995. *The Survey Instrument*. 1st ed. Thousand Oaks, CA: Sage.

Herndon, Peter, and Charles McClure. 1986. "Unobtrusive Reference Testing: The 55 Percent Rule." *Library Journal* 111 (April 15): 37-41.

Leedy, Patrick. 1989. *Practical Research: Planning and Design*. 4th ed. New York: Macmillan.

Powell, Ronald R., and Lynn Silipangi Connaway. 2004. *Basic Research Methods for Li-brarians*. 4th ed. Greenwich, CT: Libraries Unlimited.

Chapter 3

Content Analysis

Content analysis consists of procedures for defining, measuring, and analyzing both the substance and meaning of texts or messages or documents. Over the years, the definition of content analysis has evolved to embrace larger contexts. Bernard Berelson, an early pioneer of the methodology in social science research, defined content analysis as a "technique for the objective, systematic, and quantitative description of manifest content of communication" (1952, 74). Writing a half century later, Kimberly Neuendorf (2002, 10) described the methodology as primarily quantitative:

> Content analysis is a summarizing, quantitative analysis of messages that relies on the scientific method (including attention to objectivity-intersubjectivity, a priori design, reliability, validity, generalizability, replicability, and hypothesis testing) and is not limited as to the types of variables that may be measured or the context in which the messages are created or presented.

It is important to keep in mind, however, that content analysis can be either quantitative or qualitative. When researchers take a quantitative approach, they focus on numerically measurable objectives. Their research questions are typically stated as hypotheses, they use standardized instruments of proven reliability and validity, and they use inferential statistical techniques in data analysis. Although Neuendorf firmly believes that this methodology can only be quantitative, not all content analysis research concerns itself with the counting of things. Klaus Krippendorff (2004, 87) points out that "quantification is not a defining criterion for content analysis." In fact, he notes that "[u]sing numbers instead of verbal categories or counting instead of listing quotes is merely convenient; it is not a requirement for obtaining valid answers to a research question." Both quantitative and qualitative approaches to content analysis are valid and coexist within the social sciences and within library and information science research. They are simply different ways of examining the same problem. We will look at both quantitative and qualitative content analysis studies within this chapter.

Content analysis has been used in social science research for the better part of a century as a means to determine message characteristics found in a body of text. In fact, some type of content analysis has been applied to the study of texts for several centuries. Then and now, most content analysis research has focused on the news media. In the seventeenth century, the Catholic church conducted some of the earliest content analysis studies because they feared that newspapers—then a relatively new communication medium—were spreading irreligious information. In the nineteenth century, with the dramatic increase in mass-produced newspapers, many social critics conducted content analyses on the types and the tone of newspaper articles. Some studies measured the number of column inches devoted to religious, scientific, and literary topics, as opposed to stories dealing with sports, gossip, or scandal; other studies focused on the numbers of significant and wholesome stories versus those that were deemed to be cheap, frivolous, or immoral. Although early efforts in content analysis may now seem simplistic and decidedly biased, content analysis has evolved as a research methodology over the past century to become rigorous, grounded in theory, and standardized in its procedures. Throughout the twentieth century, the methodology experienced an intellectual growth as social scientists expanded their studies to different types of texts and began asking new kinds of questions. In the mid- to latter part of the last century, the methodology spread to other disciplines such as psychology, linguistics, sociology and, not surprisingly, library science.

Beginning in the 1940s and continuing for the next forty or so years, volumes of *Library Literature* indicate content analysis as a popular methodology for thesis and dissertation research. Bernard Berelson, an early pioneer in the development of content analysis as a research methodology, served as dean of the Library School at the University of Chicago from 1946 to 1951. It was primarily due to his influence, as well as overall trends in social science research during the mid-part of the twentieth century, that library science began using content analysis as a research methodology. From 1943 to 1963, 62 percent of all theses and dissertations listed in *Library Literature* used content analysis. One of Berelson's students at the University of Chicago was Lester Asheim, whose dissertation compared the content of novels and the motion pictures made from them, and conducted many other research projects that dealt with themes or social issues found in specific media (book reviews, popular magazines, children's and young adult literature).

The methodology is still one of the more popular ones within the field. In a 2004 study on research in library science, Denise Koufogiannakis and Linda Slater found that content analysis is one of the top five preferred methodologies in library science literature. (For a broad historical overview of content analysis, see Krippendorf [2004, 3–17] and Berelson [1952, 21–25], which provide a brief overview of early twentieth-century content analysis research conducted in the United States.)

In conducting a content analysis study, a text's content is revealed by looking at it in a manner different from the ordinary reading of the text. Note also that the term "text" is considered in its broadest sense. Very loosely defined, a "text" consists of any material type that communicates meaning. Consider the range of texts that can be studied using content analysis:

- *Written materials:* books, journals, magazines, newspapers, advertisements, official documents.
- *Visual items:* films, documentaries, television programs or advertisements, photographs, works of art, clothing.
- *Sound texts:* music lyrics, operas, musicals, songs, polkas.
- *Combinations of types of materials:* Web pages, performance art, or computer programs that combine visual, text, and sound elements.

The "content" of a given text is anything (words, phrases, pictures, ideas) that can be communicated within the text. To illustrate how the content is drawn out of and studied within a body of texts, take for example a hypothetical study of how Hollywood has depicted dog intelligence in feature films over the past 75 years. In this case, the "texts" might consist of all Hollywood-produced feature films with at least one dog in a main or supporting role. The content studied could be made up of actions, signals, behaviors or any other communication modes whereby canines have exhibited intelligence through their actions. Generally speaking, after defining and categorizing these "intelligence signs," researchers would then review all the films sampled, code them, and then compare content across films (the texts) to find similarities, themes, or trends. Researchers could analyze and comment on their findings either through reporting raw numbers and percentages or by pulling examples or quotes from the texts to illustrate main points. Another example of "texts" and "content" is Kuchi's (2006) study examining how and to whom academic libraries communicate their mission statements in the Web environment. The "texts" Kuchi studied were the library mission statements of the 111 Web-based Association of Research Libraries (ARL), whereas the "content" she reviewed consisted of the visibility of these mission statements (statements linked directly from the home page or linked indirectly from other pages) and the mission statements' intended audience (links to the mission statements from specific stakeholders' Web pages, e.g., students).

Drawbacks to conducting content analysis research are relatively few, but should be noted. In practice, content analysis can be time-consuming and labor intensive. Coding documents by hand requires time, patience and, often, assistance. Even if the researcher uses computer programs to count occurrences and frequencies, the computer program is only as good as the programmer who creates it and the person who uses it. Users of computer programs for analysis still must create and employ well-defined categories for coding content. Content analysis also cannot be used to make claims about motives, the meanings that individuals draw from messages, or the effects of those messages. It can reveal trends and themes as evidenced through the texts studied, but it does not show the cause or the result of those trends, themes or behaviors. Finally, and perhaps most importantly, "content analysis cannot determine the truthfulness of an assertion . . . it reveals the content in a text but it cannot interpret the content's significance" (Neuman 2003, 311).

Nonetheless, content analysis is a very attractive method for library researchers because it is nonreactive, unobtrusive, and not limited by geography. It is nonreactive in the sense that people themselves are not being studied; rather, textual evidence of their social behavior or actions is examined. It is unobtrusive in the sense that researchers are not directly studying human behavior; instead, the method looks at human-produced artifacts. This means that content analysis studies are often exempt from review by institutional review boards, or are subjected to more lenient review than studies using human subjects. (In fact, content analysis raises few, if any, ethical concerns, especially when the study uses publicly available texts.) The unobtrusiveness of content analysis also means that content analyses are free from the reactivity effects that human subjects often introduce into research studies; newspaper articles, after all, cannot shape their "responses" to match researchers' presumed intentions like people can.

Content analysis is not limited by time or space. Content analysis can be used to study the past through analysis of diaries, newspapers, or other archival-type records. In this way, it serves as an important learning tool, giving a peephole view on the concerns of people from past centuries. Because it is not confined to a specific area, researchers can just as easily study content produced on other continents as they can study content produced locally. Moreover, depending on the type of text under examination, there are few history or maturation effects even when the study is interrupted. Texts' unchanging format, coupled with the fact that most texts are portable, is very handy for researchers, who can then study the texts at any time and in any place. If Web sites are the object of examination, the researcher needs to take measures to ensure a tight data collection period because of their volatility. Web sites aside, most texts under investigation are in a fixed format and are not likely to change.

FINDING A TOPIC

Content analysis studies fall into three different broad categories: text-driven, method-driven, and problem-driven (Krippendorf 2004). Text-driven analyses arise out of the text itself and often begin without a specific research question in mind. They are exploratory in nature, seeking to arrive at a general understanding of the texts, or collection of texts, under analysis. And because they are exploratory, not setting up hypotheses to test or measures to apply, they are often qualitative in nature. Very few content analysis studies in library science are text-driven.

Method-driven analyses come from the researcher's wish to apply the methodology to previously unexplored areas. An example of a method-driven analysis would be taking a methodology developed to analyze gender roles in advertisements and applying it to ads appearing in library science publications.

A problem-driven analysis involves real world problems that reflect the concerns and issues within a discipline or a focus area. Epistemic in nature, problem-driven content analysis studies purposefully examine texts in the belief that a methodical examination of these will provide answers to research questions. Almost all content analysis research in library and information science within the past 20 years has been problem-driven, as is indicated by the fact that all the studies described in Figure 3-1 or mentioned in the following categories are problem-driven.

Figure 3-1: Studies Using Content Analysis Methodology

Dahl, Candice. 2001. "Electronic Pathfinders in Academic Libraries: An Analysis of Their Content and Form." *College & Research Libraries* 62 (3): 227-237.

> *Using guidelines developed for print pathfinders (Kapoun 1995), the researcher analyzed the content of 45 electronic pathfinders from 9 academic institutions in Canada. She examined the pathfinders for consistency of format within the institution, scope, readability, and usability, ranking the pathfinders in each of the 4 categories on a 1 to 3 scale. Findings show little uniformity among pathfinders within each institution and that pathfinders vary in their complexity and usefulness.*

Ellison, Jim. 2004. "Assessing the Accessibility of Fifty United States Government Web Pages: Using Bobby to Check on Uncle Sam." *First Monday* 9 (7). Available: http://firstmonday.org/issues/issue9_7/ellison/index.html

> *As a way of determining whether all 50 Web sites met federally-required accessibility guidelines, the researcher used two different computer programers, Bobby and Cynthia Says, to evaluate the White House, 2 government Web portals, Web sites from 15 executive branch departments and 32 federal agencies. Provides descriptive chart listing each government Web site, its url and type and severity of accessibility violations.*

Hahn, Karla L., and Kari Schmidt. 2005. "Web Communications and Collections Outreach to Faculty." *College & Research Libraries* 66 (1): 28–40.

> *Researchers looked at 149 SPARC member Web sites on collection development to see how libraries are communicating changes in their collections and issues in scholarly communication. They created a pilot survey to develop a coding scheme for the 4 categories used to examine libraries' collection development Web. Findings are reported in raw numbers and percentages, and researchers include charts showing responses to questions 1 through 3.*

Koufogiannakis, Denise, Linda Slater, and Ellen Crumley. 2004. "A Content Analysis of Librarianship Research." *Journal of Information Science* 30 (3): 227–239.

> *Researchers examined 2,664 articles published in 91 library science journals in 2001 as an effort to determine the prevalence of research within the profession's journal literature, the characteristics of the type of research conducted as well as the topics covered. Researchers performed independent assessments with high inter-rater reliability and found that a little over 30 percent of articles published were research. They list the top library science research journals, also charting study types by domain and the top 5 research journals by domain.*

(Cont'd.)

Figure 3-1: Studies Using Content Analysis Methodology *(Continued)*

McGrath, Eillen L., Winifred Fordham Metz, and John B. Rutledge. 2005. "H-Net Book Reviews: Enhancing Scholarly Communication with Technology." *College & Research Libraries* 66: 8–19.

> *Authors studied the differences between traditional and electronic book reviews by examining the length, content, style, timeliness, and format of book reviews appearing on H-Net in 2002 and found significant differences in length and review style of electronic reviews.*

Snelson, Pamela, and S. Anita Talar. 1991. "Content Analysis of ACRL Conference Papers." *College & Research Libraries* 52 (3): 466–472.

> *Authors examined the content of 181 papers presented at the 2nd through 4th ACRL conferences to determine whether papers were more research based than found in a former study where only one-third of the papers were research. Descriptive tables note the overall research content from each conference, major research goals, and research characteristics.*

Still, Julie. 1998. "Role and Image of the Library and Librarians in Discipline-Specific Pedagogical Journals." *Journal of Academic Librarianship* 24 (3): 225–231.

> *The author searched ERIC and conducted a page-by-page review of 13 of the journals to characterize and describe the image and role of librarians in 19 discipline-specific teaching journals. In the seven-year period under examination, 1990–1996, the author found that only 53 articles from the 13,016 listed in the 29 journals mentioned libraries or librarians. Excerpts from articles mentioning libraries are provided showing how the institution and the profession are portrayed within the literature.*

Further, content analysis studies tend to focus on one of three different topical areas:

- *Studies that are focused on the delivery of library services.* These range from the characteristics of interactive reference service via the Web (Bao 2003; Wells 2003), to commonalities in teaching Web-based full-text databases (Bernnard and Hollingsworth 1999), to online tutorials (Dewald 1999; Tancheva 2003), to materials for presenting scholarly communication and collection development information to academic faculty (Hahn and Schmidt, as listed in Figure 3-1). In service delivery studies, researchers are typically interested in identifying similarities, characteristics and themes in texts in order to improve or enhance the particular services within their own library that are embodied by those texts. For instance, in the Hahn and Schmidt study, the authors wished to discover how their collection management pages could be improved "to promote awareness of recent collection changes" (2005, 29). Similarly, Kornelia Tancheva (2003) examined library instruction tutorials to see how they adopted learning theory principles while she was working on designing an online tutorial for Cornell University's Mann Library.
- *Studies that are focused on specific resources commonly found in libraries.* Often viewed as the prototypical content analysis study in library science, resource-specific studies examine a particular type of work as a way to

learn more about how the resource or genre functions and to discover similarities with other types of resources. As shown in Figure 3-1, McGrath,
Metz and Rutledge's research on electronic book reviews is a good example
of a resource-specific study. They compared book reviews appearing on the
electronic distribution list H-Net over the course of one year with print
book reviews in order to determine how electronic book reviews differ from
those in traditional sources. Book reviews are frequent subjects for content
analysis studies, as are newspapers, especially online newspapers, which have
gained a lot of attention within the past few years because of the innovative
electronic functions they make available to users. Erdelez and Rioux (2000)
looked at the different ways online newspapers allow readers to share articles with others ("e-mail this article," "share this article with a friend") and
Doughy (2002) evaluated ten online newspapers using standard usability
guidelines. Web pages are another frequent subject of content analyses.
Ryan, Field and Olfman (2003) focused on state government home pages,
looking at how these changed over a five-year period, while Julie Still (2001)
studied university library Web sites from English-speaking countries.

- *Studies that are focused on the profession itself.* Like members of other professions, library and information scientists are concerned with the evolution and changing nature of their work and their workplace. Of particular
concern is the enormous impact that technology has had in libraries.
Nowhere is this concern more apparent than in the profusion of job-trend
studies using content analysis over the past 15 to 20 years (listed in Figure
3-2). Studies such as these benefit the profession as a whole because they
not only can serve as a bellwether for changes within the profession but
also signal possible changes in budget and resource allocations. These pro-
fession-focused studies also provide proof for those needing a scholarly article to point to as they make their case for an issue. In fact, critics of
library school curricula, as well as instruction librarians, have commonly
pointed to Lynch and Smith's (2001) study of academic librarian positions to bolster their claims that library school offerings do not correspond to workplace needs for computer and teaching proficiencies.

Although "[n]o single model is applicable to all content analyses" (Busha and
Harter 1980, 174), all content analysis studies do share common elements.
Pamela Snelson and Anita Talar's 1991 article analyzing ACRL conference papers
for research components serves as a good illustration of these common elements.
Nonreactive in its approach, Snelson and Talar's study analyzed all conference
papers presented at the second through fourth ACRL conferences to determine
whether or not "true" research was increasing within the profession. Each of the
181 papers analyzed served as a unit of analysis for the study. Because the total
number of papers, or units, was relatively small, the authors did not need to

Figure 3-2: Job Analysis Studies

Job Type	Description of study	Citation
Academic librarian	The authors updated Reser and Schuneman's prior work and tracked changes in the academic job market by examining 900 job ads published in 1996 from *American Libraries, The Chronicle of Higher Education, College & Research Libraries,* and *Library Journal.* Authors specifically examined differences in public, systems, and technical services positions.	Beile, Penny, and Megan M. Adams. 2000. "Other Duties as Assigned: Emerging Trends in the Academic Library Job Market." *College & Research Libraries* 61: 336–347.
Academic librarian	Authors culled 220 job ads from the March issues of *College & Research Libraries News* every 5th year from 1973 to 1998 to discover how job requirements have changed over time. Authors specifically examined behavioral skills required, degree requirements and faculty status, noting emerging trends in the need for computer and teaching skills.	Lynch, Beverly P., and Kimberley Robles Smith. 2001. "The Changing Nature of Work in Academic Libraries." *College & Research Libraries* 62: 407–420.
Academic librarian	Authors examined the differences in public and technical services positions found in 1,133 job ads published in 1988 from *American Libraries, College & Research Libraries,* and *Library Journal* and looked in particular at job skills, degree and foreign language requirements, and salary ranges.	Reser, David, and Anita Schuneman. 1992. "The Academic Library Job Market: A Content Analysis Comparing Public and Technical Services." *College & Research Libraries* 53: 49–59.
Academic librarian	Specifically addressing computer skills, the author reviewed 2,500 job ads posted every 5 years in *American Libraries* over a 20-year period.	Zhou, Yuan. 1996. "Analysis of Trends in Demand for Computer-Related Skills for Academic Librarians from 1974 to 1994." *College & Research Libraries* 57: 259–272.
Cataloger	In determining technology's impact on cataloging positions, the author reviewed 151 job ads appearing in *American Libraries* and *College & Research Libraries News* from 2000 to 2002 and specifically focused on position title, degree requirements, and necessary skills.	Khurshid, Zahiruddin. 2003. "The Impact of Information Technology on Job Requirements and Qualifications for Catalogers." *Information Technology and Libraries* 22: 18–21.
Cataloger	Studied changes in cataloging positions over a ten-year period by culling job postings in one issue per year in *American Libraries.*	Chaudhry, Abdus Sattar, and N. C. Komathi. 2001. "Requirements for Cataloguing Positions in the Electronic Environment." *Technical Services Quarterly* 19: 1–23.

(Cont'd.)

Figure 3-2: Job Analysis Studies (Continued)

Job Type	Description of study	Citation
Collection development librarian	Researcher drew on 433 job ads posted in *College & Research Libraries News* over 11 years to determine what type of skills and experience were required for collection development positions.	Robinson, William C. 1993. "Academic Library Collection Development and Management Positions: Announcements in *College & Research Libraries News* from 1980 to 1991." *Library Resources & Technical Services* 37: 134–146.
Electronic resources librarian	Author traced the evolution of the position over a 17-year period, from 1985 to 2001, through an examination of 298 jobs posted in *American Libraries*.	Fisher, William. 2003. "The Electronic Resources Librarian Position: A Public Services Phenomenon?" *Library Collections, Acquisitions & Technical Services* 27: 3–17.
Electronic resources/ digital librarian	Researchers examined 223 job ads appearing in *College & Research Libraries News* from 1990 to 2000, focusing specifically on job title, reporting line, duties and home department, in order to learn about the evolving nature of technology in academic libraries.	Croneis, Karen S., and Pat Henderson. 2002. "Electronic and Digital Librarian Positions: A Content Analysis of Announcements from 1990 through 2000." *Journal of Academic Librarianship* 28: 232–237.
Instruction librarian	Author used both qualitative and quantitative methods in examining LI positions posted over three-month period on LIBJOBS to determine skills and knowledge required.	Clyde, Laurel A. 2002. "An Instructional Role for Librarians: An Overview and Content Analysis of Job Advertisements." *Australian Academic & Research Libraries* 33: 150–166.
Preservation librarian	Authors tracked the evolution of preservation librarian positions by examining job titles, requirements, education and experience found in 116 preservation-type positions posted in five different publications over a 13-year period.	Cloonan, Michele Valerie, and Patricia C. Norcott. 1989. "Evolution of Preservation Librarianship as Reflected in Job Descriptions from 1975 to 1987." *College & Research Libraries* 50: 646–656.
Subject specialist librarian	Author studied 315 job announcements appearing in three different publications over eight and one-half years to see how the position has evolved and specifically looked at position title, ARL status of hiring institution, tenure requirements, salary range, duties, reporting line, and both required and desired education, skills, and experience.	White, Gary W. 1999. "Academic Subject Specialist Positions in the United States: A Content Analysis of Announcements from 1990 through 1998." *The Journal of Academic Librarianship* 25: 372–382.

(Cont'd.)

Figure 3-2: Job Analysis Studies *(Continued)*

Job Type	Description of study	Citation
System librarian	Author uses qualitative techniques to determine characteristics of systems librarian positions (job title, duties, skills, degree requirements, reporting line, salary) through an analysis of 107 announcements posted in *College & Research Libraries News* over a four-year period.	Foote, Margaret. 1997. "The Systems Librarian in U.S. Academic Libraries: A Survey of Announcements from *College & Research Libraries News*, 1990–1994." *College & Research Libraries* 58: 517–526.
Youth services librarian	In order to determine whether demand has increased for youth services librarians over time and whether changes have occurred in employment criteria and job duties, Adkins examined job titles, responsibilities, education, skills, and experience requirements found in 285 youth services positions posted in *American Libraries* from 1971 to 2001 in five-year increments.	Adkins, Denice. 2004. "Changes in Public Library Youth Services: A Content Analysis of Youth Services Job Advertisements." *Public Library Quarterly* 23: 59–73.

sample. They had already narrowed down their population by examining only three sets of conference papers. They were also fortunate in that a previous study by Coughlin and Snelson (1983) on a similar topic had already established coding categories and corresponding conceptual definitions that they could use. (As further proof that research can proceed by accretion, Coughlin and Snelson themselves drew on conceptual definitions and categories previously developed by Atherton (1975) in her study of the research methods employed in information science literature.) These "recycled" conceptual definitions provided the criteria by which Snelson and Talar judged whether or not the papers were research reports. They also furnished Snelson and Talar with previously validated categories by which to structure their analysis of the specific characteristics common to all of the units studied. Snelson and Talar tested inter-coder reliability, also referred to as inter-rater reliability, in a small pilot study where each researcher coded a sample of conference papers and achieved a .90 reliability coefficient. The variables in this study (the categories studied) were nominal, or non-numeric, categorical variables that cannot be counted (i.e., gender, race, religious affiliation are all nominal variables). Because they used nominal variables, Snelson and Talar used chi-square (χ^2) analysis as an inferential statistic to accept the null hypothesis of no significant increase in the number of research papers (chi-square and null hypothesis will be discussed in more detail later in the text).

However, as mentioned earlier, not all content analysis studies are quantitative, as Snelson and Talar's was; some studies are qualitative in nature. A good example of a qualitative content analysis study is Foote's analysis of job postings for systems librarians (listed in Figure 3-2). She took an inductive approach in identifying and analyzing job requirement categories for systems librarians. Some of these are not visible at the outset of the study but emerge as important concepts through careful analysis. Foote's study also features other important characteristics found in qualitative studies: a relatively small sample size, no statistical measures employed, and findings reported in raw numbers and quotations for the text. For a more in-depth description of the differences between quantitative and qualitative research see Chapter 4.

FORMULATING QUESTIONS

Serving as a guide to the overall research design, the well developed research question provides the infrastructure for the entire research project. Content analysts typically formulate research questions that can have several possible solutions and that deal with previously unobserved phenomena within the text studied. Like many other methodologies, a content analysis study frequently presents one or more hypotheses in addition to the research question. A hypothesis differs from a research question. A hypothesis is a declarative statement that predicts a relationship between two or more variables, while a research question asks about an observed reality. Consider these research questions and corresponding hypotheses drawn from content analysis research in library and information science:

- *Research question:* "Have requirements for entry level positions become more stringent or lax over time?"
  Hypothesis: "Over time, employers require more experience and knowledge that cannot always be gained from library school" (Sproles and Ratledge 2004, under "Methodology").
- *Research question:* To what degree has the U.S. government met its goal of rendering its Web pages accessible to people with disabilities?
  Hypothesis: The United States government has met Section 508 accessibility guidelines for all of its Web pages (Ellison 2004, Figure 3-1).
- *Research question:* Which job announcements are more likely to require that candidates possess an advanced subject degree, technical services or public services librarian positions?
  Hypothesis: "Public services jobs are more likely to require advanced subject degrees" (Beile and Adams 2000, 337, Figure 3-2).
- Research question: Do library and information science research papers differ from their science counterparts?
  Hypothesis: Library science conference papers differ from their science counterparts by being less likely to include a problem statement, literature review, hypothesis, research methodology, findings and conclusions. They are, therefore, less rigorous. (Snelson and Talar 1991, 468, Figure 3-1).

Not all content analysis research in library and information science contains formal hypotheses; however, researchers should have a hypothesis for such a project before conducting it even if they do not state it, or state it only informally. Hypotheses, whether they are stated or unstated, formal or informal, help guide the researchers' reading of the texts. Similarly, even where content analyses have hypotheses, they may report their data in raw numbers and percentages without employing tests of statistical significance to test these hypotheses. Such is the case in Cloonan and Northcott's (1989) article on the evolving role of the preservation librarian, as well as in Laurel Clyde's review of instruction librarian positions. Both studies deal with small data sets and both explore the subtle, but significant, changes in two different librarian positions over time.

An important element in developing research questions and hypotheses is the formulation of conceptual definitions for the variables within the study. Without solid, well-thought-out descriptions of categories and carefully devised coding procedures, content analysis is weak. These categories are classes of characteristics, topics, or themes that recur regularly enough to be quantified and described. Content analysts either rely on standard definitions or create their own definitions for categories. Wherever possible, researchers try to use standard definitions to increase the validity of their own research and heighten its reliability. Koufogiannakis, Slater and Crumley (2004), for example, employed a previously developed taxonomy of six separate subject domains (reference, education, collections, management, information access, retrieval and marketing) to classify the topics in library science research articles published in 2001 (described in Figure 3-1). However, where standard definitions do not exist, researchers must construct their own. For example, in studying how academic libraries communicate their mission statements via the Web, Kuchi (2006) created definitions and categories for direct links from the library main page; indirect links from the library main page; and the labels used to identify the link to the mission statement. Regardless of whether researchers create their own definitions for categories or rely on standard definitions, it is essential that the definitions be exhaustive and mutually exclusive. This is because the definitions form the basis for the codes, which will be later applied to the data set. If clearly defined categories are absent in a study, the project loses its conceptual framework and, essentially, loses its raison d'etre. For similar reasons, good definitions are required for the researcher to implement an objective and systematic counting-and-recording procedure that produces "a quantitative description of the symbolic content in a text" (Neuman 2003, 211).

DEFINING THE POPULATION

Population definition actually occurs at several steps within a content analysis research project. It is sometimes inherent in the topic selection mechanism when the study is purposely limited by date, by type of text, or by group within the research question. Dahl (2001) uses population definition as a way of simultaneously selecting a topic by focusing on electronic pathfinders from nine Canadian libraries (listed in Figure 3-1). By looking only at *electronic* pathfinders, she has narrowed down the entire universe of pathfinders to focus on those appearing in a specific format. Even more specifically, Dahl looks at Web-based pathfinders—not all electronic pathfinders. She further defines her population to include pathfinders from "the library web sites of top ranking Canadian universities according to the annual ranking conducted by *Maclean's* in 1999" (Dahl 2001, 229). She thus limits her focus by geographic region as well as institution type. (Moreover, her use of a well-recognized external source such as *Maclean's* helps to ensure the validity of her project.) Similarly, Hahn and Schmidt in their analysis of faculty outreach and communication on collection development Web pages narrowed their population early on by asking their research question only of Scholarly Publishing and Academic Resources Coalition (SPARC) member Web sites. (SPARC was developed by the Association of Research Libraries and is "an alliance of universities, research libraries, and organizations" whose purpose is to serve as a "constructive response to market dysfunctions in the scholarly communication system." www.arl.org/sparc/about/index.html.) They singled out SPARC member institutions, in part because SPARC members are at the forefront of addressing major issues in scholarly communication but also because they recognized that this group was small enough (149 members at the time of the study) to comprise a workable dataset.

However, not all content analysis studies in library science simultaneously define their populations at the research question development phase. Ellison's (2004) study, for example, asked how well U.S. government Web sites complied with Section 508 accessibility guidelines. Even with this question (which was limited to U.S. government Web sites as opposed to all Web sites), Ellison still needed to further define the population because of the high number of U.S. government sites. He ultimately used purposive sampling (see below) to select 50 home pages—chosen to reflect a balance between executive departments—from the approximately 20,000 U.S. government home pages (2004, Under "Methodology").

Even when topic selection does not also determine population selection, the topic under examination guides the library researcher in limiting the population. The job trend studies listed in Figure 3-2 limit their populations by position type as well as by time period and by publication. Zhou (1996) pulled job ads appearing only in *American Libraries* over a 20-year span; Clyde (2002) limited her analysis to job ads posted on the electronic distribution list, LIBJOBS, for three months; Beile and Adams (2000) selected a year's accumulation of academic library job ads published in four major professional journals. One might wonder why these authors took three separate approaches when addressing similar research questions. Researchers typically limit the time period for the practical reason of not wishing to collect more data than they can possibly analyze. If studying the ways a particular job has evolved over a period of time or if looking at how the demand for particular skills within job positions has evolved, researchers often opt for a lengthy time span because the passage of time is an integral component of the research study as a whole. On the other hand, if researchers are comparing the skills and knowledge needed in a specific job title, the date range is not as important as is collecting many advertisements for the same job type. Again, the research question drives the data collection method!

When content analysts are faced with studying a large population and must satisfy the need for generalizabilty, they often select a representative sample to study. Before doing so, a sampling frame is created. This frame consists of all the items within the population from which the sample will be drawn. Researchers should always consider the way they order their initial list, or sampling frame. Will the sampling frame be in alphabetical order? If not, will the list have any order at all? Will the order of the list have a significant impact on sampling if the order is not standardized? From this frame, content analysts draw their sample either randomly or non-randomly (see Chapter 7).

Among random sampling methods, content analysts have several choices:

- *Simple random sampling* is similar to a lottery, or drawing items out of a hat. Content analysts might list each item in their sampling frame on a separate slip of paper, put the slips in a container, and withdraw slips one by one until they have enough for their sample. Or, using a less whimsical method, they might number all items within the sampling frame and use a table of random numbers to select units.
- *Systematic random sampling* is where the researcher selects every *nth* unit. In his study of the increasing need for computer skills in the library workplace, Zhou (1996) selected librarian position advertisements appearing every five years over a 20-year period. Lynch and Smith (2001) similarly examined only the March issues of *College & Research Libraries News* at five-year intervals over a span of 25 years to study the changing nature of academic positions.
- *Cluster sampling* occurs when a researcher selects a specific set of texts and then studies all the units within that set. An example of cluster sampling is Still's 1998 study (listed in Figure 3-1) on how librarians and libraries are depicted in discipline-specific pedagogical journals. To find mentions of libraries or librarians, Still searched a predetermined list of 29 pedagogical academic journals (i.e., *History Teacher, Journal of Chemical Education,* etc.) in the *ERIC* database using the truncated keyword *library?* She then conducted a page-by-page analysis of over seven years' worth of 13

randomly selected journals from the original set of 29 to discover any mention of libraries.

- *Stratified sampling* is employed when content analysts wish to divide up the sampling frame into categories in which they are interested. For example, Bao (2003) took all 1,402 institutions of higher education in the U.S. and, using the Carnegie Foundation's classification scheme, first divided these institutions into three major categories and then, within these major groups, further divided them into categories of public or private to arrive at six stratified categories. From these categories, Bao applied proportional sampling based on the total number of institutions in each category.

Two main types of nonrandom sampling methods are employed in library and information science content analysis research.

- *Purposive sampling* entails making a judgment regarding which units to include in a study. Ellison (2004) used this type of sampling when he selected 50 U.S. government Web sites to see if they met accessibility guidelines. He chose the 50 Web sites for his sample by first dividing all U.S. government sites into three general categories (Web portals, federal agencies, and executive branch departments). He then selected Web sites from each of these three categories based on the percentage of Web sites represented by each. He rounded out his selection of two Web portals, 15 executive branch departments, and 32 agencies by adding the White House. Johnson (2003) also used her own judgment when she decided to examine 70 different academic library instruction Web sites. Taking a Google-like approach, Johnson compiled her list of Web sites based on the activity level of instruction librarians as evidenced through their electronic discussion list postings, presentations at discipline specific conferences and professional service at the national level. Thus, Johnson's list was made up of Web sites from academic libraries with high producing, high energy library instruction librarians. On the surface, Johnson's choices might seem questionable. However, her research study was project-oriented. She was developing a library instruction Web site for her institution and chose Web sites created by a group of peers she admired and wished to emulate. Like Johnson, researchers using purposive sampling must plausibly justify their selections so that they are credible.
- *Convenience sampling* consists of using what is readily available. This raises an obvious question of whether this is really sampling at all, since the whole concept of sampling entails choosing to include or exclude items. Because convenience sampling does not make these choices, it is questionable whether the texts under analysis are representative of the phenomena as a whole. Despite concerns about the representativeness of

convenience samples, though, there are reasons researchers might use them. Sometimes researchers cannot obtain a random sample because the population they are sampling is so small that they must resort to analyzing the only items they can find. Such was the case in a cheat sheet study conducted several years ago by faculty at Troy State University (Pullen, Ortloff, Casey and Payne 2004). Intrigued by frequently finding discarded cheat sheets in various public areas (such as garbage cans) near and around their building, the authors began to collect the cheat sheets, cataloging the time, date, and location of their discovery. Cheat sheets do not represent an easily obtainable, public data set like Web sites or job announcements. Thus, because of the nature of the content studied, the authors made a compelling case for adopting a convenience sample. They also admitted that their study was not completely generalizable because "the sampling method used is easily contaminated by external biasing factors such as the researcher's daily travel pattern, and unknown differences in inclination that students in different disciplines have to use cheat sheets" (Pullen et al. 2004, 619).

SELECTING A RESEARCH DESIGN

Content analysis research design begins with choosing units of analysis to study; constructing a coding scheme for these units; and developing an enumeration system, in the case of quantitative analyses. Generally known as operationalization, many of the basic procedures used in selecting a research design and measurement instruments in other types of research apply equally to content analysis. What sets content analysis apart from other methodologies in research design is coding construction. For this reason, this section deals primarily with coding and codebooks, their construction and execution.

As previously discussed, the sampling unit consists of texts selected for analysis. These sampling units might be Web pages, pathfinders, job advertisements, cheat sheets, conference papers, databases, or a myriad of other types of texts. The unit of analysis, or variable, is what is actually counted and measured. A unit of analysis can be the same as or smaller than the sampling unit, but it can never be larger than the sampling unit. For example, Dahl's (2001) sampling unit consisted of 45 electronic pathfinders. Her units of analysis comprised four different "best practices" characteristics in pathfinders: consistency, scope, readability, and usability. The variables measured in Dahl's study are the four pathfinder characteristics. Similarly, Ellison (2004) used predetermined categories enumerated in Section 508 of the U.S. Rehabilitation Act as his unit of analysis.

Once the units of analysis are determined but before coding any text, the content analyst must carefully develop and clearly define all variables to be analyzed. Each conceptual definition for a variable will then become part of the codebook. Not all studies can draw on established conceptual definitions like Dahl and Ellison were able to do in their studies. Sometimes researchers need to create their own conceptual definitions because none exist. In these scenarios, researchers take an investigative, testing approach in identifying variables to study and in developing their codebooks and coding procedures. Such is the case in the code definitions shown in Figure 3-3. These particular definitions, which in turn formed the codebook for the study, originated in a transaction log study that examined the types of repair strategies online catalog users employ to fix their search errors (Turner and Beck 2002). The codebook charts out, in shorthand form, the types of repairs used by those searching a library online catalog, providing codes and explanations for each category. This was an exploratory study, evolving from a preliminary set of online catalog transaction logs where the researchers noticed interesting patterns in the ways users tried to recover from their search errors. Consequently, the repair strategy categories as shown in Figure 3-3 did not originate from a standardized external source of repair strategies.

Although many content analysts create their own unique categories that are specifically designed to meet the needs of the particular texts they are studying, this type of approach requires that the researchers start from scratch. This approach may appeal to highly creative and control-oriented researchers, but it has several drawbacks. Despite achieving high coding reliability coefficients (see Chapter 5), the study itself remains unique and is not comparable to others. In order to make contributions to existing knowledge, content analysts might be better off relying on previously applied and successful conceptual definitions.

The codebook is an instructional guide for coders, as well as a record of the entire coding project. A good codebook ensures that coders can complete their task with relatively few problems. It also helps guard against inconsistencies over time and among coders. Certainly the codebook can and should be modified as the lead researcher and the coders redefine any murky categories.

The hypothetical codebook shown in Figure 3-4 represents a job trend analysis research project loosely based on a 2001 study by Lynch and Smith. Note that all variables (job category, year posted, institutional classification, degree requirements, and so on) are fixed and finite. For example, under "Degree Requirements" only four responses are possible. Although some categories contain an "unable to determine" coding, all categories are fully described with only one logical way to code each.

Thorough coder training is a very important step in ensuring both the quality and the replicability of the project. The content analyst needs to formulate clear instructions for coders so that they are not only working together but also thinking alike.

Figure 3-3: Sample Categories for a Study of Online Catalog Search Repair Strategies

Level	Code	Type	Example
Word *(Repairs occur at word level only)*	WS	Spelling/Word Stem Change	multi-meter → multimeter 18th → eighteenth agriculture → agricultural
	WP	Plural/Singular	duns → dun group → groups
	WC	Capitalization	Doll → doll
	WY	Synonym	logging → deforestation
Concept *(Repairs involve the concept[s] searched. A concept is typically multi-word or else is a phrase and can be multi-concept)*	CP	Punctuation: Add/drop punctuation	city of ladies → "city of ladies" women's intentions → womens intentions
	CB	Broaden: Drop concept/word	How to use a digital multimeters → digital multimeters
	CC	Change to another concept	Decline and Fall of Rome → Edward Gibbon
	CN	Narrow: Add concept/word	"puerto rico" → "puerto rico""English" pizan → pizan city of ladies
	CR	Rephrase	Ireland travel → Ireland guidebook
Search *(Repairs show knowledge of search types or knowledge of specific functions within search types)*	SI	Invert words/names	Edward Gibbon → Gibbon, Edward
	SA	Add/drop article	A Doll House → Doll House
	ST	Switch search type	A Doll House (Subject) → A Doll House (Title) tf 140 s73 (Keyword) → tf 140 s73 (Call Number)
	SL	Limit search	Home care → home care (limited to specific library location) Africa → Africa (limited to media type—videotapes)
	SB	Switch field in Boolean search/divide phrase into two fields/combine into one field	Norway (title) → Norway (subject) Management consulting (keyword) → consulting (keyword) AND management (keyword) Japan (subject) AND family life (subject) → family life in Japan (subject)
Other	R	The exact same search is retyped	Ibsen, Heinrik → Ibsen, Heinrik

Figure 3-4: Sample Codebook

Academic Job Analysis

Unit of data collection: Each academic librarian job ad posted between 1980 to 2005 that appeared in at least one professional publication

Job number: Fill in the job number as listed on the photocopy

Coder name: Fill in your name

Date: Today's date

Job category: Indicate the job category based on the title; if that isn't possible, base it on the content of the ad

1. Administrative (deans, directors, associate university librarians)
2. Administrative Other (personnel officer, grants, public relations, fund raising)
3. Head of a subject library
4. Department head
5. Reference (general and subject specific)
6. Instruction
7. Outreach/Distance education
8. Technical services (acquisitions, serials, cataloging)
9. Collection development
10. Specialty areas (government documents, maps, special collections, archives, rare books, media)
11. Systems (information systems, network, automation)
12. Other

Year posted: List the year of the job ad

1. 1980   4. 1995
2. 1985   5. 2000
3. 1990   6. 2005

Institutional classification: Assign institutional classification based on *The Classification of Institutions of Higher Education* by the Carnegie Foundation

1. Research Universities   4. Baccalaureate Colleges
2. Doctoral Universities   5. Associate of Arts Colleges
3. Master's Universities

Degree requirements: List the degrees required

1. None listed   3. ALA accredited MLS
2. MLS, ALA accreditation   4. Second Master's degree
   not specified

Professional experience required: List, if any, number of years of professional experience required

1. None, entry level   4. 5 or more
2. 1–2   5. Unable to determine
3. 3–5

Preferred degrees: List degrees preferred

1. None listed   3. ALA accredited MLS
2. MLS, ALA accreditation   4. Second Master's degree
   not specified   5. Doctorate

Faculty status: Note whether or not position has faculty status

1. Yes
2. No

If this does not occur, their results will not be comparable. In order to make sure that the study is replicable, coder instructions should include:

- descriptions of all training materials used
- job descriptions for all coders listing any qualifications required
- operational definitions for all variables and their categories with examples on how to identify them and distinguish one category from another
- copies of all forms used in the study (e.g., coding form, spreadsheets, etc.)

While it is best to keep the codebook succinct to guard against possible coder exhaustion (discussed later in this chapter), it is also better to specify too many categories for a given variable than too few. Defining as many categories as possible before gathering the data ensures that researchers do not have to define categories halfway through the coding process, when doing so would be time-consuming and require backtracking—and could even call into question the entire research design. (Note also that the hypothetical codebook shown in Figure 3-4 relies on external, standard definitions for institution type, drawing on types as outlined by the Carnegie Foundation. Researchers strengthen and increase the validity of their research design by relying on conceptual definitions or frameworks that have been previously tested or are widely recognized as standard sources.)

An important factor in codebook design and in developing clear and sensible coding sheets is the enumeration for each variable. All of the variables and specific categories outlined in the codebook in Figure 3-3 and the coding sheet in Figure 3-5 are nominal, meaning that the numbers assigned to each category have no true numerical value. Nominal variables comprise just one type of measurement scale used in content analysis.

There are four levels of measurement in content analysis research, given in order of complexity:

- *Nominal scale* is the lowest level of measurement and consists of a set of categories that are distinct from one another. Numbers are representative and are only used for labeling purposes. Other methods such as letters or words could also be applied. For example, the codebook in Figure 3-3 uses letter codes instead of numbers. Also, the numerical ordering is unimportant. Gender is an excellent example of a nominal variable. It has no numerical value but it can be assigned a number in cases where a researcher wishes to measure gender in relation to other variables.
- *Ordinal scale* is made up of a set of categories that are rank-ordered on some type of continuum. Although the numbers do not always indicate equal distance between categories, in an ordinal scale, each point is ranked "more than" or "less than" other points on the scale. A teacher who separates essays into three piles ranging from very good/excellent to poor/atrocious while grading is essentially using an ordinal scale.

- *Interval scale* also represents an ordering of categories, but one that reflects the distance (or interval) between categories within that ranking. Categories in interval scales are represented by numbers that can be calculated in the normal, mathematical sense. An interval scale assumes that all points, or categories, on the scale are equidistant. Examples of interval scales are test scores, years of experience, and annual salaries.
- *Ratio scale* is not used much in the social sciences but is worth mentioning when discussing measurement scales. This type of scale always has a zero value, whereas the other three scales do not require it. Also in a ratio scale, the points or categories are precise multiples of other points on the scale. Age is an example of a ratio scale. Zero age is possible in humans: babies, when they are born, are at age zero. Equally possible is calculating averages and ratios with human age. For instance, a researcher might want to calculate the average age of first-year librarians in a demographic profile of entry level librarians within a specific job or within a specific library type.

The sample codebook in Figure 3-4 represents relatively simple manifest coding, where few, if any, texts analyzed require judgment calls about categories (e.g., institutional classification, degree requirements, year posted) because these categories are present in the data. But what about situations where the researcher is studying latent content or its underlying structure looking for implicit markers within a text? An example of latent content is where the category is not spelled out in the data (such as job title, year posted, degree requirements), but relies upon the coder's judgment in assigning it to a specific category. In coding latent content, how do researchers go about constructing well-defined variables and creating clear and consistent guidelines in their codebooks?

Dahl's pathfinder study is a good example of possible answers to these questions. She analyzed electronic pathfinders according to four variables (consistency,

Figure 3-5: Sample Coding Sheet

Academic Job Analysis
Job Number _____   Coder Name _____
Date _____
Job Category (1–11) _____
Year Posted (1–6) _____
Institutional Classification (1–6) _____
Degree Requirements (1–4) _____
Professional Experience Required (1–5) _____
Preferred Degrees (1–5) _____
Faculty Status (1–2) _____

scope, readability, and usability) previously defined by Kapoun in his 1995 analysis of print pathfinders. For the first variable, consistency, all pathfinders from a specific institution were compared and ranked by how closely these institution-specific pathfinders shared the same design characteristics, document structure, reading level and audience. Only Dahl (2001) decided the level of consistency, making holistic judgments based on coding guidelines, not on concrete matches in the data such as those found in the codebook shown in Figure 3-3. For the other three variables, pathfinders were examined and ranked individually using a three point ordinal scale, with one as the lowest score possible. For each category, coders assigned a one when the pathfinder was judged to be poor overall, assigned a two when the pathfinder showed both positive and negative aspects, and assigned a three when the positive aspects outweighed the negative. Dahl's study demonstrates how researchers can use variables representing latent content—those that require value judgments—in deciding whether a text contains or does not contain certain values and converting these to a numerical scale.

GATHERING DATA

Quality control is of utmost importance in gathering and coding data analyzed in content analysis research. Because the primary goal of content analysis is to identify and document relatively objective characteristics of a text, reliability is vital. Most library and information science content analysis studies use human coders who, in turn, could possibly introduce subjectivity in their coding. Therefore, content analysts need to take steps to reduce coding problems, such as subjective coding. And it is not just the problem of the *possibility* of human coder subjectivity that needs to be guarded against but also the *appearance of the possibility of subjectivity*. If researchers do not take care of these issues, red flags of suspicion may be raised by peer reviewers, colleagues, and readers. Additionally, if researchers cannot establish reliability for the measure, the validity of that measure is also in question because, while reliability does not guarantee validity, it is a necessary condition for validity. In the context of a content analysis study, reliability is often obtained through conducting agreement-tests between coders. The higher the agreement, the stronger the reliability.

It is precisely because of these quality control issues that content analysts wish to achieve acceptable levels of inter-coder reliability. Content analysts want to achieve a basic validation of their coding scheme or their measurement tool, so that different coders can arrive at similar results time after time. Therefore, in any good content analysis study, even if the lead researcher does all the coding, she must also conduct a reliability test with a second coder. Otherwise, the resulting measures could be deemed idiosyncratic, subjective, and merely the end result of one coder's interpretation. Failure to validate the coding scheme can undermine the entire project.

What is an acceptable level of inter-coder reliability? Unfortunately, content analysts do not agree on this point. Neuendorf (2002) lists varying interpretations from leading social scientists in her discussion of five different rules of thumb for acceptable inter-coder reliability levels. While most analysts generally accept coder agreements of .90 or higher, there is little, if any, agreement regarding the acceptability of those falling below .80, and agreements below .70 are suspicious enough to warrant that researchers undertake steps to ensure a higher agreement level.

Inter-coder reliability tests are frequently used in both the pilot and final phases of the research process. If the pilot test uncovers problems in the coding scheme, then the scheme needs to be revised, and results from the pilot study are not included in the final analysis of data. In the final phase, inter-coder reliability is conducted on a randomly selected sample, and the results of this test are then reported in the results. This test also represents the coders' overall performance. Both tests are important and serve different purposes. The pilot reliability test helps to identify poorly formed or poorly communicated variables in the codebook. If the pilot test shows reliability problems, the researcher needs to take one or more of the following steps to remedy the problem:

1. Initiate more coder training that includes providing further definitions of and concrete examples for the problematic variable.
2. Rewrite the codebook instructions to clarify how that problematic variable is measured.
3. Combine categories within a problematic variable.
4. Dissect the problematic variable into two or more distinct and understandable variables.

However, no number of remedies can equal good coder preparation. Coder training is especially important because it helps to synchronize the coders with the overall project. It also helps to fine tune the coding scheme, giving it higher viability. Revisions to the coding scheme at the pilot stage are often inevitable. Content analysts need to be aware of threats to reliability and deal with them if they arise. Four of these are outlined in Figure 3-6 along with suggestions on how to deal with these pitfalls. The first two listed constitute the most frequently encountered pitfalls. Fortunately, a need for more training and coding scheme revisions are two problems that are easily solved. The final pitfall described in Figure 3-6, that of the rogue coder, is one that all researchers wish to avoid. Happily, it is also one that does not occur very often. Content analysts should only remove the coder from the study as a last resort.

Two common methods of calculating inter-coder reliability are shown in Figure 3-7. The first method, percentage agreement, is used with nominal scales and is the most popular coefficient used to calculate inter-coder reliability, probably because it is easy to calculate and is widely accepted. One of its disadvantages, though, is its inability to account for chance agreement. It also requires a precise

Figure 3-6: Coding Pitfalls

Problem	Remedy
1. Insufficient or ineffective training	Ensure that coders undergo several training sessions and practice coding text prior to the pilot test. In these sessions, address misunderstandings and clarify procedures, making sure that all coders have a solid understanding of all definitions, all categories, and are familiar with the project.
2 Inadequate or incomplete plan	Create a carefully worded set of instructions and ensure that your categories are thoroughly defined. Test these with coders at practice sessions. Implement changes in the plan, as needed, both before and after the pilot test.
3. Exhaustion	Be sure that you are not asking your coders to do too much. Consider and guard against situations like tackling too much during one session or giving them unrealistic time frames. Build some breathing room into your schedule.
4. Rogue coders	Ensure you and your coders are in sync. Sometimes a coder cannot code reliably even after many training sessions and alterations in the coding scheme. If this happens, it is best to get a new coder.

match in scoring. Two different coefficients, Scott's *pi* (Scott 1955) and Cohen's *kappa* (Cohen 1960), provide ways for the researcher to calculate agreements that are beyond chance for nominal scales. Other coefficients such as Spearman's *rho* and Pearson's correlation coefficient are used for ordinal, interval, and ratio measurement scales. Readers wishing to use these calculations should consult a text on descriptive statistics. Alternatively, Kimberly Neuendorf's *Content Analysis Guidebook* (2002) provides excellent instructions on calculating these coefficients.

What happens in cases where an acceptable level of reliability cannot be achieved for a specific variable even after all reliability testing has been completed? Let's say that the content analyst has made several changes to the coding scheme, has conducted many training sessions for the coders, and has calculated inter-coder reliability coefficients for all data. However, time after time one particular variable consistently achieves a coefficient of .30 or less. What then? In these troubling scenarios, content analysts have two options: get rid of the variable entirely, or completely rewrite it with better defined categories. Although neither may be easy, researchers need to prepare themselves for the possibility of this rather infelicitous event and know how to deal with it. If this does occur and the variable is removed from the study, the researcher needs to address this issue in the research report and describe how the problem was handled.

Finally, content analysts need to consider the time frame in gathering and interpreting data, especially when working with Web pages. As a freely available

Figure 3-7: Inter-coder Reliability Coefficients

1. Percentage Agreement

Two coders have coded 10 different repair strategies according to the codebook shown in Figure 3-5.

The formula is $PA = A/n$ PA= Percentage agreement
  A = Number of agreements
  n = Total number coded

Unit	Coder A	Coder B	Agree?
1. marine environmentalists (keyword) → marine conservation (keyword)	CR	CR	Y
2. marine conservation (keyword) → marine conservation groups (keyword)	CN	CN	Y
3. marine conservation groups (keyword) → marine conservation groups (keyword)	R	R	Y
4. marine conservation groups (keyword) → marine conservation group (keyword)	WP	WP	Y
5. marine conservaton (keyword) → ocean conservation (keyword)	CR	CR	Y
6. decline and fall (keyword) → Edward Gibbon (author)	CC & ST	CC & ST	Y
7. Edward Gibbon (author) → Gibbon, Edward (author)	SI	SI	Y
8. 1880 and Norway (subject) → Victorian and values (subject)	CR	CC	N
9. Victorian and values (subject) → "A Doll House" (subject)	CP & CC	CP & CC	Y
10. "A Doll House" (subject) → "1880 and history" (subject)	CC	CC	Y

Total n=10   9 (Y)

Percentage Agreement = A/n = 9/10 = .90 agreement (90%)   1 (N)

2. Holsti's method (1969)

In the same study as above two coders have each coded the same 1,002 search repairs.

They agreed on 989 analysis units.

Holsti's formula is $PA = 2A/(n_1 + n_2)$

A = Total agreements
n_1 = total units coded for coder 1
n_2 = total units coded for coder 2

Percentage Agreement = 2,989 / (1,002 + 1,002) = .987 agreement (98.7%)

data repository, the Web is an excellent data choice for a nonreactive research project, and many library and information science researchers have mined Web data for their content analysis studies. However, the Web and its contents constitute a non-fixed medium. It goes without saying that Web pages are volatile; their content changes just as the society that produces them changes. Because of Web instability and mutability, researchers need to acknowledge this constraint and take measures to gather Web data consistently and all within the same time frame. Examples of content analysts heeding this very important limitation are common in the literature:

- "To gauge the comparison fairly, all data were collected during April 2000, as a reflection of Web sites at one given time. Data collection over a longer period of time might be muddied by changes in Web design" (Still 2001, 162).
- In a study of common characteristics found in Web-based interactive reference services in academic libraries, "the author accessed a sample of university and college home pages and 'virtually' visited each institution's library home page between March 16 and May 11, 2001" (Bao 2003, 253).
- "To assess the frequency with which SPARC member sites were providing information on local collection changes, all members' library Web sites were surveyed between October 2003 and February 2004 using the membership list posted on the SPARC member Web site" (Hahn and Schmidt 2005, 30).
- "In December of 2003, the home pages of 50 Federal Web sites were evaluated with the online version of Bobby 5.0, using the Section 508 evaluation option" (Ellison 2004, under "Procedures").
- In a study of the design characteristics of ready-reference and e-mail reference pages on the Web sites of 110 academic libraries in the Association of Research Libraries, "data were gathered during the week of February 8 to 12, 1999" (Stacey-Bates 2000, 66).

INTERPRETING THE EVIDENCE

Content analysis studies typically report findings in terms of raw numbers, percentages, and frequencies. A few of the studies that we have examined in this chapter contain formal research hypotheses and employ statistical tests of significance to test these hypotheses (Snelson and Talar 1991; Sproles and Ratledge 2004; Beile and Adams 2000). Most library and information science content analysis research, however, does not include these formal research characteristics. This may be due to a number of reasons: the study may be more practitioner-oriented, the data set may be too small for tests of statistical significance, or the study may be exploratory or problem-driven.

All reports of findings must directly address the research question. Koufo-giannakis, Slater, and Crumley used simple bar graphs to describe findings for each of their research questions. Their bar graphs showed the top ten library journals publishing research articles, the number of articles by type of research performed, and the number of articles by area of focus. Similarly, Hahn and Schmidt used simple tables noting the different ways libraries inform faculty about library collection changes. In these tables, they also list every method of communication and how many libraries employ these. For example, in one of their tables that addresses the particular types of information that academic libraries communicate to faculty regarding library collections (information on gifts, on the approval plan, on the materials budget, on digital collections), Hahn and Schmidt (2005) list every information type they encountered (23 in all) and provide percentages reflecting how many sites overall offered that information type. Bao also presents his findings on the presence of Web-based interactive reference services as percentages and does so in table format. Turner and Beck's (2002) search repair study reported its findings in tabular format, as shown in Figure 3-8. Even researchers using qualitative methods in their content analysis research employ numbers to point out trends or changes or similarities within their datasets. Cloonan and Norcott (1989) took a qualitative approach to data analysis in their study of the evolving nature of preservation librarianship because of wide variance in preservation position titles and because their sample size was too small to apply statistical tests. Even so, throughout their interpretation of the data, Cloonan and Norcott discuss their findings numerically.

In all of the above examples, although the researchers display their findings in table format, the bulk of their analysis is devoted to explanations and interpretations within the text. And this is where researchers need to think seriously before committing to hasty pronouncements as to "why" the data indicate a certain tendency. In the findings from the search repair study shown in Figure 3-8 (with the referring codebook shown in Figure 3-3), Turner and Beck were initially surprised that over 50 percent of all search repairs occurred at the concept level. Concept level repairs are where searchers semantically alter their search by broadening, narrowing, or changing concepts. Concept level repairs reflect cognitive level decision making, where searchers rephrase or refocus their perception of what they are looking for. However, in looking at the results a bit more closely, Turner and Beck (2002) noticed that 27 percent of the time, searchers employed one specific type of repair: changing the search type. This involves keeping the same search but adjusting the search from, for example, a keyword to a title search. Upon further examination, they found that most searchers were changing their search type from a keyword search to other types of searches. This finding drove the authors to examine other reasons why searchers were moving from the broader keyword search to more specific search types and

Figure 3-8: Results Reported in Basic Frequencies

	Repair Code	Repair Type	% of all Repairs	TOTAL (n=1002)
Search Repairs by Repair Type				
Word Level Repairs	WS	Spelling	8.2%	82
	WP	Plural/Singular	1.3%	13
	WC	Capitalization	2.3%	23
	Total Word Level Repairs		11.8%	118
Concept Level Repairs	CP	Punctuation: Add/drop punctuation	3.0%	30
	CB	Change to broader concept	11.8%	118
	CC	Change to another concept	10.4%	104
	CN	Narrow: Add concept/word	13.2%	132
	CR	Rephrase	14.6%	146
	Total Concept Level Repairs		52.9%	530
Search Level Repairs	SI	Invert words/names	2.3%	23
	SA	Add/drop article	0.9%	9
	ST	Switch search type	27.2%	273
	SL	Limit search	2.2%	22
	SB	Boolean Syntax Change	2.7%	27
	Total Search Level Repairs		35.3%	354

forced them to look at areas such as search screen design for the online catalog, as well as the display order and explanations of all the search types available.

The few content analysis studies in library and information science that do employ tests of statistical significance almost all rely on chi-square tests. Chi-square measures whether there is an association between nominal (non-numeric) variables. In their study on changing requirements within the academic library job market, Beile and Adams (2000) used chi-square to test several of their hypotheses, all of which dealt with whether technical or public services job announcements are more likely to require a specific skill or experience. They found statistically significant differences between technical and public services positions in computer skills and additional educational requirements but did not find statistically significant differences in other areas examined. These findings, coupled with their use of a statistical measure, helped to strengthen the

Beile and Adams study. Chi-square is discussed more in depth in other chapters within this book, but it is a fairly easy statistic to calculate. In fact, it is one of the few that can be easily calculated on a handheld calculator.

TELLING THE STORY

Content analysts can rely on major content analysis texts (Krippendorff 2004; Neuendorf 2002), as well as general texts on social science research methods, to guide them in writing up their research and displaying their data. They have many interesting examples to draw on in discussing their findings and need not limit themselves to the traditional structure of discussing their findings one by one in relation to each research question. When content analysts choose to present their findings visually in tables, graphs or charts, it is important that the visual displays chosen clarify and enhance findings. Nothing is worse than including visual information that is unintelligible. If using abbreviations in tables due to space restrictions, make sure to include a key or legend explaining these. It is best to follow regular conventions in reporting statistical findings. Knowledge of these conventions is easily picked up through reading of content analysis literature.

Because content analysis deals with coding texts, inclusion of sample coding sheets is highly recommended and descriptions of coding categories is a must. These need not be elaborate, especially when researchers are using preexisting standards or guidelines. But in cases where researchers are constructing their own categories and corresponding definitions, such as the study represented in Figures 3-3, 3-7, and 3-8, researchers owe it to their readers, as well as to the integrity of the study, to describe their categories in detail. These can be represented in appendices or in figures. This inclusion of authentic research documents helps present as complete a picture of the research project—given space limitations—as possible. If researchers have taken a qualitative approach, such as Cloonan and Norcott (1989) did in their analysis of preservation librarian job announcements (described in Figure 3-2), they need to describe and summarize their categories as thoroughly as possible so that readers gain a deeper understanding of the study. In describing the variance in job announcements, Cloonan and Norcott gave verbatim examples drawn from the job announcements text to illustrate these variances.

Although it may go without saying, any research report must provide convincing evidence that the results can be reproduced. Many scholarly journals require proof of the reliability and statistical appropriateness of the research findings. Content analysts can assuage many concerns or doubts on the part of readers by clearly explaining reliability measures taken in coding the data set. They also need to establish validity for any inferences they draw by making convincing arguments and by retracing their steps in the research process, justifying their decision making all the while. Content analysts can expect that their findings may be received with some skepticism if they have not explained their procedures in a clear and organized fashion. Even though they perceive their findings to be clear, valid, and obvious, it is highly likely that not all share that view; therefore, content analysts need both to anticipate these doubts and to offer conclusive arguments for the validity of their inferences.

REFERENCES

Atherton, Pauline. 1975. "Research in Information Science: An Assessment." In *Perspectives in Information Science: Proceedings of the NATO Advanced Study Institute on Perspectives in Information Science*, 1973, edited by Anthony Debons and William J. Cameron, 665–683. Leyden, Netherlands: Nordhoff.

Bao, Xue-Ming. 2003. "A Study of Web-based Interactive Reference Services via Academic Library Home Pages. *Reference & User Services Quarterly* 42: 250–256.

Berelson, Bernard. 1952. *Content Analysis in Communication Research*. New York: Free Press.

Bernnard, Deborah F., and Yolanda Hollingsworth. 1999. "Teaching Web-Based Full-Text Databases: New Concepts from New Technology." *Reference & User Services Quarterly* 39: 63–70.

Busha, Charles H., and Stephen P. Harter. 1980. *Research Methods in Librarianship: Techniques and Interpretation*. New York: Academic Press.

Cohen, Jacob. 1960. "A Coefficient of Agreement for Nominal Scales." *Educational and Psychological Measurement* 20 (1): 37–46.

Coughlin, Caroline, and Pamela Snelson. 1983. "Searching for Research in the ACRL Conference Papers." *Journal of Academic Librarianship* 9 (1): 21–25.

Dewald, Nancy H. 1999. "Transporting Good Library Instruction Practices into the Web Environment: An Analysis of Online Tutorials." *Journal of Academic Librarianship* 25 (1): 26–32.

Doughy, Roger. 2002. "Evaluating Online Newspapers Using Established Web Design Guidelines." Master's thesis, University of North Carolina.

Erdelez, Sandra, and Kevin Rioux. 2000. "Sharing Tools on Newspaper Web Sites: An Exploratory Study." *Online Information Review* 24: 218–228.

Johnson, Anne Marie. 2003. "Your Virtual Front Door: Making Your BI Website Welcoming and Valuable to Faculty and Students." In *Managing Library Instruction Programs in Academic Libraries*, edited by Julia K. Nims and Eric Owens, 97–100. Ann Arbor, MI: Pierian Press.

Kapoun, Jim. 1995. "Re-thinking the Library Pathfinder." *College & Undergraduate Libraries* 2 (1): 93–105.

Koufogiannakis, Denise, Linda Slater, and Ellen Coumley. 2004. "A Content Analysis of Librarianship Research." *Journal of Information Science* 30 (3): 227–239.

Krippendorf, Klaus. 2004. *Content Analysis: An Introduction to Its Methodology*. 2nd ed. Thousand Oaks, CA: Sage.

Kuchi, Triveni. 2006. "Communicating Mission: An Analysis of Academic Library Web Sites." *Journal of Academic Librarianship* 32 (2): 148–154.

Lynch, Beverly P., and Kimberly Robles Smith. 2001. "The Changing Nature of Work in Academic Libraries." *College & Research Libraries* 62 (5): 407–420.

Neuendorf, Kimberly. 2002. *The Content Analysis Guidebook*. Thousand Oaks, CA: Sage.

Neuman, Lawrence W. 2003. *Social Research Methods: Qualitative and Quantitative Approaches*. 5th ed. Boston: Allyn and Bacon.

Pullen, Robert, Victor Ortloff, Saundra Casey, and Jonathon B. Payne. 2004. "Analysis of Academic Misconduct Using Unobtrusive Research: A Study of Discarded Cheat Sheets. 2004." *College Student Journal* 34: 616–625.

Ryan, Terry, Richard H. G. Field, and Lorne Olfman. 2003. "Evolution of US State Government Home Pages from 1997 to 2002." *International Journal of Human-Computer Studies* 59: 403–430.

Schmidt, Dean, and James Swanton. 1980. "Qualifications Sought by Employers of Health Sciences Librarians, 1977–1978." *Bulletin of the Medical Library Association* 68 (1): 58–63.

Scott, William A. 1955. "Reliability of Content Analysis: The Case of Nominal Scale Coding." *Public Opinion Quarterly* 19: 321–325.

Sproles, Claudene, and David Ratlege. 2004. "An Analysis of Entry-Level Librarian Ads Published in *American Libraries*, 1982–2002." *Electronic Journal of Academic and Special Librarianship* 5 (2–3). Available: http://southernlibrarianship.icaap.org/content/v05n02/sproles–c01.htm (accessed May 17, 2007).

Stacey-Bates, Kristine K. 2000. "Ready-Reference Resources and E-mail Reference on Academic ARL Web Sites." *Reference & User Services Quarterly* 40 (1): 61–73.

Still, Julie. 2001. "A Content Analysis of University Library Web Sites in English Speaking Countries." *Online Information Review* 25: 160–164.

Tancheva, Kornelia. 2003. "Online Tutorials for Library Instruction: An Ongoing Project Under Constant Revision." In *Learning to Make a Difference: Proceedings of the Eleventh National Conference of the Association of College and Research Libraries, April 10–13, 2003, Charlotte, North Carolina*, edited by Hugh A. Thompson, 267–279. Chicago: Association of College and Research Libraries.

Turner, Nancy B., and Susan E. Beck, 2002. "Search and Rescue: Repair Strategies of Remote Users Searching the Online Catalog." Paper presented at the eighth annual Reference Research Forum, American Library Association Conference, Atlanta. Available: http://ala.org/ala/rusa/rusaourassoc/rusasections/rss/rsssection/rsscomm/rssresstat/search.ppt (accessed May 17, 2007).

Wells, Catherine A., 2003. "Location, Location, Location: The Importance of Placement of the Chat Reference Button." *Reference & User Services Quarterly* 43 (2): 133–137.

Chapter 4

Interviews and Focus Groups

Since the 1920s, interview research, be it conducted individually or with groups, has been a core methodology in social science research. Initially, researchers at the University of Chicago used interviews to answer big picture questions about the human condition. It was not until after World War II, however, that interview methodology experienced a split between quantitative and qualitative approaches. During that time many researchers, especially those in market research, political science, and mass communication, took the macro view, focusing on survey research techniques that gathered opinion data from a cross section of respondents. This particular branch of interview research stressed the use of non-biased sampling methods and employed tightly structured, fixed response questionnaires for its data collection instruments. Meanwhile, anthropologists and sociologists, taking the micro view, continued to further refine qualitative interviewing techniques wherein researchers engaged participants in conversations as a way to explore and understand the topic from their point of view. Within the field of interview research, both quantitative and qualitative approaches continued to grow apart, developing their own characteristics and techniques. (Platt [2001] provides a basic overview of the history of interview research methods.)

In this chapter, we focus on the qualitative approaches to interview research methodologies, noting their use in library science research. Before jumping into the particulars of interview and focus group methodology, though, we first need to examine qualitative research, investigate its purposes and uses, and note how it differs from quantitative research.

Qualitative research is "an inquiry process of understanding based on distinct methodological traditions of inquiry that explore a social or human problem. The researcher builds a complex, holistic picture, analyzes words, reports detailed views of informants, and conducts the study in a natural setting" (Creswell 1998, 14). Qualitative research takes a sense-making approach to interpreting data and phenomena. The desired outcome of a qualitative study is to understand how people think about processes. To put it another way, in a qualitative research project, researchers attempt to capture people's explanations for how things happen. For example, a researcher might examine a situation within a specific culture and then attempt to explain how it is understood, interpreted, and experienced by that group. Often referred to as naturalistic research because it studies phenomena in their natural settings (as opposed to laboratory settings), qualitative research uses language, not numbers, as its primary data source. Case studies, interviews, personal experiences, focus groups, observations, and think-aloud protocols all use both participants' and researchers' words and phrases as their main data sets. Within a qualitative study, field work is a key tenet in data gathering. The researcher, as primary data collector, mingles with, is among, and is part of the study's participants. A qualitative study takes an inductive approach, looking at specifics to make generalizations. It does not start with a big picture view of reality that it imposes on the situation. Rather, a qualitative study creates its view of reality by aggregating the pieces of that reality which participants provide. A qualitative study is context-specific because the research is conducted within the environment in which the phenomenon occurs and the participants reside.

Good qualitative research uses rigorous data collection and analysis procedures. A fundamental characteristic of qualitative research is "evolving design" (Creswell 1998, 21) that presents multiple realities. It also differs from traditional, "scientific" research studies in two significant ways. First, in qualitative research the researcher is the primary instrument of data collection. Second, the focus of the research is the participant's viewpoint. Because of this focus on the intimate, on human experiences and behaviors, researchers often write up their study in an informal personal style so that readers feel they are "in the picture" with the participants. Figure 4-1 provides an outline of essential characteristics of qualitative research.

Researchers choose a qualitative approach because their topic and their research question demand it. Answering "yes" to any of the following eight questions should prompt library researchers to strongly consider qualitative research (Creswell 1998, 17-19):

1. Does your research concern a "how" or "what" question? These types of questions seek in-depth descriptions or explorations of processes or situations. For example, a research question that asks, "How do high school students use the Web to find information for their assignments?" (Lorenzen 2001, listed in Figure 4-5), provides a good basis for a qualitative research project.

2. Is your research project a close-up analysis instead of the panoramic view that is typically found in quantitative studies? Kuhlthau's study (1988) of high school seniors' library research processes is one such microscopic study. She focused on 26 students enrolled in two advanced placement

Figure 4-1: Qualitative Research Characteristics

Naturalistic—Data collection occurs in natural settings, where humans reside and not in laboratories or any other "un-natural" settings.

Researcher is part of the project—The researcher is the primary instrument in data collection. An external instrument such as a test or a treatment is not the primary method of data collection.

Linguistic/descriptive data—The data set consists of words and sometimes visuals but generally not numbers.

Emergent theory—The research design is not a priori. Theories or hypotheses are not established beforehand; rather, these arise out of the data analysis.

Process oriented—The research design focuses on the process as well as the outcome. In qualitative research, the researcher wants to know how things happen.

Inductive data analysis with a focus on specifics—The interpretation is idiographic, with analysis conducted on the particulars of a case or situation rather than on generalizations.

Concentrates on participants' views, behaviors, actions—The point of the research is to understand multiple realities, in how humans make sense of their lives, their perceptions, and their realities.

Informal writing style—The researcher reports the study in an informal style, often using the first person narrative to put the reader directly into the research story.

English classes at the same high school. Here, Kuhlthau learned a good deal from a small group instead of taking a broader approach with a much larger population, in which she could have learned a little about a larger number of students.

3. Do you have enough time and resources to dedicate to data collection? Qualitative research can be a time-consuming, detail-oriented project, requiring access to audio taping and transcription equipment and mandating a well-organized data storage method.

4. Will your project "work" only if conducted in a natural setting? If you took participants out of their usual environment, would the study be flawed? Again, Kuhlthau's study explored high school students' library research activities within the natural setting of their school library media center. If she had interviewed them in foreign surroundings, such as an impersonal conference room distant from school grounds, she might not have gathered the rich data that she was able to retrieve.

5. Do you wish to bring yourself into the narration of the study? Some people do, because they are acutely conscious of how the researcher's identity shapes the research process. If you don't, don't let your answer put you off. Not all qualitative research tells the research story in the first person. Many studies refer to the primary researcher as "the author."

6. Are you willing to participate actively in data collection? Would you accept taking on the role of student in exploring and explaining your findings from a participant's viewpoint?
7. Are you conducting this research project because no theories exist that explain participant behaviors or phenomena?
8. Is your discipline and its readership open to and interested in a qualitative approach? A quick glance at the current scholarship in library and information science indicates that, yes, qualitative research is a recognized approach that has a place at the table in library and information science research.

Another way to define qualitative research is to contrast it with its quantitative cousin. Although both are currently accepted and respected methods of inquiry, this was not always the case. As in any situation where new movements challenge traditional views, the dominant forces try to quash the insurgency. This was the case with qualitative methods that differed from the traditional positivist view. Resorting to marginalization and ridicule, tactics that Lyotard (1984) labels intellectual terrorism, those in both camps advanced criticisms of their opponents that often dissolved into "four legs good, two legs bad" disputes. Although most of those arguments are in the past, differences between qualitative and quantitative methods are substantial and deserve to be examined.

Quantitative research differs from qualitative research greatly in its overall approach, philosophy, and methods. Known as the scientific method and also referred to as *positivism*, quantitative research is objective, uses deductive techniques, tests hypotheses, and employs instruments that reduce data to numbers. The experimental studies profiled in Chapter 6 are quantitatively based. These employ a priori research designs that the researchers follow throughout the projects. In a quantitative study, researchers often use data collection instruments that result in numerical data. Data sets are frequently subjected to statistical tests to determine whether there is a significant relationship between variables. In contrast, qualitative research uses an open and evolving plan that is flexible and can be adjusted throughout the research process. That is not to say that qualitative research is without rigor in its methodology and analysis. Rather, it uses different techniques to realize that rigor. Most often, researchers collect several different types of data so as to be able to view the research problem from multiple perspectives. In interview and focus group research, researchers ask open-ended questions as their method of data collection so that the participants shape the research. Because researchers have questions about the life worlds of their respondents, they must allow their respondents to express themselves fully in order to study those worlds. In contrast, a quantitatively based survey or poll is tightly controlled and uses pre-selected responses. And just as a survey or questionnaire is not the best instrument to use when researchers wish

Figure 4-2: Quantitative and Qualitative Methods Compared

Quantitative Methods	Qualitative Methods
Objective	Subjective
Deductive	Inductive
Tests hypotheses	Uses grounded theory
Employs instruments that reduce data to numbers (multiple choice instruments, structured questionnaires)	Employs instruments that produce linguistic information (unstructured interviews, focus group responses, observations, usability tests)
Results reported as numbers, statistics	Results reported in words and phrases
Researcher is removed, distant	Researcher is involved, often becoming part of the community studied
Research design fixed from the beginning and is typically not adjusted	Research design evolves and adapts as needed throughout the research process

to examine fully a group's thoughts on a situation or a concept, it follows that an intense and lengthy one-on-one interview is an unsuitable method to learn about who is the preferred political candidate for a specific office.

It helps to think of research methods as a toolbox from which the researcher selects the appropriate tool to fit the research problem. When researchers are faced with research questions requiring a close, in-depth view of a phenomenon that can be explained only by questioning or observing one or several different participants, a qualitative approach is warranted.

Researchers who conduct qualitative research are particularly vulnerable to questions regarding ethical conduct because their research almost exclusively involves humans, either individually or in social groups. Although many of these ethical issues are discussed in-depth in Chapter 10, they need additional mention here. First of all, in dealing with human participants, researchers need to guard against deceiving or harming participants in any way, either purposefully or inadvertently. Deception can take the form of not informing participants of:

- any risks involved in participating in the research project
- the nature of the research project
- the identity of the researcher

These last two points were hotly debated in academic circles recently with the publication in 2005 of Cathy Small's book, *My Freshman Year*, an account of Small spending a year as an undergraduate and interviewing students about their lives as a way to understand undergraduate behavior and attitudes, a phenomena the author found increasingly perplexing. Small wrote under the pseudonym of Rebekah Nathan. Her true identity was revealed within less than a year of the book's publication by a reporter at the *New York Sun*. The nature of the research and self-disclosure controversies arose because Small did not reveal her true identity to the students she interviewed. For obvious reasons, she did not say, "Hi, I'm Dr. Cathy Small, on leave from my faculty teaching job for a year to do research on undergraduate behavior and values. Can I ask you some questions?" She did, however, tell students that she was conducting a research project on undergraduate life and that she was going to publish her findings. Some have argued that because she was enrolled as a freshman and taking classes, her life situation directly contradicted her revelation of conducting a research project. According to Small's critics, her fellow students really believed that Small *was* a student. Thus, her conducting *publishable* research was entirely implausible to them, meaning that they "consented" to be interviewed with the view that these interviews likely meant nothing. Although she revealed her identity to one student who questioned her research project and she told a few students with whom she had developed close friendships who she really was, Small deliberately chose not to reveal her identity. Supporters of Small argue that Small had received clearance from her institution's research board to go forward with the project as well as support from her university's administration. Additionally, none of the students interviewed have objected.

Certainly this is not a cut-and-dried case of an ethical research lapse, but it is one worth bearing in mind. Those defending Small's semi-disclosure note that "[p]articipant-observation is like life, dynamic and changing. As in human relationships, sometimes you do keep secrets" (Farrell and Hoover 2005, 36). Others take a harder line, believing that Small could have achieved the same results even if she had disclosed herself. Because she violated the "informed" component of "informed consent," they counter that her entire study is cast in a questionable light. This controversy shows us that extra care should be taken in any type of research that deals with human subjects. When in doubt, err on the side of caution.

One of the most egregious ethical violations a researcher can commit is revealing a respondent's identity to the public at large or to other interested parties who have some control over that person's well-being, livelihood, or domestic or public situation. Consider the following ethical issues researchers must consider when conducting studies involving human subjects:

- *Revealing information about participants* that could possibly cause psychological, social, or economic harm. For example, in a hypothetical study researching library staff members' knowledge of and dedication to the library's new strategic plan, a staff member might reveal job search plans and activities that could be detrimental to the employee if the researcher provided this information to supervisors without masking names or other potentially identifying information.

- *Courts can subpoena research data.* Researchers should keep this point in mind when deciding on the questions that they ask (for example, questions regarding downloading music on library computers or wholesale photocopying of library materials not yet in the public domain) and how they store their data for future retrieval.
- *Confidentiality protections may be in place* that constrain the collection of sensitive data.
- *Data should be well organized and stored securely.* Data must be stored so that it can be easily retrieved and also in such a way as to ensure against damage or loss. Researchers need to have a logical and well-planned storage scheme and need to make back-up copies of computer and paper files.

With a general understanding of qualitative research, we will now turn our attention to interview and focus group research methods. When first established as a research method in the early part of the twentieth century, interviewing was merely a purposeful method to secure information about individuals or about other people or situations known to the participant (Odum and Jocher 1929, 366). Soon after, researchers looked beyond the basic reporting-out function of interviews, finding other benefits:

> The personal interview is penetrating; it goes to the "living source." Through it the student . . . is able to go behind mere outward behavior and phenomena. He can secure accounts of events and processes as they are reflected in personal experiences, in social attitudes. He can check inferences and external observations by a vital account of the persons who are being observed. (Young 1939, 175)

Interview research can be divided into two different types: structured and unstructured. A structured interview is often referred to as survey or questionnaire research, where researchers ask questions in a fixed order with predetermined responses as choices. The interview is short in duration, typically lasting no more than half an hour. The questions are written in advance, and the researcher reads these verbatim to respondents, also providing them with fixed response choices. One of the aims in structured interview research is to gather a large unbiased sample with a low margin of error so that the results are generalizable, representing a larger group at a fixed point in time. Structured interviews are commonly used in market research and political polling, as well as in social science research in general. Structured interviews are a quantitative method and are numbers based. Although not covered in-depth in this book, much has been written about the design and execution of structured survey interviews. Figure 4-3 lists several excellent sources to consult when designing such a project.

Unstructured interviews use a qualitative approach. The interviewer asks open-ended questions and allows participants to respond in their own words.

Figure 4-3: Suggested Works on Survey Research

Buckingham, Alan, and Peter Saunders. 2004. *The Survey Methods Workbook: From Design to Analysis*. Cambridge, UK: Polity Press.

> This interactive book is divided into three parts: "Research design," "Data collection," and "Data analysis." The authors assume no prior background with conducting surveys or knowledge of statistics. A good starting point.

Fink, Arlene. 2003. *The Survey Kit*. 2nd ed. Thousand Oaks, CA: Sage.

> Each of the slender volumes in this ten-volume set provides the basics in conducting survery research of all types. They guide the researcher in writing survey questions, interview techniques, sampling, reporting, and many other topics.

Nardi, Peter M. 2003. *Doing Survey Research: A Guide to Quantitative Methods*. Boston, MA: Allyn and Bacon.

> Writing at the introductory level, Nardi guides the reader through the entire research process.

Patten, Mildred L. 2001. *Questionnaire Research: A Practical Guide*. 2nd ed. Los Angeles, CA: Pyrczak Publishing.

> Patten initiates the reader in good survey research practice, showing how to plan for a project, write quality questionnaire items, effectively test items and select a respondent population, analyze and communicate data through tables and figures, and craft written reports of research.

These in-depth and intensive interviews may be a half hour to three hours in length. Like structured interviews, unstructured interviews typically use scripted questions. The similarity ends there. During an unstructured interview researchers need not repeat the question verbatim. Overall, the goal is to have a conversation in which researcher and respondent explore a topic as thoroughly as possible given both the limits of time and the conversants. Gorman and Clayton (2005, 127) further divide unstructured interviews into three different types:

- *Standard*—In this type of interview, the interview script or schedule requires researchers to pose the questions verbatim and in exact order so that answers can be compared across all respondents. Because the interview schedule is rigid, the interview session may be somewhat inflexible and lack spontaneity. If the topic under discussion is a delicate one, the interviewer may lose out on eliciting important data because the respondent might not feel comfortable about revealing information without additional questioning that departs from the interview script.
- *Guided*—The guided interview schedule lists specific areas to focus on, but the actual wording of questions is not controlled. This allows interviewers to ask questions in any manner they feel can best communicate the topic and elicit rich responses. With guided interviews, the conversational flow is more relaxed and natural, and researchers can gather very detailed information.

- *Exploratory*—The exploratory interview is the most unstructured of the three types. It consists of an informal conversation where the questions arise through the discussion of a topic or series of topics. In this type of interview, the topic leads the conversation more than the interviewer does. Because an exploratory interview is so unstructured, it requires that the researcher be fairly experienced in the techniques of both interviewing and data collection.

Focus group interviewing has its foundations in the pioneering methods of social scientists Paul Lazarsfeld and Robert K. Merton in their studies at Columbia University during World War II of audience reactions to military training and wartime propaganda films. Merton and Kendall (1946) and Merton, Fiske and Kendall (1956) continued to perfect the method in the years following the war; Merton (1987) provides a detailed personal account of the birth of focus groups.

Soon, this methodology was embraced by market researchers. The focus group interview is still a primary data gathering method for researchers of consumer product preferences, but it has also been adopted by researchers in the fields of education, health care, public policy, communication studies, and other fields, including library science.

A focus group is a type of interview that has its own specifications and uses. It is designed to uncover insights and perspectives from a small group of participants that are not retrievable by other methods. It allows participants to express themselves in their own words in describing their behavior, beliefs, viewpoints, and preferences. Almost always made up of a selected, homogenous sample, a focus group session is conducted by an experienced moderator who leads participants in a discussion using a sequenced script of questions that address very specific, predetermined topics. Optimally, focus group moderators channel the ebb and flow of the discussion, acting as deft and benign conversation traffic cops and demonstrating limited, but firm, control over the discussion as they move it from one topic to another. The goal of a focus group session is to discover both *what* people feel and *why* they feel that way. Most often, focus groups are exploratory sessions that seek to examine, in detail, participants' perceptions of services, situations, people, or products so that researchers can evaluate how their views shape behaviors. A focus group study generates a range of opinions, experiences, and viewpoints from its participants. A focus group study is qualitative in nature and may be used both as a primary and as an ancillary research method.

Focus group research is also inductive because its primary tenets are exploration and discovery. This is evident in its earliest use in library science research when, in the early 1980s, researchers began using focus groups to study subject retrieval in online catalogs (Kaske and Sanders 1980). A few years later, Markey (1983) employed focus groups to explore respondents' general perception and use of online catalogs. Since that time, focus group interviews have been conducted fairly frequently in library science research. Most studies fall into two broad groups:

- *Product development studies* that concentrate on gathering users' impressions of resources or new services. In a system improvement study, Connaway, Johnson and Searing (listed in Figure 4-6) asked users to evaluate their library's online catalog. Crowley, Leffel, Ramirez, Hart and Armstrong (listed in Figure 4-6) took the same approach and convened focus groups to help them understand why users found the library's Web site so confusing. Similarly, Henner and Charles (2002) asked groups to discuss their information needs as a way of developing a Web site for public health professionals. And Leighton, Jackson, Sullivan and Dennison (2003) asked both students and faculty for their thoughts in redesigning the navigational structure of their library's Web site.
- *Library service evaluation* is another area appropriate for focus group research. As a way to determine whether the library was meeting user needs, Massey-Burzio (featured in Figure 4-6) asked six different user groups to think back and talk about their thought processes and activities while using the library. Young and Von Seggern (listed in Figure 4-6) asked users to talk about the services they used to gather information in order to ascertain whether their library was current in technology. D'Esposito and Gardner (1999) and Chase and Alvarez (2000) both explored participants' usage of the Internet as a research tool.

Focus groups provide instant feedback for library researchers who are exploring new ideas or services. The data collected can be highly detailed, and the environment gives researchers the flexibility to probe and clarify participant responses, to ask follow-up questions, and to pursue side topics as they arise. Focus groups have high face validity because they gather real life data in a realistic setting. They are synergetic in execution as participants' responses typically play off one another.

Focus groups are a good choice for speedy data collection since the length of a session is relatively short, lasting between one and a half to three hours. Considering the time involved in most qualitative studies, devoting only several hours for a session is a small time commitment. They provide an excellent opportunity to collect a large number of viewpoints on a topic within a relatively short time frame. Focus groups also can provide a relatively low cost solution in terms of time, energy, and money compared with one-on-one interviews. If using a professional moderator, however, focus groups can be costly.

FINDING A TOPIC

Interview research is an excellent method to use when tackling research problems that explore respondents' beliefs, experiences, opinions, or knowledge structures since the most obvious way to find out someone's views is to ask them. Questions such as "what factors contribute to teaching faculty members supporting library instruction?" (Manuel, Beck and Molloy 2005) or "how do the elderly go about finding information and do the resources they use differ depending on the type of information they are seeking?" (Wicks 2004) both explore topics from the respondents' viewpoint in order to arrive at a more robust and detailed understanding of the situation. Essentially, interviews help researchers investigate causation—why people behave a certain way. Interviewing is also useful when little or no research has been done on a topic, or when not much is known or understood about a specific group. For example, Barrett, in the study described in Figure 4-5, found that while faculty and undergraduates' information seeking habits had been examined in great detail, graduate students' behaviors had not yet been studied. Because graduate students represent a significant percentage of academic library users, Barrett chose to focus on this particular group to find out whether their information seeking habits were distinct enough to separate them from undergraduates and faculty. Other advantages to using interview research are that researchers get immediate responses to their questions and can adjust their thinking about their research topic as they collect data. This instant response is not possible with more structured interviews, such as mail or Web surveys, because responses often trickle in while the researcher is engaged in other activities. Another benefit of in-person interviews is the ability to collect a great deal of data rather quickly, especially when audio taping the interview.

As with any methodology, library researchers should consider some of the disadvantages before undertaking interview research. The research question may not lend itself well to this particular method. For example, when Topsy Smalley (2004) wanted to determine whether high school students whose schools have library media teachers do better in a library research course than students enrolled in schools without librarians, she did not interview the students about their experiences. Instead, she examined objective measures and compared students' grades and class rankings. Researchers should also avoid using interviews when they cannot gather a group of individuals to interview. Potential respondents may not have enough time, the topic may be sufficiently controversial to scare off participants, or the researcher may not have access to a particular group. For example, conducting in-person interviews or focus groups with storytime participants, aged one to three, might be a challenge insofar as gathering reliable data or even gathering comprehensible data!

Another reason not to use interviews is that researchers have limited time or funds. Transcribing and then analyzing taped conversations is time-consuming and can be expensive. After transcribing, researchers must sift through a huge amount of data to pick out the salient points. Finally, researchers should carefully consider trends within their discipline and their readership before embarking on an interview project. If one's reading audience or discipline shows a marked preference for quantitative research studies, then a qualitative interview will neither inform nor impress.

Focus groups are used as both a stand alone method and in combination with other research methods. (For a lengthy discussion of the uses of focus group research in library and information science, see Connaway [1996]). Focus group interviewing has been a particularly appropriate method in library science research because of its concentration on participant perspectives. Focus group interviewing provides an immediate feedback loop and thus lends itself to studying specific user groups, to testing out new services or products, and to evaluating those already established. Focus groups can also replace questionnaires or surveys in studying user preferences. They are particularly useful in needs assessment and community analysis. Library researchers can use focus groups as a way to study groups not easily reached, such as non-library users, specific minorities, or even children (provided they are able to talk intelligibly). Essentially, any research project with the aim of understanding both what people think about a topic and why they think that way is an appropriate candidate for a focus group study.

Some of the practical difficulties of focus groups are the difficulties of scheduling a time for the focus group and problems with recording equipment. A good moderator who is skilled in social dynamics and facilitating conversations is of utmost importance. Sometimes one participant will dominate the group, not allowing others to talk or persuading group members to think in a certain way. Focus groups have a tendency towards "groupthink" in cases where most or all participants are risk averse and do not wish to disagree or to reveal their true thoughts. There is also the possibility of two or more members taking a strong dislike to one another. A skilled moderator should be able take care of all of these problems. Results from a focus group study are typically not generalizable; however, there are ways to control for this problem, and we will explore them later in this chapter.

There are several types of research studies in which focus groups are not especially useful. First of all, it is not always useful to build consensus among group members—especially when the act of orchestrating agreement counteracts the real purpose of the study, that is, eliciting everyone's opinions and impressions. It is also not a useful instructional method, nor is it a good way to test participant knowledge or abilities. Researchers certainly would not use a focus group to make statistical inferences. In cases where confidentiality of any sort is of utmost importance, a focus group is not appropriate. If participants do not trust the sponsoring agency, a focus group would probably not yield rich data because of participants' fear of disclosure. Finally, focus groups should not be used to study a highly controversial or emotionally charged topic. Take, for example, a situation in which a university library must offset a 12 percent budget

Figure 4-4: Benefits and Drawbacks of Interview and Focus Group Research

INTERVIEWS	
Benefits	**Drawbacks**
• Immediate response to question • In-depth exploration of topic • Investigates causation • Personal emphasis in data collection • Speedy data collection	• Labor intensive • Lacks selectivity • No anonymity • Potential bias creep
FOCUS GROUPS	
Benefits	**Drawbacks**
• High face validity • Low cost (unless using an expensive professional moderator) • Highly detailed data • Synergetic • Flexible	• Potential scheduling hassles • Problems with dominant personalities • Deciding what is a typical group • Non-generalizable results • Potential technological glitches • Possibility of groupthink • Possible effects from a bad moderator • Possible high costs with incentives and expensive professional moderator

cut mandated by the state legislature. To achieve that unfortunate goal, the library has developed a novel approach—they will be canceling all serial subscriptions directly linked to the top grant-producing academic programs and their respective faculty. Since these folks bring in the most dollars, they can divert a percentage of their research dollars to fund their serial subscriptions for the library. In this hypothetical scenario, the university library would do well *not* to convene a focus group of academic faculty, and especially not one made up of faculty receiving the most research dollars through their grant efforts. Just picture the outbursts in such a group and the angry letters to the school newspaper.

Within the field of library science research, qualitative interviews and focus group studies have been used increasingly over the past 20 years. Interview research has most often been used to study specific user groups and their behaviors, but it has also been applied to studies of non-user groups. For instance, Jean Major's study, as listed in Figure 4-5, analyzes librarians and their relations with academic faculty.

Interview research generally arises from researchers asking themselves specific "why" questions about a population or topic or incident. These questions can originate in several ways. If we take a look at the origin of several studies we see that our library researchers came from a variety of departure points to arrive at their research topics:

- *On-the-job research project:* Seamans (2002) wanted to find out how freshmen acquire and use information during their first year so she could effectively design relevant instructional programs and offer appropriate services. Her research study, listed in Figure 4-5, grew out of a combination of an on-the-job information gathering project (i.e., designing a program) and her dissertation topic.
- *Challenging popular assumptions:* Shoham (1998) investigated a long-held belief that libraries charging fees for service will suffer a decline in service. Shoham's study focused on Israel, where public libraries typically charge a fee to borrow books. Antell (listed in Figure 4-5) challenged commonly held beliefs regarding college students' preference for using public libraries, instead of their academic library, for their research projects.
- *Thought-provoking question from a job interview:* During a job interview, Walter (in press) was asked at what point he ceased to be a teacher and became, instead, a librarian. Puzzled because he still saw himself as a teacher, he decided to explore how librarians think of themselves as teachers and how they develop a "teacher identity" as opposed to a librarian identity.
- *Critiquing the critics:* In reaction to library instruction critics' charge that librarians should not teach the research process or are doing a poor job of teaching it, Fister (listed in Figure 4-5) decided to interview the students themselves to discover the processes they undergo when engaged in a research project.
- *Outgrowth of another research project:* Valentine (listed in Figure 4-5) reanalyzed data collected in a study conducted several years previously, following the thematic threads of students' beliefs, activities, and behaviors regarding research strategies.
- *Mandate from a professional organization:* In response to a 1991 charge from ACRL that sought to promote outreach to teaching faculty, Major (listed in Figure 4-5) began her research on mature librarians' collegial relationships with academic faculty.

Major's study provides a solid example of characteristics typically found in a qualitative interview study. Major wanted to study a phenomenon that she had noticed in her professional life: successful relationships between academic faculty and librarians. She wished to gain an in-depth understanding of how these relationships evolve and thrive, so she chose to interview 18 mature librarians, asking them about their relationships with academic faculty. During her interviews, she specifically asked respondents about their close working relationships

Figure 4-5: Sample Studies Using Interviews

Antell, Karen. 2004. "Why Do College Students Use Public Libraries? A Phenomenological Study." *Reference & User Services Quarterly* 43 (3): 227–236.

Interviewed 17 college students that use public libraries for their research assignments to determine why they chose to use public rather than academic libraries. Appendix includes interview responses grouped by five major categories and 20 subcategories.

Barrett, Andy. 2005. "The Information-Seeking Habits of Graduate Student Researchers in the Humanities." *Journal of Academic Librarianship* 31 (4): 324–331.

In an exploratory study, the author interviewed ten masters and doctoral candidates in the humanities to determine whether this group demonstrated different information-seeking characteristics than their faculty or undergraduate counterparts.

Fister, Barbara. 1992. "The Research Process of Undergraduate Students." *Journal of Academic Librarianship* 18 (3): 163–169.

To find out whether undergraduates employ the same search strategies as taught in library instruction sessions, the author interviewed 14 students recently completing successful research projects. Interview schedule provided.

Lorenzen, Michael. 2001. "The Land of Confusion? High School Students and Their Use of the World Wide Web for Research." *Research Strategies* 18 (2): 151–163.

Nineteen students at a private high school were interviewed to learn about how they use the Web for their research assignments. The author reports that students use a variety of sources for their research and that they needed assistance in evaluating the information they did find when traditional authority checks were not present.

Major, Jean A. 1993. "Mature Librarians and the University Faculty: Factors Contributing to Librarians' Acceptance as Colleagues." *College and Research Libraries* 54 (6): 463–469.

The author explored the factors contributing to the acceptance of librarians as colleagues within an institution by interviewing 18 mature librarians considered to be colleagues of teaching faculty.

Seamans, Nancy H. 2002. "Student Perceptions of Information Literacy: Insights for Librarians." *Reference Services Review* 30 (2): 112–123.

Using ACRL's Information Literacy Competency Standards as a framework, the author interviewed nine students from a freshmen composition course as well as the course instructor to determine the type of services appropriate for that group.

Seiden, Peggy, Kris Szymborski, and Barbara Norelli. 1997. "Undergraduate Students in the Digital Library: Information Seeking Behavior in a Heterogeneous Environment." In *Choosing Our Futures: Eighth National Conference, Association of College and Research Libraries, April 11–14, 1997.* Available: http://ala.org/ala/acrlbucket/nashville1997pap/seidenszymborski.htm (accessed May 18, 2007).

Authors interviewed 42 undergraduates to determine how they decided which resources to use, the search strategies they employed, and the problems they encountered. Authors present novice and expert models of user behavior based on their findings.

Valentine, Barbara. 2001. "The Legitimate Effort in Research Papers: Student Commitment versus Faculty Expectations." *Journal of Academic Librarianship* 27 (2): 107–115.

Using data from an earlier study where the author interviewed 31 undergraduates and five faculty from several colleges and universities, this study concentrates on the differences between students' actions and faculty expectations in learning and applying the research process. Author offers five recommendations to librarians in helping students with their research projects.

with faculty and how these were built and maintained. In Major's (1993) study, the phenomenon under scrutiny was the "successful relationships with academic faculty." In reporting on her findings using library faculty's own words, she found that frequent librarian involvement in the "university's governance structure ... [and] ... a reputation for effective performance" (468) to be main themes that emerged from her analysis of the data. Inductive in its approach, Major's study shows that her theories on the evolution and sustenance of strong librarian-faculty relationships come out of the data itself and not from testing hypotheses.

FORMULATING QUESTIONS

Obviously, some research questions naturally lend themselves to conducting interviews with individuals or groups. For example, Walter's (in press) research question of "To what extent and in what ways do academic librarians develop a teacher identity?" is best explored by directly asking the librarians themselves and not by using a predefined measurement instrument. Remember that the research question governs the methodology employed and not the other way around. Thus, research questions that require interviews are those that:

- Seek to understand, or at least explore, complex and nuanced human issues.
- Require prose instead of numerical description. This is especially important when little is known about the topic.
- Aim to explore a phenomenon or behavior, looking for themes. Seamans and Lorenzen (both listed in Figure 4-5) were the first researchers to look at how their respective informants perceived specific issues or situations. Thus, interview research is typically exploratory in nature and takes a personal approach.

Because the approach is exploratory, interview and focus group research questions take a reflective tone, in which researchers wonder what is going on, who could help them best describe and understand that situation, and what are essential themes that underlie the situation. These questions are "open-ended, evolving, and non-directional" (Creswell 1998, 99). Consider these interview research questions drawn from six model studies profiled in Figure 4-5:

- How do freshmen gather and use information, how do "they organize and make sense of it, and what role [does] it play in their lives"? (Seamans 2002)
- Why do college students use public libraries for their assignments instead of their own university library? (Antell 2004)
- Are humanities graduate students' information-seeking habits different from models already defined for faculty or undergraduates? If so, how do their habits differ? (Barrett 2005)

- How does the research process employed by undergraduates compare with that frequently taught in library instruction sessions? (Fister 1992)
- How do high school students use the Web for their research projects? (Lorenzen 2001)
- How do undergraduates describe learning to do research? What was their prior library and computer experience? Why did they choose database searching over other research methods? (Seiden, Szymborski and Norelli 1997)

Although focus group studies are equally concerned with exploring human reactions to library resources or services, they are also frequently pragmatic and action oriented with an on-the-job problem to be solved. Let's look at several research questions from studies profiled in Figure 4-6:

- *Purpose:* To improve Web site design to make it more intuitive and user-friendly.
  Research question: How do users navigate the library's Web site? What obstacles do they find and how would they re-design the Web site? (Crowley, Leffel, Ramirez, Hart and Armstrong 2002)
- *Purpose:* To assess effectiveness of reference and instructional services for foreign students.
  Research question: How do foreign students use the library to complete their research projects? What problems have they encountered and how were those problems resolved? (Li 1998)
- *Purpose:* To evaluate and assess the library's services in meeting users' needs in light of recent technological changes within libraries.
  Research question: How are users dealing with rapid technological changes in the library? How helpful are staff members in meeting user needs? (Massey-Burzio 1998)

DEFINING THE POPULATION

Many methodologies require unbiased, random samples for their population, and structured interviewing is one such methodology. It seeks the most representative sample possible so that its results are generalizable to a broader population. Not so with qualitative interviewing and focus group methodologies. In fact, much of the success of these studies hinges on the purposeful selection of participants. A random sample is not the goal.

Before deciding *who* you sample among the target population, it is important to explore the *characteristics* that make up a good sample. Sometimes researchers need not worry about figuring out the desired characteristics for their sample because these are already embedded in the research problem. For instance, Antell's (2004) research project (featured in Figure 4-5) required input from

Figure 4-6: Sample Studies Using Focus Groups

Connaway, Lynn Silipigni, Debra Wilcox Johnson, and Susan E. Searing. 1997. "Online Catalogs for the Users' Perspective: The Use of Focus Group Interviews." *College & Research Libraries* 58 (5): 403–420.

> *The authors conducted focus groups with undergraduates, graduates, and faculty to uncover strengths and weaknesses of library's online catalog and to gather user priorities for system improvement. Authors provide in-depth description of the research process (planning, recruitment, question development) and evaluate focus group use. They also consider the reliability of the methodology.*

Crowley, Gwyneth H., Rob Leffel, Diana Ramirez, Judith L. Hart and Tommy S. Armstrong. 2002. "User Perceptions of a Library's Web Pages: A Focus Group Study at Texas A&M University." *Journal of Academic Librarianship* 28 (4): 205–210.

> *Due to user difficulty using the library's Web site, the authors decided to convene focus groups to help them discover how users perceive the Web site. In total, 26 participants, ranging from undergraduates to graduates, university staff to teaching faculty, formed the focus groups, with a group made up of each of the six types. Five general themes outlining user confusion are presented in the findings section which in turn led to several changes to the Web site.*

Frank, Polly. 1999. "Student Artists in the Library: An Investigation of How They Use General Academic Libraries for Their Creative Needs." *Journal of Academic Librarianship* 25 (6): 445–455.

> *In order to discover how and why studio art students use libraries, the author conducted 19 focus groups with over 180 students over a three-year period. Findings are discussed in depth.*

Li, Suzanne D. 1998. "Library Services to Students with Diverse Cultural Backgrounds." *Journal of Academic Librarianship* 24 (2): 139–143.

> *The author conducted three different focus groups with foreign students to assess library services regarding the research needs of this culturally diverse group. Results of the study gave rise to eight library improvements for this group. Appendix includes questions posed during group sessions.*

Massey-Burzio, Virginia. 1998. "From the Other Side of the Reference Desk: A Focus Group Study." *Journal of Academic Librarianship* 24 (3): 208–215.

> *Author recruited library users to discover how users "think and behave as they seek information" and to determine whether library services and programming are on target in meeting their needs. Figures and text boxes provide users' representative comments regarding reticence in asking questions, not understanding basic research principles, and rationale why library instruction is not useful.*

Young, Nancy J., and Marilyn Von Seggern. 2001. "General Information Seeking in Changing Times: A Focus Group Study." *Reference & User Services Quarterly* 41 (2): 159–169.

> *Arising from a desire to evaluate reference service in light of recent changes in technology, the authors conducted many focus group sessions over a six-month period. The authors used The Ethnograph, a computer software program to assist with data analysis that yielded seven thematic areas which the authors explore. Appendices include focus group script and a demographic chart of each focus group.*

college students who fell into a specific category: those that regularly and almost exclusively used their public library for their academic work.

Antell did not use a scientific method to select her sample; instead, she asked 18 library users who had identified themselves as college students if they would be interested in participating in her study. All but one of the students she approached agreed to participate. Her sample, though, contained a mix of students attending five different schools in three different cities. Frank's (1999) research (described in Figure 4-6) on how art students make use of the library's general collection also contains population characteristics within the research problem. With the help of college and university art faculty, Frank enlisted students who were enrolled in studio art classes in Minnesota colleges and universities and who had used academic libraries for their art projects.

Not all interview populations are so clear-cut. Sometimes researchers must revisit the problem more than once to determine the most desirable respondent attributes for a population that will yield the most relevant information. In her first study on students' experiences in conducting library research, Valentine (1993) asked library student assistants about their experiences. However, since there was no uniformity among students' assignments, it was difficult to make comparisons. She reworked her design and in a subsequent study (2001, in Figure 4-5) interviewed students enrolled in the same courses.

Typically, in interview research studies within the social sciences, researchers select a stratified purposive sample, one that contains participants possessing representative characteristics of the population under investigation. A stratified purposive sample of a library staff might include administrators, middle managers, librarians, classified staff, and long-term employees, as well as those recently hired and including both men and women. A stratified purposive sample is helpful when researchers wish to obtain a variety of viewpoints or perspectives from different folks within an institution. Not all researchers are lucky enough to gather stratified purposive samples, often because they do not have a large group of respondents from which to select a stratified sample. Much of the interview and focus group research in library and information science relies on basic purposive samples or a mix of purposive and convenience samples.

Convenience sampling is defined as using what is available. It is quick and easy, but the potential for bias is strong. Many researchers use convenience samples for pilot tests instead of the final study because they produce "homogeneous data which are highly unlikely to provide enough sources of understanding and ways of looking at a situation or a problem" (Morse and Richards 2002, 70). If you are using a convenience sample, it would be a good idea to triangulate your data collection with other methods or sources of data. Researchers engage in triangulation (also known as cross-examination) when they use multiple methods within a single study to double or triple check results. Researchers can be more confident with a result if different methods lead to that same result. Seamans (listed in Figure 4-5) employed triangulation in her study of freshmen and information literacy. Hers was a convenience sample in that she had access to a freshmen composition class; however, to offset the one-sidedness of her sample, she triangulated her data collection methods. She not only conducted face-to-face interviews with the students but also asked them to complete an open-ended survey instrument. Her third and final method consisted of electronic conversations via e-mail to elicit students' experiences with libraries and in finding and using information during their first semester for their course assignments. Seiden, Szymborski and Norelli (1997) employed triangulation in their study by first conducting a pilot study of ten students, which led to a revision of their interview schedule. Then the authors conducted face-to-face interviews with 32 students as well as several group interviews with the same 32. Finally, the authors specifically selected juniors/seniors who had just completed a senior thesis/major project to interview. We will discuss ways for researchers to triangulate their study later in this chapter. The topic is also addressed in Chapter 8.

In deciding on the number of people to interview, most researchers stick with a small sample for a variety of reasons. First of all, it saves time and energy to sift through transcripts of 30 interviews instead of 300. Also, because they are dealing with a smaller data set, researchers are better able to focus their energies on discovering nuances, themes, and categories in their data. What is a small sample? Looking over the studies featured in Figure 4-5, you will notice that the number of interviewees is mostly in the ten to 30 range, with a few outliers. Seamans (2002) interviewed only nine students, whereas Seiden, Szymborski and Norelli (1997) interviewed 42. There is no formula that dictates a requisite number of interviewees. Instead, researchers should ask themselves each time they interview new participants whether these participants offer new or novel insights that relate to the research question. Once researchers arrive at a point where participants contribute no new information to their understanding of the research problem, they have reached saturation and can stop interviewing. One very practical concern in choosing the number of interviewees is the amount of time researchers wish to devote to transcribing the data. There are obvious budgetary concerns in both researcher time and labor. A final point to consider in deciding how many people to interview dovetails with saturation and that is the research problem itself. Researchers need to keep the focus of the research always at the front and center of project development.

In focus group research, defining participant characteristics is very important. Library researchers need to figure out who has the most insight on their topic. As they figure out the "who," they need to make decisions about a wide variety of participants' attributes such as age, background, income bracket, occupation, and gender. Another way to approach defining one's population is to work backwards. What type of people does the library researcher wish to be able to say something about in the final report or study? The studies profiled in Figure 4-6 all include library users, but a few zero in on library users' specific characteristics (i.e., Frank and studio art students; Li and foreign students) as dictated by their research topic. Other studies are more broadly based and include a mix of characteristics (faculty, graduate students, undergraduate students, university staff). Often researchers have very specific requirements as to which types not to include. Connaway, Johnson and Searing (see Figure 4-6) wanted to have "typical" library users in their study of the online catalog, so they screened potential participants to weed out very knowledgeable catalog users.

After deciding on participant characteristics, focus group researchers then face several decisions:

- How many total participants will the study include?
- How many groups with there be?
- How many participants will be included in each group?
- Should each group include a mix of participants or should each group be homogeneous?

As always, the research problem itself primarily drives the answers to these questions through its purposes and goals. The researcher's budget also drives the answers to these questions by establishing the maximum number of groups within the project's budget. Other focus group studies can also help the researcher to figure out how many total participants and groups to include. Massey-Burzio (listed in Figure 4-6), for example, included 38 participants divided into six groups (each of which averaged six or seven participants); Li (listed in Figure 4-6) included 30 participants divided into three groups (each of which contained ten foreign students); and Connaway, Johnson and Searing (1997) included 49 participants divided into six groups. A typical focus group includes between six and ten participants, although sometimes groups can contain as few as four and as many as twelve. If the group is too large, it will be hard for the group to discuss the topic thoroughly with everyone's participation, but if the group is too small, library researchers may not get the variety of viewpoints needed. Finally, in determining the total number of participants and groups, researchers should also be alert for saturation. Once groups begin repeating the findings of prior groups, the saturation point has probably been reached.

Whether the groups are homogeneous also depends upon the research question and upon whether the researchers wish to contrast different groups' responses or to analyze the data across groups. In their study of users' responses to the library's Web page, Crowley, Leffey, Ramirez, Hart and Armstrong (listed in Figure 4-6) split their participants into six different groups (consisting of teaching faculty, library faculty, university staff, graduate students, freshmen, and upper-level undergraduates) because they wanted their participants to feel comfortable in sharing their viewpoints. A student would probably not feel comfortable in sharing his viewpoints in front of his professors. Li (1998) included a mix of different genders, nationalities, and ages in her study of foreign students, but considered her groups homogeneous because they shared relatively the same level of expertise with the topic (the library). And because all participants were equals as students, no one in the group had power over another. As Li's method suggests, power differentials are crucial factors in determining group composition. It is best not to include in the same focus group students and their teachers, children and their parents, staff and their supervisors, or a combination of boys in high school and in seventh grade. "Mixing" of individuals with different power levels typically counteracts the synergistic group effect and stifles the free flowing communication that is the strength of a focus group. Beyond being homogeneous in their relevant demographic characteristics and power differentials, the only other thing that group participants need share is a willingness to participate in the conversation, a feeling of comfort in doing so, and some interest in or knowledge of the topic under discussion.

Once library researchers have figured out who they want to include in their focus groups, they then need to figure out a way to encourage people to attend the session. Recruiting participants can be a struggle, as Connaway, Johnson and Searing (1997) note in their study. They made nearly 180 phone calls, but only 49 participants showed up for the group sessions. Library researchers need to consider the business of participants' schedules, gauge participants' motivation level, and adjust as needed. Krueger and Casey (2000) recommend personalizing the invitation and following up with an equally personal phone call. Other researchers (Ho and Crowley 2003; Connaway, Johnson and Searing 1997) sent non-personalized calls for participation by e-mail or flyers and get decent results. Sometimes library researchers need to offer incentives to lure participants to the sessions. Connaway, Johnson and Searing offered undergraduates ten dollars apiece for an hour and a half session, and Massey-Burzio (1998) enticed students with fifteen dollars for an hour and a half of work. For faculty participants, she offered food, not cash. These incentives add up, so frugal researchers should budget for incentives when planning the entire project.

SELECTING A RESEARCH DESIGN

In preparing for an interview or focus group project, researchers need to follow a series of steps. First they need to decide what data needs to be collected to best answer the research question. Then, they need to develop data collection instruments and chart out methods to collect the data. These first and second steps are closely entwined in interview and focus group research because both deal with constructing questions to ask during the sessions. In interview research, the data collection instrument is referred to as either the interview schedule, for structured interviews, or the interview guide, for semi-structured interviews. The interview schedule is a list of questions that the interviewer will ask verbatim and in exact order. It also contains a set of instructions to the interviewer for how to proceed in asking the questions during the interview. The interview guide is more loosely constructed, allowing for flexibility. The guide may or may not list the exact questions researchers intend to ask, but it does list the topics to be covered, all of which are relevant to the research problem. Library and information science interview studies traditionally use the more formal interview schedule in both interview and focus group studies. Many of the model studies shown in Figures 4-5 and 4-6 include their questions in figures, appendices, or within the text. When constructing the interview schedule, library researchers need to be sure that all aspects of the research problem correlate to an interview question. Researchers may use a theory or a set of standards as a framework for their questions. Kuhlthau (1989) used both Belkin's anomalous state of knowledge and Kelly's personal construct theory to study the cognitive and affective aspects of high school students' information search processes; Valentine (1993) used Kuhlthau's Information Search Process as a framework for her interview questions; and Seamans (2002) based her interview questions on the Association for College and Research Libraries' *Information Literacy Competency Standards for Higher Education*. Researchers need not pack their interview schedule with a lot of questions. It is better to ask between five and eight questions that will generate significant data than to ask a long list of very detailed questions. Researchers ought to construct the interview schedule as a data collection instrument that allows for field notes. See Figure 4-7 for an example of an interview schedule. It is a good idea to ask a few colleagues to look over the interview questions to make sure all research questions are covered in the interview schedule, as well as to weed out any ambiguities in wording, any duplication in questions, or any questions that do not directly relate to the research problem. Another test to make sure the project is on sure footing is to carry out a pilot study with participants possessing the same characteristics as your target group. This is also a good way to test recording equipment and functionality. Note any difficulties and correct them before embarking on the big project.

Question development is very important in focus group research. Researchers should use open-ended questions to elicit rich detailed data, avoiding the dead-end "yes" and "no" questions. Another tactic to avoid is asking participants why they think a certain way or believe something, because this can make people feel defensive. Researchers should allow latitude in participants' responses to the questions and elicit involvement by asking them to compare, or sort, or rate something. Questions should also be phrased to help elicit participants' experiences, so asking them to recollect or "remember the time" can be very effective. In developing the entire schedule, researchers should organize questions so that they move from general to specific and should build in transition phrasing such as "now I would like to move on to another topic" so that the session has a seamless flow to it.

In planning the data collection process, researchers have many elements to consider: deciding how to collect the data, scheduling the sessions, selecting a facility, choosing a moderator for the focus group, and offering incentives. Data can be collected in several different ways. Field notes of the session are useful to

Figure 4-7: Example of an Interview Schedule

Interview # _____   Name: _____

Date: _____   Interviewer: _____

1. Tell us about when you first began incorporating librarian-provided information research instruction into your courses and how long you have been doing this?

2. Why do you think it is important that your students be taught library research skills and information sources?

3. Why do you ask a librarian to teach your students library research skills and information sources?

4. Tell us about your best and worst experiences with librarian-provided information research instruction. What made these "best" and "worst" experiences stand out?

5. Please recall some concrete examples of library instruction experiences that made a difference (positively or negatively) for you and/or your students.

6. Beyond these concrete examples, please tell us about your perceptions of the effects (short- and/or long-term) of librarian-provided information research instruction on the students in your courses.

Source: Manuel, Kate, Susan E. Beck, and Molly E. Molloy. 2005. "An Ethnographic Study of Attitudes Influencing Faculty Collaboration in Library Instruction." *The Reference Librarian* 89/90: 139–161.

researchers with poor memories and might be used alone if participants do not wish to be taped.

Most researchers use a combination of field notes and either audio or video-tapes. Audio taping is the most commonly used method. It is relatively inexpensive and fairly effective in accurately capturing the participants' speech—provided, of course, that researchers are using good equipment and high quality tapes. If non-verbal communication such as gestures, facial expressions, and body movements are important to the research question, then researchers ought to consider videotaping the sessions. Videotaping equipment can be a bit more expensive than a tape recorder and require an experienced operator. This method is more frequently used in focus groups than in one-on-one interviews because of the need to study group dynamics and the synergistic effects of the session. Whether using audio or videotaping, researchers ought to test out the equipment before-hand and do so in the room where the interviews will take place. If researchers are conducting interviews over the telephone, then the audio taping setup needs to be tested thoroughly before the interviews begin.

Internet chat offers another data collection method. Although it has not yet been used widely in interview research in library and information science, Inter-net chat presents researchers with an exciting and attractive opportunity because the transcripts are immediately available.

When researchers schedule their interview sessions, they need to gauge ap-proximately how long the sessions will last in order to give themselves and the participants an idea of what to expect. Most interviews and focus group sessions last anywhere from one to three hours. Another scheduling concern with focus groups is aiming for a time that will draw high attendance. Weekends and evenings are often bad choices, but breakfast or lunch hours can draw full atten-dance, especially if food is offered as an enticement. Also, it is a good idea to check out the facilities ahead of time, if using an unfamiliar space, to deal with heating or cooling problems, lighting, seating, and to test out equipment.

Interview researchers often note that they have followed a certain approach in their research design. Whether called phenomenological, ethnographic, case study or grounded theory, the mention of any of these in a research article can confuse a reader unversed in that particular type of approach. Authors would do well to provide a short explanation of their approach in their article and perhaps reference authoritative sources. All these approaches share a qualitative origin, but their focus and purpose differ.

The focus of a phenomenological study is to understand a phenomenon or a situation and how individuals experience and define that phenomenon. Antell's study of college students' use of their public library for their academic assign-ments and Major's research on strong working relationships between academic faculty and librarians are both phenomenological in their approach because they look at an occurrence or observable fact that is experienced by a specific group.

A case study, such as Seamans' (2002), takes a specific area or environment for its focus. The focus for Seamans' case study was a freshmen composition class. In a case study, the researcher needs to gather a wide variety of informa-tion about the case in order to get a well-rounded multidimensional view. To this end, Seamans collected her data in a variety of ways: questionnaires, e-mail discussions, and face-to-face interviews.

In a grounded theory study, researchers wish to develop a theory about the research problem (Strauss and Corbin 1998). Using open coding as they analyze the interview data, researchers develop their theory that is "grounded" in the data, as well as "grounded" in daily life. Thus, the theory emerges from the data;

Figure 4-8: Four Approaches to Research Design

Activity	Phenomenology	Case Study	Grounded Theory	Ethnography
Purpose of study	To understand a phenomenon or a concept from the viewpoint of those who have experienced that phenomenon	To gain an in-depth understanding of a specific environment or case	To develop a theory through close analysis of the data	To understand the behaviors and beliefs of a specific group in order to describe that culture
Who/what studied	Many individuals who have experienced that phenomenon	A specific area, event, process, or activity	Many individuals who have experienced or have participated in an event, project or situation	Members of a specific group or culture
Sampling	Find individuals who have experienced that phenomenon	Find a specific case	Find a homogeneous sample	Find a specific culture group of which the researcher is not a member
Type of data collected	Interviews	Interviews, observations and other documents	Interviews	Interviews, observation and other documents

Based on information from John W. Creswell. 1998. *Qualitative Inquiry and Research Design: Choosing Among Five Traditions.* Thousand Oaks, CA: Sage.

it is not confirmed by it as in much scientific, a priori research. Many information-seeking studies take a grounded theory approach. For example, Barrett's study of how humanities graduate students seek out and find information, Fister's analysis of undergraduate research processes, and Valentine's research on differences in student and faculty's perceptions of the research process all employ grounded theory in their approach.

An ethnographic approach focuses on studying the behaviors, beliefs, and experiences of a specific group in order to describe and define that culture. Manuel, Beck and Molloy (2005) used an ethnographic approach in their study of teaching faculty that support and respect library instruction. A chart outlining these four approaches is shown in Figure 4-8.

A final consideration in planning the research project is striving to ensure internal validity through triangulation, a process already mentioned in the previous section. Triangulation refers to the way researchers obtain "multiple perspectives through completed studies that have been conducted on the same topic and that directly address each other's findings" (Morse and Richards 2002,

76). Triangulation requires that researchers employ different approaches to the research question and can be accomplished in a variety of ways. In their analysis, researchers can contrast different data types and methods that illuminate the same question. As noted above, Seiden, Szymborski, and Norelli (see Figure 4-5) triangulated their study by conducting focus groups and one-on-one interviews of different groups of students (students currently completing a research assignment, upper-level undergraduates working on a major research project) and discussing their research strategies in using electronic resources. They also had groups respond to a questionnaire that asked students to discuss resources they would use to answer six different research questions. What is important in their evolving research design was that they not only used three different data collections methods (e.g., questionnaires, focus groups, and one-on-one interviews) when they examined how students go about learning to use electronic resources in their research projects but that they also tracked this process in several different groups of students at various stages in their undergraduate careers. They analyzed findings from each data collection group and used these to provide a well-rounded view of the research problem in their analysis.

GATHERING DATA

Collecting data in an interview or focus group study involves interrelated activities that pose several challenges for researchers. Some of these activities have been discussed in earlier sections, but here we consider them in the context of actually collecting data. The activities can be organized into six broad categories: (1) selecting the site and participants; (2) making contact with participants; (3) employing purposeful sampling; (4) collecting the data; (5) resolving problems during data collection; and (6) storing the data. These steps need not be strictly followed in the order that they are given. For example, researchers might want to first employ purposeful sampling before site selection. Once the first three activities are taken care of, researchers need to decide exactly how they will collect the data. These collection techniques can range from audio taping to videotaping to writing field notes to using e-mail or Webcams. Once researchers have decided on their data collection strategy, they need to think through and be prepared for any problems they might reasonably encounter during the interview or focus group sessions and plan on how to deal with these challenges. The most common challenges are listed in Figure 4-9. Finally in dealing with ways to store data, researchers are advised to:

- develop a master list of all of the types of information collected
- always back up computer files
- label audio or videotapes for quick identification and retrieval
- mask identity of participants within the data to protect anonymity

Figure 4-9: Challenges in Data Collection

Logistic	Interview Specific	Data Maintenance	Focus Group Specific	Ethical
• Making initial contact with participants to ensure they will consent to be interviewed • Scheduling interview times suitable for both interviewer and participants • Finding a place to conduct session devoid of noise, interruptions, and other distractions • Ensuring recording equipment is in good working order and that tapes function well in the machine • Having batteries for the tape recorder in case there is no electrical outlet • Taking adequate and appropriate notes during the interview	• Creating an atmosphere of trust • Getting participants to open up • Keeping interviewer talk to a minimum • Lacking confidence in interviewing • Handling interruptions and getting the interview back on track • Handling an interview of two participants at once: Challenges of balance, pace and staying on track • Dealing with emotional outbursts • Coping with interviewees who do not wish to be audio or videotaped • Getting interviewees back on track after straying from the topic	• Understanding the financial, labor and human energy costs of transcription • Hiring a good transcriber • Securely storing data from the project so that it can be easily located • Dealing with backup computer files • Protecting participant anonymity in files • Developing a quick and visual means for identifying and locating data stored	• Finding a time for all participants to attend the session • Hitting upon an incentive that will attract and secure participants • Ensuring conversation balance among participants • Handling experts, dominant talkers, obnoxious or shy participants • Pacing the session so that all topics are covered • Ensuring that each participant is not rushed through a reply and that everyone has the opportunity to talk	• Protecting the anonymity of participants • Deciding whether or not to disclose the nature of the project to participants and if so, to what depth • Deciding how to handle "off the record" information disclosed during the interview that is potentially volatile • Deciding whether or not to share personal experiences with participants

More and more frequently, researchers use e-mail or chat to collect data, or conduct virtual focus groups. If you choose any of these electronic data collection methods, you must assess the logistics of collecting this type of data and devise solid procedures for recording and storing it. Although considerably less costly to administer and transcribe, electronic interviewing has its special challenges, advantages, and disadvantages (Meho 2006). Library and information science practitioner-researchers have not yet used electronic interviews or virtual focus groups to any significant degree. For this reason, we do not cover these topics in-depth in this chapter. However, librarian-researchers are strongly urged to explore these new data collection methods because they offer exciting opportunities for researchers.

Interview research data collection can be broken down into a series of steps:

1. *Identify participants:* Make final decisions regarding who will make up your list of respondents based on purposive sampling procedures.
2. *Decide on interview type:* Decide which interview type to use in gathering the information needed to answer the research question:
   a. *Phone interviews:* These are best when the researcher cannot have a face-to-face session, but they do not allow the researcher to note any non-verbal communication such as gestures, facial expressions, or overall participant affect.
   b. *In-person interviews:* One-on-one interviews allow for all communication types to be gathered and observed, but if respondents are shy or in some other way cautious or uncertain about speaking to the interviewer, then another method should be used.
   c. *Focus groups:* As already noted, focus groups are helpful when researchers wish to gather information that is the fruit of respondent interaction, when researcher time is limited in data collection, and, as in the above case, when individuals might not wish to be interviewed one-on-one due to shyness or uneasiness in being singled out. However, researchers need to be skilled in allowing all participants to talk and should guard against one or a few respondents who may monopolize the session.
3. *Make final decision on facilities:* Figure out where to conduct the interviews. Will it be in one specific room, as is done for focus groups, or will the interviewer travel to hold the interview sessions? If using one room, check out heating and cooling operations and room lighting, and make sure that shades or curtains are available if strong sunlight is an issue. For focus group sessions, if offering meal or food incentives, make sure there is adequate space for self-service food trays and beverages. Ensure that participants will have enough space to eat and talk. This might not be a problem if there is a large table in the room but if not, find some way for participants not to have to hold plates in their laps and drinks in their hands.
4. *Checkout equipment:* Ensure that all recording devices work. Even though electrical outlets may be available in the room you are using, check the battery supply for the recording devices and purchase more if needed. Tour the facility and make sure that electrical outlets are available and functioning. Test out any microphone equipment and cassette or video tapes in the recording devices to ascertain their clarity.

5. *Design interview schedule:* Develop an interview schedule or a list of questions that has ample space for note taking.

6. *Obtain consent:* Before starting the interview, obtain formal signed consent from participants. This can be done in advance of the interview or focus group session and can serve to collect pre-session demographic information from participants.

7. *Pace the interview:* While conducting the session, follow the interview schedule, or question list, carefully. Make sure you are giving adequate time for each question and ensure the respondent does most of the talking.

8. *Follow proper protocol:* At the close of the interview, thank the respondents, tell them how the data will be used and offer to share the results with them once the study is concluded.

The steps in a focus group session are similar, but also require that researchers concern themselves with a few other points in data collection. If researchers are not able to hire an experienced moderator, then moderator training is important. The moderator sets the tone of the session, and the success of the session hinges on the first minutes of the session when the moderator introduces the session. The moderator needs to strike a balance between ease and formality that encourages the free flow of information but that also requests that participants take the session seriously. A model pattern to introduce the session includes the following:

1. welcome and introductions
2. overview of the session
3. setting of ground rules
4. begin with first question

Moderators should pace the focus group session so that it moves at a good clip while still covering all topics. It is important to ensure that all participants' views are included. One way to do this is for the moderator to pause five to ten seconds after a response to elicit another viewpoint. When participants are too noncommittal in their answers, nodding their heads and murmuring short bleats like "I agree," moderators can use gambits such as, "Would you explain further?" "Can you give me an example?" or a more formal, "Please describe what you mean" to elicit richer information. If too many participants are echoing the same ideas, moderators can ask, "Are there other points of view?" or "Does anyone see this differently?"

All focus groups are different and unpredictable because they are composed of people with different backgrounds and experiences. Some specific types of people can pose real challenges for the moderator.

- Dominant talkers often will not yield time for others to make their points. Some dominant types are aware of their tendency to dominate, and others are entirely oblivious of how they come across. Suggested strategies for moderators to use in toning down the dominant talker are to sit right next to the person and employ subtle controls with body language or to shift the conversation to another participant by diplomatically saying, "Thanks, Beth. Does anyone have another point of view?"

- Long-winded participants may use a lot of words and even more time to get to their point. A participant like this can use up much valuable time. Avoidance body language—such as not making eye contact, paper shuffling, turning away—can help the long-winded types to slow down for a pause. When the participant pauses, a skilled moderator needs to jump in and direct the conversation to another participant.

- The next problem type is the expert. They are especially challenging because they have a tendency to intimidate others, shutting down all voices but their own. These people may truly be experts in their field, but that does not mean that no one else is an expert. Moderators can remind the group that "everyone is an expert" to help put others at ease and, at the same time, remind the self-appointed experts to turn down the volume. Another way to avoid introducing the theme of individual expertise into the discussion is to have people introduce themselves at the beginning of the session by giving only their names, rather than their positions or background in the topic.

- Another troublesome type is the offensive or argumentative participant. Fortunately, such participants are rare in focus groups, but all moderators should be prepared with effective ways to handle them. The first thing to do is to point out the problem verbally. "Charlie, we are inviting everyone's comments today about the reading marathon program and are not going to discuss anyone's political affiliations or their religious beliefs, so I am asking you to stick to the topic at hand." If that strategy does not work, then ask the troublemaker to leave: "Charlie, you don't appear to want to discuss the citywide reading marathon program so I will let you go ahead and leave." Follow the person outside; give him or her the promised incentive along with a handshake and a "thanks for coming." This tough but fair stance may be hard for moderators to adopt, but will make the difference between a successful session and a failure.

- A final difficult participant type is the shy person. How does the moderator draw out comments from someone who does not wish, or is too timid, to contribute? One way to encourage shy people to speak up is for the moderator to make eye contact with the individual and use encouraging body language. Moderators might want to call on the shy person by name to draw them out. "Judy, what are your thoughts on asking the mayor to kick off the reading marathon program?"

In closing the focus group session, good moderators provide a quick summary of the session, hitting on the main points. Once the session has been summarized, moderators then solicit for any other comments, corrections or amendments, by asking something like, "Did we miss anything?" After assembling any last comments, it is time to thank everyone for coming, hand out any incentives, and then wish all a speedy and safe trip.

INTERPRETING THE EVIDENCE

Analyzing qualitative data is a deliberate, continuing process that is systematic, is done sequentially, and uses verifiable procedures. Undertaking qualitative data analysis demands that researchers be at ease with both a bit of ambiguity and the unexpected as they try to make sense of their data and discover themes therein. At this phase of the research project, researchers need to be open to new possibilities found in the data that they might not have previously thought about. For example, Seamans found themes within her data that came from topics students wished to discuss (such as the electronic use of information sources) and not from those that she was particularly interested in (i.e., the costs of information). Thus, Seamans needed to shift gears from her preliminary focus and concentrate on topics that the data provided. Another example of researchers finding surprises in their data is where Manuel, Beck, and Molloy (2005) discovered that a third of teaching faculty interviewed use library instruction to affirm what they are teaching in the classroom by pulling in an outside expert, the librarian, to testify on their behalf. This was a surprising revelation to the researchers, and it was something that they discovered only after analyzing the interview transcripts. This process of discovery is an exciting part of qualitative research.

In fact, interview and focus group data analysis is all about discovery. Those taking a grounded theory approach employ what is called open coding, and this is used by many library researchers in their data analysis (see Antell, Barrett, and Valentine in Figure 4-5). In open coding, researchers read their interview data, first finding, and then dividing, the data into specific categories. They constantly compare the data with the emerging categories to ensure that their categories are in line with the data they are looking at. If not, researchers need to reassess their categories, perhaps dividing them into two or more separate categories, or else they need to redefine one category to include the new information. In her grounded theory study of why college students use their public library for their research assignments, Antell found five major themes: personal convenience, materials, ease of use and familiarity, staff, and subjective appeal. She further divided these five categories into 24 subcategories, organizing participant quotes within each subcategory. Each quote defines and explores the subcategory and its parent category in ways the author could not do in her own words because her participants so eloquently tell the story for her. Her well-structured and thoughtful analysis of a large amount of data provides novice researchers with an excellent model to follow in both organizing and presenting their data.

Often, novice researchers collect more data than they can meaningfully analyze. This can lead to frustration, feelings of being overwhelmed and, in some cases, panic. When this happens, researchers are advised to step back and review their research problem, thinking seriously about what exactly they wish to know. By going back to square one and defining their fundamental purpose in collecting all this data, researchers can then sift through the daunting pile of data, excluding anything that does not fit the research question. Novice researchers should also be aware that not everything is worthy of analysis, or even can be analyzed. Researchers need to make choices at every step of the research project, and they should place their attention on the data that is most relevant.

Before embarking on analyzing one's corpus of data, researchers are advised to take a few, very important security measures. Foremost is taking care of the original data. Your originals are both the tapes (in the case of electronic interviews, these are data files) of the interviews and the transcripts. Researchers should organize and securely store these originals. In their data analysis, researchers should be working with copies of the original transcripts so that if they make mistakes, they can toss the copy and begin again. It is best to think of the original transcripts as just that, the original. These originals should be treated as gold and securely stored. They should not be marked up, altered or edited in any way.

In transcribing the data, researchers need to decide whether to do it themselves or hire a transcriber. If selecting the latter, note that most charge by the hour and not by the job due to the variety in sound quality of the tapes and differences among interviews or groups. Without knowing how much a transcriber will charge for the entire job, it is difficult to manage a budget. Also, it is difficult finding experienced transcribers who will do an accurate and thorough job. If working at or living near a university with graduate programs in the social sciences, researchers might be able to find a skilled graduate student, but this is not always possible.

If researchers decide to tackle the transcriptions themselves, they should follow a few simple rules of thumb:

- Use a consistent style. Use the same style regarding font, margins, line spacing, page numbering, header and footer information. The transcripts should be internally consistent.
- Identify speakers when roles change. Always identify the interviewer or the moderator through some sort of consistent style such as using bold or a different font or just the initials Q and A.

- Focus on accurate recording of the meaning rather than stylistic perfection. People rarely speak in complete sentences. It is best to put in the punctuation where it makes sense. Equally, transcribers need not type up a linguistically accurate transcription where all pauses, or changes in intonation and pitch are accurately recorded using specialized characters and conventions. This is not that type of transcription. What is important, though, is that the transcription is a verbatim account of what was said. Researchers should not attempt to change participants' words to make the interview "read" better or alter the speakers' grammar. If words are unintelligible after several attempts at comprehension, type in the ellipsis (. . .) to indicate that something is missing. Alternatively, researchers might wish to use the term *[unintelligible]* in brackets to indicate that a word or phrase cannot be understood.
- Allow sufficient time for transcription (two to four hours per half hour tape) and type the transcript in a place with few interruptions or distractions.
- Use high quality playback equipment to ease frustration and to help speed along the transcription process.

Let us now look at eight steps researchers should take in trying to make sense of their transcripts (Tesch 1990, 142–145):

1. *Do a first pass.* Read through all of the transcriptions carefully to gain a general sense of the data. Jot down ideas as they come to mind instead of waiting to do this at a later stage of the analysis. Often, "out of the blue" ideas may be real epiphanies.
2. *Focus on one interview.* Pick one transcript—the most intriguing, the shortest, the first one you come to, whatever. Go through it, asking, "What is going on here?" Do not think about the specific content of the information or how it was phrased; instead, think about its underlying meaning, its overall topic. Be sure to write down your thoughts.
3. *List and organize.* Once several transcripts have been reviewed, make a list of all topics found so far. Compare all topics and cluster together any similar ones. Form these topics into columns. These can be organized as major topic, unique topic, and "leftovers." Then choose a name for each topic. These can be taken directly from the participants' words; they can be catchy phrases; they can be any word or phrase that succinctly describes the topic as a whole.
4. *Analyze all of the data.* Take your list of topics and go back to the data. Researchers might want to abbreviate topics and assign them a code or a number. As researchers make a close reading of the data, they need to write the codes next to the appropriate segments of the text. It is a good idea to test out this preliminary organizing scheme on just a few documents to see whether new categories and codes emerge.

5. *Describe your topics.* Describe all topics as succinctly as possible and turn them into categories. Think about reducing the total list of categories by grouping topics that relate to each other. Perhaps draw lines between the categories to show interrelationships.

6. *Decide on your codes.* Make a definitive decision on the abbreviation for each category and alphabetize these codes. Now make sure that all of the data has been coded and that every significant area has a category and a code.

7. *Put it all together.* Assemble the data materials belonging to each category in one place and perform a thorough analysis. Look at each category and decide whether it can stand alone or if it can be merged into another category. Also make sure that a category is not too broad and, if so, be prepared to subdivide the category and recode. Be sure that every research question maps to a category. Also, make sure that categories do not overlap too much, but also check that they are not overly narrow. If the organizational scheme of categories does not seem to work, researchers are then faced with recoding the data using a revised scheme.

8. *Recode the data?* This last step might not be necessary but if researchers do need to scratch their initial efforts, they should not throw out all the work done up until now. They might need to set the data aside for a few days and then pick it up again. They may also want to ask a colleague to offer thoughts on some particularly difficult categories from the first round. Fresh eyes on a document are always valuable.

Many researchers in the social sciences use computer software to help them organize and make sense of the massive amounts of information they have collected. Computer programs can assist researchers not only in speeding up the data analysis process but also in providing an organizational structure for accessing and storing the data. Weitzman and Miles (1995) note that computer programs help to:

- Code data by attaching keywords or specific tags to sections of text that can be retrieved and organized at a later date.
- Link data by making connections through relevant codes from one section of text to another.
- Store data and keep it organized.
- Search and retrieve relevant data that is similarly coded.
- Count data, looking for word or phrase frequencies or sequences.
- Display data graphically showing in a network or map structure where coded data occurs.

Some of the drawbacks to using a computer program for data analysis are fairly obvious. Researchers need to learn how to use the software program before employing it to analyze and store their data. Of course, some learn computer programs much faster than others, so researchers ought to take their own computer knowledge and skills into account before deciding to use a specific program. It is easy to assume that the computer will "do" all the work in analyzing the data. Not so! The researcher still needs to make the decisions between what is important and what is not. It is the researcher who must set up the categories or codes to analyze the data set. Once those categories are established in a computer program, researchers might be wary of changing them. However, as we have seen, qualitative data analysis is a continually evolving process, thus researchers need to be able to make these changes within their computer program. A final point to remember about computer data analysis programs is that they cannot analyze what is not there, and sometimes the absence of information is just as—or even more—important than its presence. This maxim is illustrated in Lorenzen's (2001) study of high school students' use of the Web for research (see Figure 4-5). Many of the students he interviewed hesitated and had a difficult time answering the question of how they knew whether the information from a Web site was reliable or appropriate for their assignment. Their stumbling about for an answer made it clear to Lorenzen that "the students have given very little thought to how to evaluate what they found on the Web" (Lorenzen 2001, 156). If coding solely by computer, a researcher might not have caught this highly informative—yet nonverbal—clue to students' Web evaluation skills. Overall, computer data analysis programs are useful for the things that they do well: storing, organizing, linking, searching, and counting. Researchers need to consider carefully the programs available, comparing the programs' functions to the needs of their research project, before committing both their budget and their energy to one program. To help researchers begin this deliberation, Figure 4-10 lists several commonly used and well-known programs.

We mentioned at the beginning of this chapter that qualitative research, although focused on the specifics, is not without rigor, but that it uses different methods to attain that rigor. In quantitative research, rigor is established

Figure 4-10: Commonly Used Data Analysis Programs

- *Atlas.ti*, ATLAS.ti Scientific Software Development GmbH, Berlin, Germany, www.atlasti.com
- *The Ethnograph*, Qualis Research Associates, P.O. Box 50437, Colorado Springs, CO 80949, www.qualisresearch.com
- *HyperQual*, HyperQual, 9723 Boerne Haze, Boerne, TX 78006, http://home.satx.rr.com/hyperqual/
- *NUD*ist*, QSR International, www.qsrinternational.com
- *NVivo7*, QSR International, www.qsrinternational.com
- *Qualus*, IdeaWorks, www.ideaworks.com

through the validity and reliability of a study. Within qualitative research, there are several strategies that researchers can employ to address their study's internal and external validity as well its reliability.

Internal validity, or face validity, is about the accuracy of the information collected and analyzed and how well it matches up with reality. To establish internal validity, researchers can use several different strategies. First, researchers can discuss how they used triangulation in their study. Remember that one way to triangulate a study is to collect and analyze different types of data to look at the research question; another method is to interview different groups about the same topic. Another way to check internal validity is to share categories or themes with participants and ask whether conclusions are on the mark. External validity, or generalizability, is how well the research study represents the problem in general and whether the results of the study can be applied to similar studies. In a way, this premise is in direct contradiction to the essence of qualitative research since one of the main tenets of qualitative research is to present a unique interpretation, not a generalizable one. Nevertheless, researchers can address generalizability in a limited fashion by discussing the data collection procedures and the methods employed to discover categories or themes. Reliability is the extent to which the study can be replicated and, in doing so, will produce the same results. As with external validity, reliability and qualitative research seem to be in opposition, as the uniqueness of a study seems to deny its replicability. But if researchers discuss the components of the study, such as the study's theoretical constructs, participant selection, and data collection methods, then they improve the chances that their study can be replicated in another setting.

TELLING THE STORY

Qualitative researchers use much the same overall structure as quantitative researchers in presenting and publishing their findings. Researchers chart out their projects via the general headings of introduction, review of the literature, methodology, analysis, results, discussion, and conclusions or recommendations. Researchers do not necessarily need to use these exact words for the headings, and they may wish to add sections or subsections. Nevertheless, most qualitative research sticks to the typical research report structure. In the introduction or methodology sections, the researcher may wish to discuss any underlying assumptions, theories or frameworks they have adopted. In the methodology section, researchers discuss sampling methods to select participants. They present their interview or focus group questions and match these up to the study's overarching research questions. In the methodology section, researchers also describe where the interviews took place, how long they lasted and any problems the researcher encountered during the sessions. Within the analysis section, researchers should note what approach, if any, they adopted to the research design. And if researchers are taking a specific approach (i.e., phenomenological, case study, grounded theory, ethnography), they need to use the vocabulary of that particular approach in presenting their research project. It is also within the analysis section that researchers typically explain and define the themes they uncovered in analyzing and coding the data. The results and discussion sections are those that most often use rhetorical devices unique to qualitative research, and we will look at those in-depth just a bit later.

One consideration in telling the research story is whether researchers wish to use the first person in their narrative. Most library and information science interview and focus group research studies take the more formal approach and present the researchers distantly as "the authors" within the text. In contrast, Seamans (listed in Figure 4-5) uses the first person and inserts herself throughout the text of her study; however, her style is very formal and she uses the vocabulary of the qualitative researcher so that her research does not read as an informal account. Because telling the research story through the lens of the researcher is such an integral part of qualitative research, those in library and information science who are doing or interested in doing a qualitative study are encouraged to describe their research from the "I" perspective. Doing so in greater numbers aligns the profession more closely with qualitative research norms within the social sciences and that in itself can lend face validity to the study in a small but significant way. Researchers are encouraged to examine the work of Seamans (2002), Kuhlthau (1988, 1989), and Mellon (1990), who all use the first person in their research studies.

Much qualitative research uses rhetorical devices to pull the reader into the research scenario, taking the reader by the hand, like Dante's Virgil, to point out evidence and findings in answer to the research question, by having the participants speak. Most studies described in Figures 4-5 and 4-6, and in most interview and focus group studies generally, employ direct quotes from interview or focus group participants to illuminate a theme found within the data. Denzin (1989: 83) calls this technique "thick description," where the narrative "presents detail, context, emotion, and the webs of social relationships" and where "the voices, feelings, actions, and meanings of interacting individuals are heard." Looking carefully at the results and discussion sections, readers will notice that most researchers describe and group their findings according to themes they have uncovered. Some researchers incorporate their quotes from participants within the text while others indent participants' quotes in block style to emphasize a point. Some researchers are lucky enough to use a participant quote as a way to frame a theme or a section of discussion. Major (described in Figure 4-5) thus frames her results and discussion section in a way that is helpful and informative to readers (i.e., "Are There Some Faculty Whom You Consider Colleagues?," "Contacts with Faculty," "Attitude—The Basis for Acceptance"). However, because this structure does not follow her interview questions, she then must knit together her findings with the research questions in the conclusion section in a comprehensible fashion. And because she reports her findings in ways that are compelling for readers, her approach plays an important role in narrating the research "story." We cannot and should not lose sight of our readership, nor can we overlook how best to tell the story. Researchers need to ask themselves "What is the most compelling way to frame the telling of the tale?" And it may not be the easiest or most logical way.

A final point in writing up the research story is that researchers must balance the need to identify participants in ways that enhance the storytelling with the need to protect participants' anonymity. If interviewing a group of homogeneous individuals, such as students, researchers may wish to lump them all together into one category of "student," and when introducing a comment can write, "one student notes that..." In studies where participants fall into different groups or where the researcher has described characteristics of the sample in specific ways (community college students, four-year university, private college, etc.) researchers may want to introduce participants' comments using those attributes. Manuel, Beck and Molloy (2005) introduce their faculty members' comments by referring to faculty members' departments (one English professor, a professor of business, an English-as-a-Foreign-Language professor, and so forth) as a descriptive and identifying element. These devices can enrich the study by providing the reader with a glimpse into who the participants are without revealing their identities. They also serve as an engaging storytelling device. In the final analysis, it is both the story of the research itself and the ways that the researcher tells that story that make a compelling, interesting, and worthy research study.

REFERENCES

Chase, Lynne, and Jaquelina Alvarez. 2000. "Internet Research: The Role of the Focus Group." *Library and Information Science Research* 22 (4): 357–369.

Connaway, Lynn Silipigni. 1996. "Focus Group Interviews: A Data Collection Methodology for Decision Making." *Library Administration and Management* 24: 231–239.

Creswell, John W. 1998. *Qualitative Inquiry and Research Design: Choosing Among Five Traditions*. Thousand Oaks, CA: Sage.

Denzin, Norman. 1989. *Interpretive Interactionism*. Newbury Park, CA: Sage.

D'Esposito, Joanne E., and Rachel M. Gardner. 1999. "University Students' Perceptions of the Internet: An Exploratory Study." *Journal of Academic Librarianship* 25 (6): 456–461.

Farrell, Elizabeth F., and Eric Hoover. 2005. "Getting Schooled in Student Life." *Chronicle of Higher Education* 29 (July): 36.

Gorman, G. E., and Peter Clayton. 2005. *Qualitative Research for the Information Professional: A Practical Handbook*. London: Facet.

Henner, Terry, and Patricia Charles. 2002. "Using Focus Groups to Guide Development of a Public Health Web Site." *Medical Reference Services Quarterly* 21 (4): 15–22.

Ho, Jeannette, and Gwyneth H. Crowley. 2003. "User Perceptions of the 'Reliability' of Library Services at Texas A&M University: A Focus Group Study." *Journal of Academic Librarianship* 29 (2): 82–87.

Kaske, Neal K., and Nancy P. Sanders. 1980. "On-line Subject Access: The Human Side of the Problem." *RQ* 20 (1): 52–58.

Kuhlthau, Carol Collier. 1989. "Information Search Process: A Summary of Research and Implications for School Library Media Programs." *School Library Media Quarterly* 18 (5): 19–25.

—————. 1988. "Developing a Model of the Library Search Process: Cognitive and Affective Aspects." *RQ* 28 (2): 232–242.

Krueger, Richard A., and Mary Anne Casey. 2000. *Focus Groups: A Practical Guide for Applied Research.* 3rd ed. Thousand Oaks, CA: Sage.

Leighton, H. Vernon, Joe Jackson, Kathryn Sullivan, and Russell F. Dennison. 2003. "Web Page Design and Successful Use, A Focus Group Study." *Internet Reference Services Quarterly* 8 (3): 17–27.

Lyotard, Jean François. 1984. *The Postmodern Condition: A Report on Knowledge.* Trans. by Geoff Bennington and Brian Massumi. Minneapolis, MN: University of Minnesota Press.

Manuel, Kate, Susan E. Beck, and Molly Molloy. 2005. "An Ethnographic Study of Attitudes Influencing Faculty Collaboration in Library Instruction." *Reference Librarian* 89/90 (3/4): 139–161.

Markey, Karen. 1983. *Online Catalog Use: Results of Surveys and Focus Group Interviews in Several Libraries.* OCLC Research Report Series no. OCLC/OPR/RR-83/3, text-fiche ED 231403.

Meho, Lokman I. 2006. "E-mail Interviewing in Qualitative Research: A Methodological Discussion." *Journal of the American Society for Information Science and Technology* 57 (10): 1284–1295.

Mellon, Constance Ann. 1990. *Naturalistic Inquiry for Library Science: Methods, Applications for Research, Evaluation, and Teaching.* New York: Greenwood.

Merton, Robert K. 1987. "The Focused Interview and Focus Groups: Continuities and Discontinuities." *Public Opinion Quarterly* 51 (4): 550–556.

Merton, Robert K., Marjorie Fiske, and Patricia L. Kendall. 1956. *The Focused Interview: A Manual of Problems and Procedures.* Glencoe, IL: Free Press.

Merton, Robert K., and Patricia L. Kendall. 1946. "The Focused Interview." *American Journal of Sociology* 51 (6): 541–557.

Morse, Janice M., and Lyn Richards. 2002. *Read Me First for a User's Guide to Qualitative Methods.* Thousand Oaks, CA: Sage.

Odum, Howard W., and Katharine Jocher. 1929. *An Introduction to Social Research.* New York: Holt.

Platt, Jennifer. 2001. "The History of the Interview." In *The Handbook of Interview Research: Context and Method,* 33–54. Thousand Oaks, CA: Sage.

Shoham, Snunith. 1998. "Fees in Public Libraries." *Public Library Quarterly* 17 (1): 39–47.

Smalley, Topsy N. 2004. "College Success: High School Librarians Make the Difference." *Journal of Academic Librarianship* 30 (3): 193–198.

Strauss, Anselm L., and Juliet Corbin. 1998. *Basics of Qualitative Research: Techniques and Procedures for Developing Grounded Theory.* Thousand Oaks, CA: Sage.

Tesch, Renata. 1990. *Qualitative Research: Analysis Types and Software Tools.* New York: Falmer Press.

Valentine, Barbara. 1993. "Undergraduate Research Behavior: Using Focus Groups to Generate Theory." *Journal of Academic Librarianship* 19 (5): 300–304.

Walter, Scott. In press. "Librarians as Teachers: A Qualitative Interview into Personal Identity." *College & Research Libraries.* Available: http://hdl.handle.net/2142/149 (accessed May 18, 2007).

Weitzman, Eben, and Matthew B. Miles. 1995. *Computer Programs for Qualitative Data Analysis: A Software Sourcebook.* Thousand Oaks, CA: Sage.

Wicks, Don A. 2004. "Older Adults and Their Information Seeking." *Behavioral & Social Sciences Librarian* 22 (2): 1–26.

Young, Pauline. 1939. *Scientific Social Surveys and Research.* New York: Prentice Hall.

Chapter 5

Observation and Usability

Observation and usability research studies share a common focus on human behavior and actions. They also share a common objective of systematically and scientifically examining what things people do in specific situations, as well as how and when they do them. Further, they comprise part of a mixed methods or multistrategy approach, where researchers use many different methodologies to examine an issue or a problem. They diverge, however, in their relationships to such mixed methods. Observation is commonly used as a part of a mixed method approach, within a study that also uses several other methodologies to gather data on a topic. Usability studies, in contrast, are wholes that result from the use of a mix of methods in gathering data. In practice, observation could be used as one of the methods in the "mix" of a usability study.

Often referred to as naturalistic research, observation studies typically focus on how people behave in their "real world" settings. In an observation study, researchers "quantify interactive behavior, either human or animal, by systematically assigning codes to behavioral events as they unfold over time" (Kitsantas, Ware and Kitsantas 2005, 914). In contrast to survey or interview research, observation is a more reliable indicator of how people really conduct themselves in a given situation. Surveys and interviews indicate how people think they behave or recall themselves as acting in a specific situation; however, we all know that there is a sharp difference between what people do and what they say they do or want to be seen as doing. While most users of a library catalog might describe their search for information as effective, observation of their behaviors while using the catalog could well reveal that they floundered while searching and only happened to find an appropriate source by chance. Because observation checks what people say against what they actually do, observational studies can also be used to test the validity of findings from other studies that have lead to programmatic changes. For example, an observation that most researchers did not, in fact, use the library during its new Saturday morning hours might call into question the validity of a survey that found that 56 percent of users believed the lack of Saturday morning hours was a significant defect of the library. Moreover, observation can be used not only to provide researchers with more accurate measures of human behavior but also to give researchers data with a higher degree of granularity than that obtained from surveys or interviews.

Observation studies are especially useful when researchers are interested in a specific process or when they wish to define a sequence of behaviors by objectively quantifying them through one or more observers. They can also be a valuable data collection method in situations where researchers would have difficulty directly acquiring information from participants who, for various reasons, cannot or will not discuss the topic under examination. Young children or Alzheimer's patients are participants who might prove impossible to interview because they are unable to express themselves, but their actions can be observed. Observation also works well whenever participants cannot easily discuss their behaviors, either because their activities are so routine that they are typically not cognizant of them, or because their activities are ones people have been trained not to discuss. For example, drivers may not be consciously aware of their use of traffic signals, and students are unlikely to admit to cheating on exams.

Observation can only be used to study behaviors (what a person does); it cannot be used to study cognition (what the person is thinking) or affect (how the person feels). Observation can also be expensive in that it uses up much of researchers' time and energy, especially in instances where researchers record events that last several hours. Observational studies are also especially prone to researcher bias, or misperceptions of human behavior caused by the researchers' own prejudices and expectations, unless the researchers take explicit steps to avoid or minimize the effects of bias. Observational studies tend to work well for people who are attentive and reflective; they work less well for people who feel the need to spring into immediate action once they notice a problem.

Usability research resembles observation in its concern with real life behaviors, but it is even more pragmatic in its overall purpose. A usability study is always product-driven and is not predominantly human-focused. It looks at how humans use something as a way of improving that device or process. According to Nielsen (1994), usability is one of two main elements that comprise the usefulness of the system. A system's utility is whether the system does what is needed, while its usability is users' ability to easily deal with the system's functionality. Usability can be conceptualized as part of a larger field of study, commonly known as either user-centered design or human factor design. User-centered design/human factor design is "the practice of designing products so that users can perform required use, operation, service, and supportive tasks with a minimum of stress and a maximum of efficiency," and its purpose is to "make the design to 'fit the user' as opposed to trying to make the user 'fit the design'" (Woodson, Tillman and Tillman 1992, 3). Like user-centered design/human factor design, usability studies focus both on (1) the fit between the system and its users, and (2) how well man-made objects, such as systems or programs, perform in natural settings with typical users. Usability studies look specifically at how well people are able to use the system and also examine all the various ways people interact with the system. In some ways, a usability study is a validity test because its overall question is "does this *thing* do what it is designed to do?" Usability testing employs controlled experimentation to determine how well people use the product; therefore, in investigating the product, researchers need to identify measurable goals for the product, set up test scenarios, map out how they will measure these scenarios, and determine how users' satisfaction will be measured. Usability studies can be good research projects for people who enjoy tinkering with their methods and proceeding by trial-and-error. They are less congenial for researchers who like control in the research setting or in the design or modification of systems.

FINDING A TOPIC

Observation studies can be divided roughly into three types:

1. *Participant observation:* Concerned with thoroughly studying individuals or a group of people in their natural environment over an extended time period in order to describe and understand that individual or group. Participant observation has its origins in anthropology, where it was pioneered by Bronislaw Malinowski, Franz Boaz, and Margaret Mead.
2. *Reactive observation:* Involves studying individual or group behaviors in a controlled setting in which the participants are aware that they are being observed and that the actions studied are dictated by the study's research design.
3. *Unobtrusive observation:* Often referred to as naturalistic observation. Researchers conducting unobtrusive studies observe participants in natural settings without the participants' awareness of the observation.

All three types exist in library science research, although researchers most often use modified versions of both reactive and unobtrusive observation. Strict participant observation studies, such as those conducted by noted anthropologists, are almost nonexistent in library science research due to the large time commitments required of the researcher. For instance, a science librarian might consider conducting a participant observation study that consisted of spending a semester in the Physics department observing the information and research activities of its students and faculty. In this scenario, the science librarian would need to take the entire semester off work. Similar to the Cathy Small/Rebekah Nathan study profiled in Chapter 4, where Small spent a year as a freshman at a large public university interviewing her dorm and classmates to understand college students, a researcher conducting a participant observation must devote a large time period to the study. Practitioner researchers, such as librarians, typically do not have large amounts of unstructured time to devote to a participant observation study. Unless they are granted a sabbatical or are able to take a leave of absence, participant observation research is most likely not in the cards for on-the-job library researchers.

The most notable of the unobtrusive observation studies in librarianship are those where researchers observed the reference interview in order to evaluate reference services by determining the accuracy and success of librarian responses to reference questions (Crowley and Childers 1971; Hernon and McClure 1987; Tygett, Lawson and Weesies 1996). Some people object to the validity of such unobtrusive observation studies by questioning whether they properly theorize users' motives for seeking help at the reference desk. Users may, in fact, be seeking advice or instructional assistance—not factual answers—when they visit the reference desk (Tyckoson 1992). Others criticize these studies for applying interpretative frameworks that may not accurately reflect the real world situation underlying the observational data. Many of the questions asked in the unobtrusive studies of reference service—like many of the questions asked in actual reference work— have no definitive answer, or they have a number of "correct" answers beyond researchers' predefined answers (Whitlach 2000). Such criticisms reflect the difficulties of finding a topic for an observational research project in reference. Nevertheless, unobtrusive studies remain a viable means of studying users' behavior in libraries. Unless librarians understand what their users actually do when they interact with an information resource or when they encounter a new or redesigned service, librarians cannot hope to develop resources or services to better serve that population. And the previously noted criticisms can be avoided with a carefully crafted and implemented research design. Moreover, with the advent of impersonal Internet communication tools such as instant messaging and chat, unobtrusive studies present intriguing possibilities for service evaluation. Figure 5-1 lists other model studies that use unobtrusive observational methods.

Observation studies in library science are focused on three main areas:

- *Studies that use unobtrusive methods to measure reference transactions.* As mentioned above, unobtrusive studies are often focused on librarians' behaviors and actions. Alafiatoayo, Yip, and Blunden-Ellis (1996) examined both the general reference processes employed in libraries and reference librarians' roles. They conducted unobtrusive studies at two universities and also sent out questionnaires to reference librarians at 22 different libraries in Great Britain. Childers (1980) studied 57 public libraries in New York asking the same 20 questions over a six-month period to determine the preparedness of library staff to negotiate the question. Hernon and McClure (1987) sought to determine the correct answer rate in both general and government documents reference services offered at public

Figure 5-1: Studies Using Observation

Fitzgerald, Mary Ann, and Chad Galloway. 2001. "Relevance Judging, Evaluation, and Decision Making in Virtual Libraries: A Descriptive Study." *Journal of the American Society for Information Science and Technology* 52 (12): 989–1010.

> *The researchers used a mixed methods approach of interviews, observations, transaction logs and think-aloud procedures in studying ten undergraduates searching Georgia's GALILEO virtual library, specifically focusing on users' critical thinking in the context of relevance judgment, source evaluation, and decision making. Appendices provide examples of users' relevance and evaluative strategies.*

Larkin-Lieffers, Patricia A. 2001. "Informational Picture Books in the Library: Do Young Children Find Them?" *Public Library Quarterly* 20 (3): 3–28.

> *The author evaluated children's access to informational picture books at ten public libraries using unobtrusive observation of children's use of these collections. The author noted book location, types of shelving, shelf height, and book display method as determinants in children's choices in book selection in the structured observation phase. To explore children's rationale in book selection, the author mapped collection locations and browsing routes in the unstructured phase.*

Norlin, Elaina. 2000. "Reference Evaluation: A Three-Step Approach—Surveys, Unobtrusive Observations, and Focus Groups." *College & Research Libraries* 61 (6): 546–553.

> *Researcher conducted a three-semester evaluative study of reference services using a mixed methods approach where over 100 students completed intake surveys, conducted unobtrusive observation of the reference staff, filled out observation worksheets and participated in focus groups. Findings are reported by semester, by user groups and their tendencies, by positive behaviors reference staff exhibited, and by areas of improvement.*

Ross, Johanna. 1983. "Observations of Browsing Behavior in an Academic Library." *College & Research Libraries* 44 (4): 269–276.

> *The author studied browsing over one academic quarter and intersession to see how the Physical Sciences Library collection was browsed as well as the average number of Items browsed per collection, the average number of browsers, and the areas of the collection users browsed. Basing her research design on that of Simon and Fussler, the author conducted random samples by 15-minute intervals of randomly sampled shelf ranges.*

Ward, David. 2004. "Measuring the Completeness of Reference Transactions in Online Chats: Results of an Unobtrusive Study." *Reference & User Services Quarterly* 44 (1): 46–56.

> *Researcher conducted an unobtrusive study that looked at how completely users' subject-based research questions were answered in chat reference sessions over a one-month period. Five proxies were trained in questioning skills and asked a total of 72 questions. Transcripts were analyzed using Childers' scale for correctness, RUSA's Guidelines for Behavioral Performance of Reference and Information Services Professionals, and the library's chat policy, which is shown in the appendices. Other information in the appendices include proxy evaluation sheets, training materials, and sample questions.*

and academic libraries. Ward (described in Figure 5-1) investigated how completely subject-based research questions were answered in a chat reference service. Tygett, Lawson and Weesies (1996) used mixed methods to test the accuracy and completeness of the reference answer, employing unobtrusive observation, an evaluation worksheet, and focus groups to probe information gleaned from the worksheets.

- *Studies that analyze patron or librarian behaviors in the library.*
  Some of these studies originate from a sense that an area or a specific service needs improvement and that the library can better meet user needs by better understanding user or librarian behaviors. Ross (described in Figure 5-1) studied user browsing patterns in her physical sciences library in order to make recommendations for off-site storage. In another browsing study, Larkin-Lieffers (2001) examined which physical and display factors contributed to young children's use of the picture book collection. In her study of librarians' approachability, Radford (1998) unobtrusively observed librarians' nonverbal signals at two academic libraries in order to determine the importance of these signals in helping patrons assess librarians' approachability.

- *Studies that examine patrons' use of resources or tools.*
  Most patron usage studies focus on how library resources meet users' needs, as well as how specific patron groups use specific library resources. For example, Arrigona and Matthews (1988) contrasted reference librarians' and patrons' use of the reference collection through tally sheets and table counts, noting that each group uses the collection in different ways. Slone (2000) was interested in public library users' strategies in searching the online catalog. Similarly, Thorne and Whitlach (1994) looked at user success in locating materials in the online catalog, and Tenopir, Wang, Pollard, Zhang and Simmons (2004) examined how various students and faculty searched the *ScienceDirect* electronic journal system for class-related topics provided by the research team.

Usability studies have been widely used in library research for the past decade or so, as libraries have become more and more in command of launching their own Web sites. They have also been used in local efforts to customize libraries' many commercially produced online catalogs, electronic resource management systems, chat reference systems, and bibliographic and full text databases. All of these are commercially purchased or licensed products that allow library administrators to tweak various system functions and decorate the interface so they are locally relevant. Usability tests are also pertinent to other library "products" such as home-grown online tutorials, self-checkout systems, shelving configurations, and sets of instructions that detail new projects or programs. The list of potential topics is endless, but Figure 5-2 provides a description of some model usability studies in library science.

A usability study should not be undertaken without careful planning. Nor should researchers assume that a product will never need any future refinements simply because a usability test was once conducted and the system had been

Figure 5-2: Studies Using Usability Testing

Augustine, Susan, and Courtney Greene. 2002. "Discovering How Students Search a Library Web Site: A Usability Case Study." *College & Research Libraries* 63 (4): 354–365.

Researchers studied the ease of navigation and clarity of their library's recently redesigned Web site through hour-long usability tests consisting of 20 tasks each with 12 participants. Findings indicate that despite clear site design, users are still very unaware of library tools and resources and their use.

Cockrell, Barbara J., and Elaine Anderson Jayne. 2002. "How Do I Find an Article? Insights from a Web Usability Study." *Journal of Academic Librarianship* 28 (3): 122–132.

Authors wished to learn the navigational paths users took in searching for articles on the library's Web site as one part of a usability study. Fifty participants representing faculty, graduate and undergraduate students completed three separate tasks and were asked to "think aloud" their actions and decisions. Findings include specific recommendations to improve the library's Web site. Appendix lists the 20 task questions for the usability test.

Graham, John-Bauer, Jodi Poe, and Kimberly Weatherford. 2003. "Functional by Design: A Comparative Study to Determine the Usability and Functionality of One Library's Web Site." *Technical Services Quarterly* 21 (2): 33–49.

In order to evaluate how well the library's redesigned Web site helped users to find materials with ease, the authors asked 30 participants through an online survey to find three types of library materials on both the old and the new Web sites and then rate the usability of each. Survey included in the appendix.

Travis, Tiffini Anne, and Elaina Norlin. 2002. "Testing the Competition: Usability of Commercial Information Sites Compared with Academic Library Web Sites." *College & Research Libraries* 63 (5): 433–448.

As a way to determine whether design features in commercially produced electronic research Web products can be used to enhance the usability of a library's Web site, the researchers conducted usability tests on two academic library and two commercial electronic research Web sites. In their study the researchers asked nine participants to complete three to five tasks per Web site. Findings indicate libraries need to increase advertising of their services, that they should avoid the "librarian knows best" model of Web design and navigation, and that they must regularly conduct user-centered usability tests on their Web sites.

determined to achieve its overall goals. Usability testing is a test-retest venture that seeks *constant* product improvement. Also referred to as an iterative design process, usability testing needs to be employed both throughout the launch process and regularly after the product has been launched to check whether the product is still viable and of use to its primary clientele. Librarian-researchers who are considering undertaking usability research are encouraged to consult one or more of the excellent texts listed in Figure 5-3.

Most of the specific topics addressed by usability studies within library science research can be organized into four different types, each of which are used at different phases of product design (Rubin 1994):

1. *Exploratory:* These tests are conducted in the early stages of product development and are concerned with the overall purpose and usefulness of

Figure 5-3: Suggested Works on Usability

Krug, Steve. 2000. *Don't Make Me Think: A Common Sense Approach to Web Usability.* Indianapolis, IN: New Riders.

> As the title implies, Krug's work is fun, informative, helpful and down to earth. For those undertaking a team-based approach to Web site design, "Chapter 8: The Farmer and the Cowman Should Be Friends" is essential reading.

Nielsen, Jakob. 2000. *Designing Web Usability: The Practice of Simplicity.* Indianapolis, IN: New Riders.

> Nielsen is one of the usability gurus and this work leads novice and experienced designers alike through all phases of making a Web page usable: page design, content design, site design and accessibility issues for users with disabilities. Nielsen's Web site at http://useit.com is full of helpful advice tips and his more recent work, Homepage Usability: 50 Websites Deconstructed, is worth reading, especially for librarians developing or reconstructing home pages.

Norlin, Elaina, and C. M. Winters. 2002. *Usability Testing for Library Web Sites: A Hands-on Guide.* Chicago: American Library Association.

> The authors are experienced in Web site usability testing and in this work they provide basic guidance in good library Web design, provide guidelines and advice in conducting and evaluating usability tests, instruct readers on involving colleagues and users in effecting change, and provide specific examples of tests.

Rubin, Jeffrey. 1994. *Handbook of Usability Testing: How to Plan, Design and Conduct Effective Tests.* New York: John Wiley.

> Rubin's work is an all around bestseller and an essential source for anyone conducting usability tests. He leads the reader step-by-step through all phases of a usability tests and provides helpful examples along the way.

the product. Since the product is often in its infancy, exploratory usability tests typically take the form of product "walk-throughs" where researchers and users explore screen shots or other paper visuals of the product. These tests are typically informal conversations, with researchers and users discussing basic functions and uses of the product. Typically, researchers record exploratory test sessions either by taking elaborate notes or by audio-taping the session. The preliminary studies in designing an online tutorial documented by Veldof, Prasse and Mills (1999) and by Veldof and Beavers (2001) are solid examples of exploratory usability studies.

2. *Assessment:* Assessment tests evaluate basic product functions. These tests are most often conducted halfway through product design and focus more on information-gathering than the verification test described below. In assessment tests, users always perform specific tasks using the actual product while researchers record specific quantitative measures (e.g., speed or accuracy).

3. *Verification:* These tests are employed in the final stages of product development for the purpose of verifying whether the product meets predetermined performance standards. Verification tests are typically quantitative.

Augustine and Greene (see Figure 5-2) verified the navigational structure of their library's Web site by comparing the average number of mouse clicks "typical" users employed in completing 20 tasks with the number of mouse clicks experts used. They also calculated the mean time it took users to achieve the task goal.

4. *Comparison:* A comparison test is not dependent on stage of product development. It is often used to compare different search interfaces, products, and design styles. Travis and Norlin (see Figure 5-2) compared two academic library Web sites with two commercially produced electronic Web research services (Questia and Blackboard) in an effort to learn whether users understand and navigate commercially produced Web sites more easily than library Web sites. Similarly, in the early stages of a Web site redesign project at University of North Texas, librarians decided to gauge user preferences by comparing their current site with three other academic library sites (Thomsett-Scott 2005).

When thinking about using observation methods or usability testing in one's research project, librarian-researchers first need to consider how suitable these methods are for their specific research problems. If researchers' topics concern how people do things in the library or how well a locally developed product might function, then, depending on the focus, either one is a good choice. If, however, the main focus of the topic concerns what users think or feel about library services or resources, then library researchers might want to seek other methods such as interviews, focus groups, or questionnaires in analyzing cognitive or affective aspects.

FORMULATING QUESTIONS

Observation studies are concerned with human behaviors; thus, their research questions focus on how individuals do something, how well they do it, how frequently, and in what ways. Similar to interview research, another naturalistic, qualitative methodology, observation studies seek to explore behaviors and, from the outset, wonder what people do in specific situations. These studies help researchers gain better understanding of the population studied. In this way, studies that seek to discover user practices and actions in relation to local systems benefit the profession as a whole by extending our common knowledge base. This is further demonstrated by considering the model studies listed in Figure 5-1:

- How thoroughly are subject-based research questions answered in a chat reference environment? (Ward 2004)
- How do young children gain access to information picture books at their public library? (Larkin-Lieffers 2001)

- What areas of the collection are most frequently browsed and what is the average number of items browsed, as well as what is the average number of browsers? (Ross 1983)
- How do users of a virtual library system critically assess, judge relevance, and decide which research items to select? (Fitzgerald and Galloway 2001)

Usability research questions are focused on practical ways to fix problems and on designing or redesigning products. To that end, a usability study does not test hypotheses; instead, it features one or more problem statements. These problem statements should be testable. Thus, the general question or problem statement for a study might be "is the library's Web site usable?" but a smaller, measurable question might be "can users find a book in the online catalog if they know its title?" It also follows that research questions in usability studies are iterative, in that they lead to further practical problem-solving questions. For example, "if given a task to find a book in the online catalog by title, which search type do users typically choose?" might lead researchers to investigate why users predominantly choose the *Quick Search* button instead of the *Title Search* button when searching for items by their title. Take, for example, the broad research problems posed in the studies featured in Figure 5-2 and some of their smaller, concretely focused questions:

- *Broader question:* Can design features found in Questia be used to enhance the usability of a traditional academic library Web site? (Travis and Norlin 2002)
  Smaller, task-focused question: How successfully can students find an article on male eating disorders in each of the four Web sites?
- *Broader question:* How clear and easy to navigate is the library's redesigned Web site? (Augustine and Greene 2002)
  Smaller, task-focused question: How many minutes, seconds, and mouse clicks does it take users to find technical help online?
- *Broader question:* How does the library's redesigned Web site help users more easily find materials? (Graham, Poe and Weatherford 2003)
  Smaller, task-focused question: When confronted with a task requiring them to find an article, can users more easily understand the headings for article databases in the previous or current version of the library Web site?
- *Broader question:* Do users experience difficulty in locating articles because they do not know the concepts and processes of bibliographic information systems, or is it because the library's Web page does not direct them appropriately? (Cockrell and Jayne 2002)
  Smaller, task-focused question: How successful are different groups of users (faculty, graduates, and undergraduates) in finding the title of a magazine article on affirmative action?

DEFINING THE POPULATION

Most observation studies in library science, especially unobtrusive studies, do not sample the population in the "normal" manner. This makes perfect sense when one considers that researchers observing human behaviors in natural settings cannot decide to randomly observe every fifth user because they might miss some really interesting and important behaviors exhibited by the second and fourth users. Instead of random sampling of people, observation studies employ either event or time sampling, and these can be random. Event sampling is where researchers have decided to study a specific activity, and when it occurs, they monitor it. For example, Larkin-Lieffers (2001) monitored activities in three children's reading rooms, noting every time a young child removed a book that faced forward, or that faced spine outward, or that was shelved at eye level. Another example is Ward's (2004) study, which looked at only subject-based research questions occurring in a chat reference environment and ignored non-subject-based questions.

In time sampling, researchers observe behaviors at different points in time for periods of predetermined duration. Ross's (1983) browsing study is an excellent example of time sampling. She divided the library's hours of service into 15-minute periods, then she used a table of random numbers to select both the time period and the day of the week to observe users browsing the collection. To indicate where observers were to begin observing, she numbered all shelf ranges and randomly assigned a shelf range for each time period. During each of the selected observation periods, observers checked the stack area, noting the Library of Congress two letter subject designation for the browser's chosen browsing area, the numbers of books browsed, and whether the browsed book was reshelved or left on a table or cart for reshelving.

In reactive observation studies, where participants are observed in artificial, test-type situations (such as those described in Norlin [2000] and Fitzgerald and Galloway's [2001] studies), researchers can and do aim for representative samples. In these two cases, both sets of researchers wanted to obtain samples that matched, as closely as possible, the overall population of their respective universities. The Fitzgerald and Galloway study contained a large number of seniors (80 percent) in their participant pool, and this may have skewed their results somewhat, although they note this drawback in their discussion. Most researchers conducting both reactive observation studies and usability tests inventory prospective subjects with a demographic survey and use this data to determine whether their sample matches the larger population. Because most researchers have difficulty obtaining participants, they often take everyone and then note any gaps or limitations in their sample in their write-up of the study. If undertaking such a study in a school, public, or special library environment, researchers will want to consider how best to solicit participants from their wider population. Some strategies for public librarians/researchers could include a mass mailing to library card holders that describes the study, offers an incentive, and includes instructions on how to volunteer. In a school library environment, librarian-researchers might want to enlist help from their fellow teachers in their school or within their school system, or work with other school librarians in their district in recruiting participants.

Researchers in usability circles have yet to agree on how many users make up a good sample. Many are familiar with Jakob Nielsen's (2000) adage that one only needs to test five users since, "[a]s you add more and more users, you learn less and less because you will keep seeing the same things again and again." Nielsen believes that researchers are better off using their research budgets to conduct several small tests with fewer users than conducting one large study with many participants. Although his point is well taken, we encourage librarian-researchers to test out their product with more than five users in spite of the redundancy factor cited by Nielsen. Aiming for a purposeful, representative sample of between ten and 20 participants is a good target. Although researchers may wish to test more than this number, they ought to avoid testing fewer unless they are conducting several small tests as Nielsen advises.

For the most part, usability studies employ purposeful sampling in selecting participants. Rubin (1994, 119) admonishes against testing the "wrong" people because the end "results will be questionable and of limited value." To Rubin the "right" people represent the typical user of the product being tested. On a college campus, the typical user of the library's Web page could be anyone from the entire campus community. The typical user of a Web-based tutorial on how to cite resources in APA style, on the other hand, would be substantially narrower, consisting primarily of undergraduate and graduate students. Rubin suggests creating a profile of the audience for whom the product is being developed as a way to guide researchers in the recruitment and selection phases of the project. Researchers can use such a profile as a baseline against which to measure whether their participant pool matches their typical user. Besides creating a profile of the typical user, usability researchers need to aim for a variety of skill levels in their user group. In any usability study it is always a good idea to include novice, less competent users along with very competent users. Many usability researchers conducting studies on searching the library's Web site, its online catalog, or research databases ask participants to fill out an intake form that not only asks for demographic information (age, status, gender) but also queries the participant's Internet and research experience.

Most usability tests are conducted on a very small sample of the larger population. Cockrell and Jayne (see Figure 5-2) aimed for a sample of 50 participants, which is a large group of participants indeed in the realm of usability studies. Other model studies shown in Figure 5-2 used smaller samples. For example, Augustine and Green (2002) tested 16 users, and Travis and Norlin (2002) tested only nine.

SELECTING A RESEARCH DESIGN

Whether conducting an observation or a usability study, researchers ought to pilot test their data collection methods. This includes any intake forms, observation logs, or matrices. Researchers should also plan in advance how they will analyze their data. It is especially important that any data collection instrument is designed so that data analysis is not overly difficult or tedious. Just as a teacher develops a test with the grading scheme in mind, so ought the researcher develop data collection instruments that ensure logical and expedient analysis.

If researchers' plans require statistical measures and they do not feel confident with their current knowledge of statistics, they should not be dissuaded from their project. As Whitlach (2000) remarks in her work on reference assessment, if you do not have experience with data analysis, find an expert who can assist you. Many colleges and universities have research or statistical analysis centers with staff who can guide and assist researchers.

Many observation studies rely on external, previously developed scales or use common definitions of primary concepts under investigation. Ward (see Figure 5-1) based his measurements of how well subject-based research questions were answered in chat reference transactions on Childers' scale for correctness, a scale that was originally developed based on an unobtrusive observation study conducted at public libraries in the 1970s. Fitzgerald and Galloway (2001), also listed in Figure 5-1, looked to major theorists in defining their concepts of relevance judging, evaluation, and decision making. Using pre-developed definitions or already created measures and scales provides an added benefit to researchers because it makes their research more valid, reliable, and comparable to other studies. A final point on the research design of observation studies is that almost all of these in library science are conducted as part of a larger research project using other methodologies. In other words, observation is not the only data collection method; researchers also use surveys and questionnaires, interview participants, and use formal tests to gauge participants' knowledge.

Any usability study incorporates the following basic elements in its design (Rubin 1994):

1. Developing problem statements or objectives, not hypotheses.
2. Using representative sample users that do not need to be random.
3. Using testing tasks that represent the actual workings of the product.
4. Controlled observation and questioning of participants during the test.
5. Collecting both quantitative and qualitative data to measure product performance and user preferences.

In setting up a usability study, researchers need to remember that usability testing is an iterative cycle of exploring, assessing, validating, and comparing. Depending on the stage of the product design each of these four tests are employed:

1. *Usefulness:* This test assesses users' reasons for using the product, concentrating on how well the product allows users to achieve their goals. All products in a usability study need to achieve the goal of usefulness. If a product is not useful but is easy to use, easy to learn how to use and users like using it, it still will not be used at all. Consider the fads of pet rocks and chia pets. Both pet rocks and chia pets are, in a sense, easy to use and to learn how to use (although some might quibble that the pet rock did not have a use). But neither object could be considered "useful" in the general sense of the term.

2. *Ease of use:* This test looks at how easy the product is to use. Ways to measure ease of use are quantitative, stipulating that a specific number or percentage of users must attain a certain performance speed or rate of error. For example, with a self-checkout system, an ease of use test could require that 90 percent of all users successfully check out two library items within ten seconds or less.

3. *Ease of learning:* This test measures how quickly and easily people can learn to use the system and how quickly and easily infrequent users can relearn how to use the system. Consider the Internet application products of the 1990s prior to Microsoft Windows applications such as telnet, Archie, and VERONICA. Most of these products were very useful because they allowed users to communicate with one another, transfer files, and search other computer networks for files of interest. However, these products had a steep learning curve, and once learned, they were still difficult to use. For infrequent users, these tools proved particularly irritating and frustrating since time had to be spent relearning the tools.

4. *Satisfaction level:* This test refers to how well users like a product and is typically measured through participant interviews that probe their perceptions, feelings, and opinions of the product. Consider a self-checkout unit that talks, similar to grocery store self-checkout systems. If the voice is irritating or gives bossy, intellectually insulting instructions, users will not like it and, consequently, will not use the product. The same could be said for a library Web site design with layout and fonts that echo a rival school's design. If users are offended or bothered by these factors, they will not enjoy using the product no matter how well it functions.

When setting up a study, usability researchers need to heed the advice of Dickstein and Mills (2000) and remember that they cannot test everything. They need to identify the tasks that are most important for their users to perform and concentrate on testing those tasks. Researchers should also remember the main goals of usability (Norlin and Winters, listed in Figure 5-3):

1. Always keep the user in mind.
2. Keep the usability test simple but elegant.

3. Remember that usability is all about improving performance through design.
4. Refine your product design and retest.

A usability test must have measurable goals as its outcome in order to ascertain whether the product is meeting those goals. These goals need to be articulated in the planning stages, often taking the form of questions. Consider the list of questions shown in Figure 5-4. Each of these questions should be accounted for in researchers' worksheets or data collection logs because each serves as an element that can be computed in calculating the overall usability of a product, in this case a Web site. In designing their own worksheets, like that in Figure 5-4, researchers need to plan carefully how they will collect, record, store, and analyze the data because any data collection instrument needs to address both the research questions as well as the ways those questions will be answered.

Most usability tests measure how well users perform in four different areas:

1. *Time on task:* The amount of time that users take to complete a given task.
2. *Accuracy:* The number of mistakes or the number of misinterpretations a user makes.
3. *Recall:* The ease or difficulty with which an infrequent user remembers how to use the system.
4. *Emotional response:* The way users respond to the tasks they have completed.

Most usability studies have very tight research designs; for instance, users may spend about an hour attempting to perform predetermined tasks on a Web-based product. Researchers often employ think-aloud protocols to get at cognitive processes, user preferences or decision making, or a combination of all three. With a think-aloud protocol, participants are asked to verbalize their thoughts, opinions, decisions, likes and dislikes as they work on a task (Ericsson and Simon 1993, 1980). As a data collection method, a think-aloud protocol is a quick way to obtain qualitative data, and it helps to identify both problems with the product and users' misconceptions. When conducting a usability study

Figure 5-4:   Questions to Guide Usability Test Construction

- Can the test participants complete the tasks successfully?
- If successful, how quickly do participants complete each task?
- If successful, how many mouse clicks does it take participants to complete each task?
- How satisfied are participants with the site?
- In the case of unsuccessful or partially successful task completion, what needs to change on the Web site to ensure that it will allow a higher degree of user success?

with think-aloud protocols, researchers should keep a log noting where users were in their navigational path and what tasks they were working on when they made particular comments so that "responses" can be mapped to the "stimuli" provoking them. Alternatively, researchers could use screen capture programs or transaction logs to match users' comments with their navigation paths.

GATHERING DATA

In unobtrusive observation studies, researchers describe exactly what occurs, including any natural changes in the environment of the interaction—regardless of whether the researchers think such changes are "important." Suppose, for example, that a researcher is observing circulation desk transactions. If birthday balloons are delivered at the circulation desk for a staff member, the researcher would note that delivery along with all other transactions. In contrast, in reactive observation studies conducted in a laboratory environment, researchers manipulate some aspect of the environment and note participants' actions or reactions. In either case, researchers need to be sure that they accurately record and evaluate participants' behaviors and achieve a high level of intercoder reliability in the analysis phase. Because of this, the coding plan needs to be clearly defined. When researchers code observational data they are recording events as they occur in time. For events to be recorded in real time, researchers must first have constructed codebooks with written descriptions of events to be observed and recorded. Codebooks should describe any rules and provide any instructions that researchers will rely upon in recording and then evaluating the observed behavior. It is useful to incorporate any preexisting, external coding systems that include known measurements so as to (1) lessen the time spent in developing such materials and (2) draw upon the validity and reliability of these instruments. Alternatively, researchers can develop their own coding and analysis schemes that reflect the concepts featured in their studies.

Observation studies are often more costly to conduct than, say, bibliometric studies because behaviors must be constantly recorded in order to guard against observer bias. Having an objective record of the observed behavior (e.g., an audio or video recording, screen captures, transaction logs) is also an excellent way to improve reliability. An objective record allows researchers to "return" and observe the event as many times as needed, which increases reliability because it serves as a permanent record of the event that external researchers can view and even code, if they wish. Moreover, most recordings allow for duplication, so that the recorded event can be used for inter-observer tests.

Usability studies are typically rigid in their data collection procedures. These procedures usually consist of an intake demographic survey; a series of tasks that participants perform in the course of a scripted session; and, sometimes, a debriefing session allowing participants to evaluate the session. Data collection procedures can also include think-aloud protocols for capturing participants' reflections on their choices and decisions; screen capture programs for charting users' navigational paths through the system; worksheets for recording information about users' navigational paths; and so on.

Researchers use a variety of different types of tests in gathering data in a usability study, depending on the phase of product development and the particular component of the product researchers are studying. The most frequently used tests are:

1. *Card sort method:* This method involves participants in ordering information for a Web site by organizing its content—represented by cards—in ways that make sense to them. Researchers create a card for each topic from the Web site and then provide participants with a stack of cards. Participants then sort the stack, grouping like cards together. After participants have sorted the cards, researchers note the groupings and may interview participants about their choices. The card sort method also helps researchers to come up with labels or names for the different groups. A particularly "catchy" word or phrase used by a participant in a card sort activity could serve as the basis for categorizing observations.

2. *Focus groups:* These are conducted as described in Chapter 4. In a usability study, a focus group helps researchers and designers understand users' reactions to product ideas. They also give researchers insights into users' beliefs, desires, and emotions about the product. Focus groups are particularly helpful as a way of debriefing participants who have just completed usability task tests such as a card sort or a guided walk through. Focus groups are also useful in initial product design stages because they gather information about users' preferences in general.

3. *Prototypes:* These are draft versions of the product (typically a Web site) either on paper or as a bare bones Web site that allows minimal navigation. A prototype test is often an excellent way to gather information from users while in the early stages of planning for and designing the product. It is also a quick and easy way for researchers to find out if they are on the right track with their plans and design.

4. *Individual interview:* The researchers and participants work together for about an hour, with the researchers probing users' attitudes and preferences in-depth.

5. *Usability tasks:* This is the typical usability test where participants are instructed to complete specific tasks, and researchers observe and record their actions. These task tests should be piloted to ensure that they can be accomplished and that they actually test those aspects of the system that researchers wish to test.

INTERPRETING THE EVIDENCE

Most observation research studies analyze and present data in the form of basic summary statistics such as frequencies or rates. Raw frequencies count how many times an event or a behavior occurred. Larkin-Lieffers (2001) uses frequencies to first determine and then to report children's usage of informational picture books by shelving method and shelf height. Ross (1983) similarly provides frequency counts of the number of items removed and returned to the shelf; browsing frequency by time of day; and time span of all observed browsing activities. Researchers can also use percentages to indicate tendencies within user behavior. Ward (2004) uses percentages to indicate the presence of instruction within the transaction and the completeness of the transaction. If time of occurrence is important, researchers can calculate mean event durations, which are obtained by dividing the amount of time observed for a particular event by the number of times the event was observed. Ross was interested to learn which subject areas in her library users browsed the most frequently and for how long; thus, she calculated mean event durations.

Whether a researcher uses frequencies, percentages and/or mean event durations is determined by the research problem itself and the ways in which the data has been collected. Ross, for example, conducted her study in anticipation of moving sections of the collection to remote storage. Her study and research question revolved around which sections of the collection were browsed most frequently in order to ensure that she did not remove parts of the collection that users browsed frequently.

Usability studies typically analyze their data sets in ways that directly address the research problem. As shown in Figure 5-4, the data collected should represent measurable goals that can be summarized. As noted under "Selecting a Research Design," the research design should specify a level of success for each criterion tested. Some researchers set this level fairly high, at 80 percent or higher, others are more lenient and content with a 70 percent success rate. Thus, in interpreting the data, it is important to focus on the tasks where users were not successful because these tasks can help to inform and perhaps improve system design. It is also important to look at the data to identify user error or confusion. If transcripts from focus groups and from individual interviews indicate that users preferred to use the "Quick Search" button instead of the "Author/Title/Subject" button in searching the online catalog because they believed that that specific search option was indeed faster, then researchers ought to consider modifying the button label. (This is especially true in cases where the search is not really quick at all because that particular option always conducts a generic keyword search where most searches retrieve hits of 10,000 items or more). Once researchers have identified specific problems in the system, they then need to prioritize these by importance. Some problems, such as the one described above, might be judged as minor labeling flaws that can easily be fixed with more accurate search labels (e.g., "Keyword Search"). Other problems—such as retrieving a "File 404" error message when clicking on the help file—indicate more important problems that can also be solved quickly.

Sometimes library usability studies uncover important problems that do not have easy fixes, though, such as those over which the library has no control or those that require programming expertise not available locally. Researchers should try to identify programming problems or problems related to vendor-supplied software before the start of their study. Otherwise, it can be very frustrating to identify a problem that cannot be fixed and can undermine the accuracy of the other results of the study.

A final part of the analysis phase of a usability study is developing a set of recommendations to report to the study group or library administration and to include in presentations or publications. Several of the model studies listed in Figure 5-2 include recommendations that address design or service issues. Cockrell and Jayne (2002) provide four overarching recommendations for Web page design that would help users search for articles by topic. Then, tied to each of the four general recommendations, they also provide specific, achievable solutions to user misconceptions of how to navigate the Web site.

TELLING THE STORY

Most observation and usability studies take the traditional form of describing the problem or the research question; examining the relevant literature to highlight similar studies and summarize critical points regarding the topic; describing the methodology used in the study; reporting findings; and making recommendations based on the findings. Most usability studies profiled in this chapter also include the task lists or test instruments in the published study. Readers' understanding of the study is enhanced if they can look at the instruments used. Including the original test instrument in the study also helps contribute to the profession's knowledge about the topic under investigation and may aid other researchers in the future. Ward (2004), for instance, provides all instruments used in his study of chat reference (evaluation sheet, training directions, sample questions) as well as the library's policy on chat reference. Just as he used Childers' scale, so might another researcher use Ward's research design and similar instruments to conduct a completeness study in a new and different type of reference environment.

Another common aspect in describing an observation or a usability study is reporting findings in a visual manner with charts or tables that help the reader to visualize the findings. Many usability studies focusing on Web sites include screen shots of Web pages that highlight critical issues or demonstrate design or navigation features of concern. Researchers who conduct interviews or think-alouds may similarly include their subjects' comments verbatim within the discussion or recommendation sections to highlight important points or to illustrate users' reactions, preferences or misconceptions of the system studied. Fitzgerald and Galloway (2001) include in their appendices user comments and questions that illustrate two of the three conceptual areas they were researching: relevance judging and evaluation. Other researchers in the future could, in turn, use some of these statements describing how users evaluate information and judge its relevance to create their own instrument that measures these two concepts in other user groups. A final consideration in writing up the findings is to note any limitations of the study and to describe any problems encountered. This helps readers to understand the real world problems encountered in doing research; it demonstrates that the researcher is aware of many of the problems with the study; and it should inform others of some real caveats and items to avoid in designing their own research projects.

REFERENCES

Alafiatoayo, Benjamin O., Yau J. Yip, and John C. P. Blunden-Ellis. 1996. "Reference Transaction and the Nature of the Process for General Reference Assistance." *Library and Information Science Research* 18: 357–384.

Arrigona, Daniel R., and Eleanor Matthews. 1988. "A Use Study of an Academic Library Reference Collection." *RQ* 28: 71–81.

Childers, Thomas. 1980. "The Test of Reference." *Library Journal* 105: 924–928.

Crowley, Terence, and Thomas Childers. 1971. *Information Service in Public Libraries: Two Studies*. Metuchen, NJ: Scarecrow Press.

Dickstein, Ruth, and Vicki Mills. 2000. "Usability Testing at the University of Arizona Library: How to Let the Users in on the Design." *Information Technology and Libraries* 19 (3): 144–151.

Ericsson, K. Anders, and Herbert A. Simon. 1993. *Protocol Analysis: Verbal Reports as Data*. 2nd ed. Boston, MA: MIT Press.

Ericsson, K. Anders, and Herbert A. Simon. 1980. "Verbal Reports as Data." *Psychological Review* 87 (3): 215–251.

Gorman, Paul, Mary Lavelle, Lois Delcambre, and David Maier. 2002. "Following Experts at Work in Their Own Information Spaces: Using Observational Methods to Develop Tools for the Digital Library." *Journal of the American Society for Information Science and Technology* 53 (14): 1245–1250.

Hernon, Peter, and Charles McClure. 1987. *Unobtrusive Testing and Library Reference Services*. Norwood, NJ: Ablex.

Hernon, Peter, and Charles McClure. 1986. "Unobtrusive Reference Testing: The 55 Percent Rule." *Library Journal* 111 (April 15): 37–41.

Kitsantas, Anastasia, Herbert W. Ware, and Panagiota Kitsantas. 2005. "Observational Studies." In *Encyclopedia of Social Measurement*, edited by Kimberly Kempf-Leonard, 913–918. Amsterdam: Elsevier.

Nielsen, Jakob. 2000. "Why You Only Need to Test with 5 Users." *Alertbox*. Available: http://useit.com/alertbox/20000319.html (accessed May 18, 2007).

Nielson, Jakob. 1994. *Usability Engineering*. Cambridge, MA: Academic Press.

Radford, Marie. 1998. "Approach or Avoidance? The Role of Nonverbal Communication in the Academic Library User's Decision to Initiate a Reference Encounter." *Library Trends* 46 (4): 699–717.

Rubin, Jeffery. 1994. *Handbook of Usability Testing: How to Plan, Design and Conduct Effective Tests*. New York: Wiley.

Slone, Debra J. 2000. "Encounters with the OPAC: On-line Searching in Public Libraries." *Journal of the American Society for Information Science* 51 (8): 757–773.

Tenopir, Carol, Peiling Wang, Richard Pollard, Yan Zhang, and Beverly Simmons. 2004. "Use of Electronic Science Journals in the Undergraduate Curriculum: An Observational Study." In *ASIST 2004: Proceedings of the 67th ASIS & T Annual Meeting: Managing and Enhancing Information: Culture and Conflicts*, edited by Linda Schamber and Carol L. Barry, 64–71. Medford, NJ: Information Today.

Thomsett-Scott, Beth. 2005. "Providing a Complete Menu: Using Competitive Usability in a Home Page Usability Study." *Technical Services Quarterly* 23 (2): 33–47.

Thorne, Rosemary, and Jo Bell Whitlach. 1994. "Patron Online Catalog Success." *College & Research Libraries* 55 (6): 479–497.

Tyckoson, David. 1992. "Wrong Questions, Wrong Answers: Behavioral vs. Factual Evaluation of Reference Service." *The Reference Librarian* 38: 151–173.

Tygett, Mary, V., Lonnie Lawson, and Kathleen Weesies. 1996. "Using Undergraduate Marketing Students in an Unobtrusive Reference Observation." *RQ* 36: 270–276.

Veldof, Jerilyn, and Karen Beavers. 2001. "Going Mental: Tackling Mental Models for the Online Tutorial." *Research Strategies* 18 (1): 3–20.

Veldof, Jerilyn, Michael J. Prasse, and Victoria A. Mills. 1999. "Chauffeured by the User: Usability in the Electronic Library." *Journal of Library Administration* 26 (3/4): 115–140.

Whitlach, Jo Bell. 2000. *Evaluating Reference Services: A Practical Guide*. Chicago: American Library Association.

Woodson, Wesley E., Barry Tillman, and Peggy Tillman. 1992. *Human Factors Design Handbook: Information and Guidelines for the Design of Systems, Facilities, Equipment, and Products for Human Use*. 2nd ed. New York: McGraw Hill.

Chapter 6

Experimental Research

In the most basic sense of the word, "experiment" denotes "a test, trial, or tentative procedure, esp. one for the purpose of discovering something unknown or of testing a principle, supposition, etc.; . . . the conducting of such operations; . . . or to try or test esp. in order to discover or prove something" (*Random House Webster's College Dictionary* 1991, 470). According to this definition, a child touching a stove to see if it really is hot is experimenting. She/he is testing whether a parent's claim about the stove being hot is true, as well as what "hot" means in reference to stoves.

Experimental research similarly engages in testing or trying for the sake of discovery or proof, but it employs more rigorous rules for testing/trying and discovery/proof than the child did. In fact, most people think of experimental methodology in terms of these rigorous rules, which govern:

- formulation of hypotheses for testing
- probability sampling of subjects for study
- operationalization of key terms in the hypothesis, or the formation of working definitions for what behaviors or objects count as evidence of the constructs being studied
- use of standardized instruments or other pilot-tested instruments of proven validity and reliability
- attempts to control for and minimize sources of error in measurement
- use of inferential statistical techniques on measurement data

Experimental research is almost always quantitative; it often generates studies described as "scientific"; and it can be terrifying for beginning researchers. This last is most unfortunate, as experimental methodology is a powerful heuristic. Some critics object that experiments, with all their controls, invoke an "artificial situation that may not reflect how people think and behave in the real world," but these controls are precisely what make experimental studies more replicable than others (Case 2002, 169). In the real world, librarians' responses to reference questions are unlikely ever to be reviewed by peers in comparison to rating criteria as a measure of their quality. An experiment that measured the quality of reference by peer review/rating criteria would not capture the complexity of reality, where librarians and patrons have their own measures of quality and often bring their feelings toward each other into their informal calculations of quality. Because the procedures for peer review and the rating criteria have been codified, however, such an experiment could be repeated easily by other researchers to see whether they get similar results. Replicability of more "real life" approaches to measuring the quality of reference answers—ones having librarians and patrons apply their own rating procedures and criteria—would, in contrast, depend upon one researcher finding librarians and patrons who chanced to have the same standards and feelings as those in another study. This latter is an unlikely possibility given the diversity of human beings!

Moreover, by "applying a theory to a particular case in an attempt to test the theory" (Case 2002, 165), experimental methodology offers clear ways to bridge theory and practice. Do the "big ideas" of theories actually hold up when tested? Can "commonsense" practices be proven to have some basis in theory? Historically, only a small percentage of studies within librarianship have used experimental methodology (Grotzinger 1981, 39ff.), and it has long been hoped that this percentage would increase with concomitant benefits to the profession if only librarians would become more familiar with the benefits and techniques of experimental methodology.

FINDING A TOPIC

Some authors emphasize other aspects in defining experimental methodology, notably planned interventions or the manipulation of changes in the environment (Case 2002; Goldhor 1972; Green 2003) or the investigation of causality (Busha and Harter 1980; Goldhor 1972; Gustafson and Smith 1994; Peng 2003). We feel, however, that it is most important to keep the focus on the twin components of testing/trying and discovery/proof contained in the basic definition of "experiment." Other guides to research methodology support our decision to focus on a broader range of experiments here, as they, too, include experiments investigating correlation as well as causation. Sometimes they describe these as ex post facto experiments, quasi-experiments, or retrospective studies. (Cf. Busha and Harter 1980, and Carey 1998.) As these guides emphasize, a "true" experiment is not always possible (Busha and Harter 1980), or may take too long or be too expensive (Carey 1998). Moreover, studies of correlation serve as a "tool for uncovering potential causal links" for future studies (Carey 1998, 31): "Indeed, if two things actually are causally linked they will be correlated, so evidence of a correlation may provide some initial reason to suspect two factors are linked" as cause and effect (Carey 1998, 10).

These two components (testing/trying and discovery/proof) are what most characterize and distinguish experimental methodology. Experimental methodology is not content with descriptions of things as they are (e.g., usage statistics on library databases); rather, it seeks to predict relationships between things (e.g., does patron status relate to database usage?) Causal relationships between things (e.g., does being a graduate student cause higher levels of database use?) are a particular focus of experimental methodology in its most rigorous form, although we include in Figure 6-1 examples of some less rigorous studies that test relationships without seeking causation because we feel that beginning researchers may find these models more helpful. Researchers should also keep the basic testing/trying, discovery/proof orientation of experimental methodology in mind because it is technically possible to employ other research methodologies within an experimental framework. For example, Young and Ackerson (1995) actually employ content analysis within an experimental framework. The testing/trying, discovery/proof can be seen in their use of experimental and control groups to discover whether "modified" library instruction led to better bibliographies in student research papers than "traditional" library instruction did. The bibliography entries were examined and scored on a rating sheet using the methodology of content analysis, but the traditional/modified comparison was experimental.

Experimental studies within librarianship, such as those listed in Figure 6-1, typically take one of three basic forms:

- *Testing to see whether a particular technique or device works in a predicted way.* Often, experiments investigate whether a technique or device (the independent variable; for instance, a particular form of library instruction) is "effective" for accomplishing a given purpose by using statistics to compare the results (the dependent variable) obtained with that technique/device to those obtained by a control group not exposed to the technique/device (e.g., Vidmar [1998]; Young and Ackerson [1995]). At other times, a model of how a technique or device works is constructed, and actual performance is measured against projected performance (e.g., Gerhart [2004]; Nowicki [2003]).
- *Testing to see which of two or more techniques or devices for accomplishing a given purpose leads to better results.* The results (the dependent variables) for groups using the different techniques or devices (the independent variables) are compared statistically with each other, and sometimes also with control groups which were exposed to none of these techniques or devices (e.g., Kenney et al. [2003]; Weston and Lauderdale [1988]).
- *Testing statistically for relationships between various characteristics of items or individuals.* These characteristics can be thought of as independent variables, or intrinsic properties of the item or individual (the age of an item,

Figure 6-1: Studies Using Experimental Methodologies

Gerhart, Susan L. 2004. "Do Web Search Engines Suppress Controversy?" *First Monday* 9 (1). Available: http://firstmonday.dk/issues/issue9_1/gerhart (accessed May 18, 2007).

"Our starting assumption is: A controversial subtopic is revealed or suppressed to the degree its URLs are recognizable in the query for the broad topic." Compared the top 100 results in three search engines and two metasearch engines for searches on broad topics, controversial subtopics, non-controversial subtopics.

Kenney, Anne R., Nancy Y. McGovern, Ida T. Martinez, and Lance J. Heidig. 2003. "Google Meets E-bay: What Academic Librarians Can Learn from Alternative Information Providers." *D-Lib Magazine* 9 (6). Available: http://dlib.org/dlib/june03/kenney/06kenney.html (accessed May 18, 2007).

Selected set of 24 questions of sort typically encountered by reference librarians for study. Got answers to questions, difficulty rating of them, from Cornell University librarians and Google Answers. Then had answers blind-reviewed by librarians based on specified quality criteria. Found that overall Cornell rated a 3.43 and GA rated a 3.39—no real difference, although they did score more differently on different sub-sets of questions.

Moore, Deborah. 2005. "GCC Research Project on Information Competency." Available: http://glendale.edu/library/instruction/documents/ICEval05.pdf (accessed May 18, 2007).

Focus on Library 191, GCC's introductory course in information competency. Matching students who took LIB 191 with a randomly selected control group on enrollment status, prior GPA, primary language, units attempted. Compared two groups over several semesters on GPA, units completed, persistence to next semester. Found that "students passing Library 191 had significantly higher GPAs and completed significantly more units."

Nowicki, Stacy. 2003. "Student vs. Search Engine: Undergraduates Rank Results for Relevance." *portal: Libraries and the Academy* 3 (3): 503–515.

Investigated end-user judgments of relevance of search engine results, as well as performance of search engines in producing results rated as relevant. Seventy-five undergraduates searched topics of their choosing in six search engines. Students' ranking of relevancy of top ten results compared to that of search engine. Found no significant correlation between student rankings and search engines.

Pask, Judith M., and E. Stewart Saunders. 2004. "Differentiating Information Skills and Computer Skills: A Factor Analytic Approach." *portal: Libraries and the Academy* 4 (1): 61–73.

Survey given to incoming first-years at Purdue to determine computer skills and IL skills provided data sets. Used factor analysis on responses to 23 questions designed to measure these skills to investigate relationship of computer and IL skills. Thirty questions divided into six areas. Found that computer literacy and IL not the same.

Smalley, Topsy N. 2004. "College Success: High School Librarians Make the Difference." *Journal of Academic Librarianship* 30 (3): 193–198.

"This study examined levels of student achievement as recorded on Library 10 grade rosters and asked: Do students from high schools in the one school district that has library media teachers do better in the Information Research course when compared to students from the high schools that do not have librarians?" (pg. 194). Tracked and analyzed for correlations information about students' high school background, midterm class rank and grade in the Information Research course, final class rank and grade in the Information Research course.

(Cont'd.)

Figure 6-1: Studies Using Experimental Methodologies *(Continued)*

Vidmar, Dale J. 1998. "Affective Change: Integrating Pre-Sessions in the Students' Classroom Prior to Library Instruction." *Reference Services Review* 26 (3/4): 75–95.

Tests whether a "pre-session [which] involves the librarian going to the classroom of the students for 10 to 20 minutes prior to the students coming to the library for an actual library instruction session" is effective in "address[ing] the affective needs of students by helping to reduce anxiety and the resistance of students" (76). Compared scores from three pairs of classes: one class from each pair was the control group, which just got LI, while the other was the experimental group, which got the pre-session.

Weston, E. Paige, and Diane S. Lauderdale. 1988. "How Do We Learn What a Database Includes? A Case Study Using Psychology Dissertations." *RQ* 28: 35–41.

Hypothesis: "... that since PsycINFO includes such a vast number of dissertation records ... surely searches in PsycINFO would retrieve the majority of the dissertations of interest on any given psychology topic and would overlap extensively with searches in Dissertation Abstracts Online." Had two librarians search 14 psychology topics submitted by doctoral candidates in psychology. Analyzed, compared the number, kinds of items retrieved.

Young, Virginia E., and Linda G. Ackerson. 1995. "Evaluation of Student Research Paper Bibliographies: Refining Evaluation Criteria." *Research Strategies* 13 (2): 80–93.

Question was: "Does a course-integrated curriculum devised to develop skills in the use of print and automated information sources ... help students access, evaluate, and use current information to write better term papers?" (83). Study over five semesters with 251 students. Used a bibliography rating sheet to standardize scoring.

the sex of an individual), and dependent variables, or non-intrinsic properties of the item or individual (the number of circulations of an item, the score on a test of library anxiety for an individual). Researchers predict and test statistically for relationships between independent and dependent variables (e.g., Moore [2005]; Pask and Saunders [2004]; Smalley [2004]).

Within these three broad categories, experimental studies display great diversity in duration, their approaches to the experimental situation, and their models of data analysis.

- Most studies are cross-sectional, or focus upon subjects at single points in time. Young and Ackerson thus measure the effects of instructional methods only over the academic term in which students received the instruction, not over the longer term of their undergraduate education. However, other studies are longitudinal and track subjects over time, as Moore does when she relates student completion of an information literacy course to GPA and persistence over community college careers.
- In some studies, researchers must create the data-gathering situation and gather data before running statistical analyses. Kenney et al. (2003), for example, needed both the production of answers to reference questions and ratings of these answers for their experiment. In other experiments, though, researchers test hypotheses by looking for statistical relationships

in preexisting data. Moore (2005) thus used data on student enrollment status, GPA, and units completed that the college registrar had already gathered.

- Experiments can also be unobtrusive or obtrusive in their design, with subjects unaware or aware of being studied. Smalley's (2004) study is unobtrusive, because researchers can easily record students' high schools, GPA, and class rank without students being aware. In contrast, Vidmar's (1998) study is obtrusive because students completing pre- and post-tests are necessarily aware of doing so—and of being studied.
- When it comes to models of data analysis, some experiments can be described as correlation studies, which establish relationships between two or more variables without establishing causation (e.g., Kenney et al. 2003); factor-analytic studies, which reduce a large set of correlated variables to a smaller set of hypothetical traits or factors underlying the correlations (e.g., Pask and Saunders 2004); or two-condition experimental studies, which manipulate variables in testing cause and effect (e.g., Vidmar 1998).

FORMULATING QUESTIONS

When experimental methodology is used, the research question should take the form of a hypothesis, or a "declarative statement about the relation between two or more variables which can be observed empirically" (Busha and Harter 1980, 10). There are several different types of hypotheses. Non-directional hypotheses predict the existence of differences between groups in an experiment without predicting which groups will perform better, while directional hypotheses predict which groups will perform better. Null hypotheses predict that there will be no differences in performance between groups. Null hypotheses are only used for testing statistical significance. That is, researchers show that the null hypothesis cannot be true. Some sample hypotheses from prior library experiments posit that:

- "both skill and confidence levels increase as a result of cumulative exposure to the library and its services" (Greer, Weston and Alm 1991, 552);
- "a given, well-known specific controversy will not be revealed" in the top results for Web search engines (Gerhart, see Figure 6-1);
- "students in the experimental tutorial group will learn as much or more than the in-class group and will also report as much or more satisfaction with the learning experience" (Nichols, Shaffer and Shockey 2003); and
- "academic procrastination is positively related to library anxiety" (Onwuegbuzie and Jiao 2000).

Ideas for hypotheses, or likely relationships between variables, come from professional experience and from reading library literature. Because your reading shapes your predictions about possible relationships, always ground your hypothesis in the literature on the topic whenever writing about your research. Weston and Lauderdale (see Figure 6-1), for example, do a good job of explaining how reading of vendor documentation and prior studies lead to their hypothesis that PsycINFO should perform as well as Dissertation Abstracts in retrieving dissertations on psychology topics.

Too many experimental studies within librarianship are, regrettably, weak in formulating their hypotheses. Sometimes the hypothesis does not limit itself to the relationship between the variables but rather attempts to prove something broader. One group of researchers used as its hypothesis the claim that "research would confirm the viability of moving to an online format for introductory information literacy instruction." (The source of this quotation and those in the next few examples are deliberately not cited here in order to protect the identity of those whose hypotheses are being critiqued.) All their experiment investigated, however, was whether students receiving library instruction via an online tutorial learned more and were more satisfied than students receiving instruction via lecture/demonstration. Viability involves more than student test scores and satisfaction. Even if scores and satisfaction were higher, a tutorial would not be viable if the library had no staff or equipment to create or maintain it. As this example shows, a hypothesis that seeks to answer a value question (Should something be done? Is this good?) can be problematic. In other cases, researchers state their hypotheses only obliquely. For example, the following text could easily be written as an hypothesis:

> The authors supposed initially that since PsycINFO includes such a vast number of dissertation records . . . surely searches in PsycINFO would retrieve the majority of the dissertations of interest on any given psychology topic and would overlap extensively with searches in Dissertation Abstracts Online.

"PsycINFO provides as comprehensive and current coverage of psychology dissertations as Dissertation Abstracts" would make a fine hypothesis here. Questions about relationships can also be written easily as hypotheses, as can statements of "research objectives" and those predicted relationships that readers are left to infer. (See Figure 6-2 for further examples). The problem with poor hypothesis formulation is that it makes it harder for both researchers and readers to determine whether the predicted relationship between the variables does in fact hold true. ("If you don't specify a predicted event precisely, there are an indeterminate number for ways of an event of that general kind to take place" [Paulos 1988, 28].)

A hypothesis is simply an informed "best guess." You should not be vague in stating your hypothesis for fear that the experiment will not support it. If not enough is known about a topic to make even an informed "best guess," conduct an exploratory study using nonexperimental methods.

Figure 6-2: Examples of Hypotheses

Original Text	Possible Hypothesis
"Do students from high schools in the one school district that has library media teachers do better in the Information Research course when compared to students from the high schools that do not have librarians?" (Smalley 2004, 194)	Students from high schools in school districts with library media teachers will score more highly in a college level Information Research course than students from high schools in school districts without library media teachers.
"The project attempted to determine if a pre-session prior to a regularly scheduled library instruction session would have any effect upon the student attitudes toward the library, the librarians, the relevance of using the library, and the effectiveness of library instruction." (Vidmar 1998, 82)	Pre-sessions prior to a regularly scheduled library instruction session will positively impact student attitudes toward the library, the librarians, the relevance of using the library, and the effectiveness of library instruction.
"The main purpose of this study was to examine whether international students' acquisition of library skills was related to their English language proficiency." (Bilal 1989, 130)	International students' acquisition of library skills will be proportional to their English language proficiency: the more proficient an international student is in English, the more library skills she/he will acquire.

DEFINING THE POPULATION

Some methodologies are designed to work with the subjects available to the researcher, or with typical rather than representative subjects. Classroom research, for example, uses existing groups of students, and content analysis can focus upon the most famous or characteristic examples of discourse on a topic. Experimental methodology is not such a methodology. Because it seeks results that are widely generalizable, it typically uses research subjects that are representative of a broader population. The population is the largest "group to which the researcher feels it is appropriate to generalize or apply the results" (Gustafson and Smith 1994, 76). Because most populations are too large for every member to be studied, researchers get subjects from the population by sampling, or selecting a portion or subset of the larger population. How many subjects are needed in a sample and how subjects should be selected are the important and difficult questions here.

We will turn to those questions momentarily, but first a caution about representativeness. "Representative" essentially means that the members of the sample match the larger population in some demographic characteristics: age, sex, income, and so on. A researcher could potentially select a sample that is representative of its population in some characteristics (age, sex, ethnicity) but that is not representative in terms of some other characteristics (e.g., income) which may actually be the major variables underlying the experimental findings. For this reason, it is not enough for researchers to say that their sample is "representative"; rather, they should specify of what population their sample is representative and why this population is relevant to the experimental focus.

Some researchers work under the misconception that 10 percent of the population represents an adequate sample size (e.g., Ware and Morganti 1986), or that larger samples are automatically better. The appropriate sample size is actually based upon the confidence level and confidence interval sought by the researcher, as well as upon the size of the total target population. The confidence level indicates the probability that subjects' responses do not represent the effects of chance alone. A 95 percent confidence level means that in only five cases out of 100 would the subjects have given that set of responses because of chance alone. In the 95 other cases, something other than chance—namely, the effects of the treatment or independent variable being studied—accounts for their responses. The lower the confidence level, the more likely the results could be due to chance alone. Ninety-five percent and 99 percent confidence levels are the most commonly used, with the 95 percent level being standard in social sciences research. The confidence interval is a plus-or-minus percentage indicating how often repeated random samples of a given size would be expected to measure a quality's "true" value. Certain confidence intervals are normally associated with certain size samples (as is shown in Figure 6-3), although the effects of target population size on sample size are somewhat more complex than can be discussed here. In general, "the larger the sample the greater our chances of getting a ratio close to that in the population [in the sample]; however, as sample size increases the chances of getting an exact match between sample and population frequencies decrease" (Carey 1998, 18). Larger samples generally mean smaller confidence intervals and hence greater assurance that the results obtained are not simply the effect of chance alone. A larger sample is also more likely to

Figure 6-3: Confidence Intervals Associated with Common Sample Sizes*

Sample Size	Approximate Margin of Error
25	+/–22%
50	+/–14%
100	+/–10%
250	+/– 6%
500	+/– 4%
1,000	+/– 3%
1,500	+/– 2%

*Based upon a 95% confidence level and a potentially infinite population.
(This figure is based on information from Carey 1998, 20.)

accurately represent the population, leading to a lower sampling error. However, bigger is not inherently better. "If the sample is poorly drawn, increasing the number of people in the sample from 1,000 to 10,000 or even to 50,000 will not make the results any more accurate" (Crossen 1996, 35). There are many tools, such as those listed in Figure 6-4, to help researchers determine appropriate sample sizes for the desired confidence levels and intervals.

How to select the sample is an even more complex question. Convenience samples are essentially samples that "come to you" (Best 2001, 55), such as those comprised of volunteers or, for instance, the first 1,000 people to enter the library building on a given day. Convenience samples are often the most easily obtained, but they yield subjects unrepresentative of the target population. Purposive samples are samples whose members are selected because researchers know they have experience related to the topics being investigated and are likely to participate in the study. They, too, are more easily obtained but are not representative of the target population. Sometimes convenience or purposive samples really are the only samples possible. Usually, however, they are not, and reliance on them, instead of on more rigorous sampling methods, can skew results. People who volunteer tend to have strong opinions on a given topic, a feature not representative of the target population, which tends to be more apathetic about the topic. Volunteers also act in an unrepresentative way by electing to participate in a research study, which is something most people do not do. As an example of this, consider two different studies—one using a convenience sample and the other using a random sample—on American attitudes

Figure 6-4: Tools for Calculating Appropriate Sample Sizes

- Sample Size Calculator, from The Survey System,
  http://surveysystem.com/sscalc.htm.
  Allows users to enter a 95% or 99% confidence level, the desired confidence interval and a population size in order to calculate the sample size needed. Can also find the confidence interval for given sample sizes, population sizes, and confidence levels. *Excellent for beginners*.

- Sample Size Calculator, from the UCLA Department of Statistics,
  http://calculators.stat.ucla.edu/sampsize.php.
  Users can enter any size population up to infinity and find out the sample size. Defaults for maximum allowable difference (0.1), confidence (.95), and variance estimate (1.0) are set. Defaults can be changed, but users would need more knowledge of statistics to know what they could/should be.

- Sample Size Calculator, from DSS Research,
  http://dssresearch.com/toolkit/sscalc/size.asp.
  Offers four different sample size calculators—for averages, one sample; averages, two samples; percentages, one sample, and percentages, two sample studies. Also has a sample error calculator and a statistical power calculator. *Great for more advanced researchers*.

toward the United Nations. *Nightline* used a convenience sample, asking volunteers to call a 900 number, when it found that "67% of Americans" favored removing U.N. headquarters from the U.S. In contrast, a random sample with 500 subjects found that 72 percent of Americans wanted U.N. headquarters to remain in the U.S., a percentage more in keeping with other studies on the topic (Crossen 1996).

Only probability samples, or samples wherein "every member of the target population has a known, nonzero probability of being included in the sample" (Fink 1995, 9), will be representative. Chance works to ensure this, provided that the sample size is adequate. Suppose, for example, you randomly selected a sample of 100 items, each item of which existed in a 50-50 rate in one of two states (e.g., red or blue in color) in the target population. Ninety-five percent of the time, the items selected for the sample would include 40-60 red items and 40-60 blue items—not too far off their 50-50 rate in the total population. Probability samples come in many types, including:

- simple random samples, where every member of the population has an equal chance of selection, and prior selections do not influence the chances of any particular member being selected
- systematic samples, where random starting points and intervals are established and subjects are selected at that interval for the sample (e.g., every 10th item starting with item number 53)
- stratified samples, where the population is divided into subgroups and subjects are randomly selected from the subgroups, with the total number of subjects taken from each subgroup corresponding to the ratio of that subgroup in the target population
- cluster samples, where naturally occurring units (e.g., schools, states) are randomly selected and all members of the selected clusters are included in the sample
- multistage samples, where clusters are selected and then a sample is drawn from the member clusters by random sampling

Researchers should carefully consider which probability sampling method works best for their needs. They can consult resources such as those listed in Figure 6-5 to learn more about various sampling models and techniques for implementing them.

Researchers should also be aware that there may be times when they will not know the full extent or demographics of the target population (Best 2001, 53–54). In the early days of the Web, for example, researchers did not know exactly who used it. This made it hard to select a representative sample of Web users in terms of variables such as age, sex, and income level. In such cases, researchers should use the best estimates of the target population, and they should be sure to justify their choices to their readers.

Figure 6-5: Suggested Works on Population Sampling

Cochran, William G. 1977. *Sampling Techniques*. New York: Wiley.

Fink, Arlene. 2003. *How to Sample in Surveys*. Thousand Oaks, CA: Sage.

Kish, Leslie. 1997. *Survey Sampling*. New York: Wiley.

Levy, Paul S., and Stanley Lemeshow. 1991. *Sampling of Populations: Methods and Applications*. New York: Wiley.

Powell, Ronald P. 1999. "Survey Research and Sampling." In *Basic Research Methods for Librarians*, 57–87. 3rd ed. Greenwich, CT: Ablex.

Stuart, Alan. 1984. *The Ideas of Sampling*. London: Griffin.

Researchers must also remember that not all members of the sample will participate in the study or yield usable data. Some members of the sample will decline to participate; others may yield data that is somehow corrupted and thus rendered unusable in the storage or analysis process. "Response rate" is the name for the percentage of sampled subjects who become respondents or actual participants in the study. Response rate is influenced by the experiment's topic, its target population, its medium of implementation, and other factors (Case 2002, 191–192). Low response rates leave findings open to the possibility of response bias—systematic differences between those who responded and those who did not (cf. Case 2002, 173). An infamous example of response bias is the 1936 poll that incorrectly predicted that Alf Landon would defeat Franklin Roosevelt in the presidential election. This poll had a response rate of only 23 percent. The people responding to it proved to be much wealthier than the general population, and to have different choices in their presidential votes (Paulos 1988, 113). Low response rates also lessen the likelihood that the findings will prove statistically significant: "The more cases of observations collected and listed, the more likely it is that a . . . t-score will emerge as significant" (Gerhan 2001, 365). For this reason, researchers should anticipate what percentage of the sample is going to be unresponsive and increase their sample size by that percentage (Fink 1995, 54). Suppose, for example, that your target population was 500, and you expected a 60 percent response rate from sampled subjects. While a sample of 217 would be sufficient for a 95 percent confidence level and a ± 5 confidence interval provided that all members of the sample responded, 40 percent of your sample is anticipated not to respond. In this case, taking 40 percent of 217 (40/100=N/217) yields 86.8 or 87, so you add 87 to 217 to arrive at a sample size—corrected for response rate—of 304. Strategies for replacing one sample member with another from the target population should be built into the research design.

As a final step, experimental researchers typically divide their probability-sampled subjects into experimental and control groups. The experimental group is exposed to the treatment, device, or procedure that the experiment is testing, while the control group is not. Sometimes a study features several different experimental groups, which are exposed to different treatments and whose results are compared, and no control group. More often, though, a control group is included along with one or more experimental groups (see Figure 6-6).

Experimental researchers prefer to use control groups because a certain amount of change between pre- and post-measures is to be expected because of chance or confounds. Control groups thus enable the researcher to compare the amount of change (pre- to post-) that results from chance or confounds with the amount of change (pre- to post-) in the experimental groups). Vidmar, Moore, Smalley, and Young and Ackerson all use control groups along with experimental groups in their studies.

Subjects should be put in control and experimental groups by randomization, or "randomly assign[ing] the subjects comprising the total sample to the experimental and comparison groups" (Powell 1999, 127). Care should also be taken to ensure that control and experimental groups are closely matched, or selected so that the experimental and control groups have subjects with similar demographic traits. Matching can never be perfect because of the immense range of differences in humans' backgrounds (Busha and Harter 1980, 36), but researchers should try to match on the personal characteristics most likely to influence experimental outcomes. Moore, for example, matches her control group to her experimental group in terms of enrollment status, prior GPA, units completed, and units attempted. (If she had not done so, differences between students' academic abilities and prior course work could not be excluded as the causes of any differences she found between groups.) Use of preexisting groups (e.g., classes) rather than individuals in studies is certainly possible

Figure 6-6: Classic Four-Cell Experimental Design

	Dependent Variable Before Treatment	Dependent Variable After Treatment
Control		
Experimental		

(e.g., Vidmar 1998), and here, too, the groups should be randomly assigned to control or experimental treatments.

Experimental studies in librarianship have sometimes shown a principled unwillingness to use control groups. Ware and Morganti (1986, 5), for example, wrote of their study that: "A control group would have meant depriving a number of students of the only formal library instruction that they might encounter during their freshman year." Such objections to control groups certainly have ethical grounds; researchers are committed to doing no harm to their subjects, and depriving subjects of their only opportunity for library instruction certainly poses harm to them. In these situations, though, it is often possible for researchers to find something of a control group, albeit one whose members are not exactly matched with or quite representative of the experimental group. Researchers have used students in another class at the same academic level and in the same subject as a control group (Brown et al. 2004), or they have used students who failed to complete the experimental treatment as a quasi-control (Fenske 1998). There are some obvious limitations to the last approach in particular, notably the possibility that the factors leading these people to drop out of the experiment (e.g., lack of motivation) also lead to their differential performance. However, as long as the authors are aware of these limitations, as Fenske is, something helpful can still be learned.

SELECTING A RESEARCH DESIGN

Key to research designs using the experimental methodology is operationalization, or the formulation of definitions (called operational definitions) of "the operations one goes though to identify an instance of what is being defined" (Best 2001, 45). Operationalization "specif[ies] what will be counted. . . . We cannot begin counting until we decide how we will identify and count instances" of the phenomena we are investigating (Best 2001, 45). For example, suppose researchers set out to measure whether collaboration with faculty in the context of library instruction "works." They might think that they and any future readers know what all these terms mean, but none of these terms are actually all that clear-cut in their definitions. What counts as "collaboration"? Is it collaboration when a faculty member sends a copy of an assignment to the library at the same time he or she gives it to students? Or is it only collaboration if the faculty member worked with a librarian in designing or grading the assignment? Are graduate teaching assistants considered "faculty"? Is teaching one-on-one at the reference desk a form of instruction, as some have argued? And, most importantly, what shows collaboration "working"? The operational definitions of key terms in the hypothesis are essential for data-gathering. Operational definitions tell what should be measured and may even give some clues as to how it can be measured.

Vidmar's article on the effectiveness of library instruction pre-sessions in lessening students' library anxiety is a model of thorough operationalization. He defines the terms "library instruction," "affect" or "affective experiences," "library anxiety," "needs assessment," "pre-session," and "instruction session" in terms of both the standard definitions within the field and his own research project. Library anxiety, for example, is defined in relation to Constance Mellon's work on the topic. Researchers are often tempted to devise their own definitions and to use non-standard definitions when operationalizing (Katzer, Cook and Crouch 1997). For instance, you might want to say that "collaboration" includes sending a copy of the assignment to the library, either because this definition covers 99 percent of what your faculty do, or because you want to show a high level of collaboration at your institution. If, however, other researchers studying faculty collaboration used a definition involving higher levels of librarian-faculty interaction in their studies, your findings will not be comparable to theirs. No field is helped by the proliferation of definitions, as multiple definitions can mean that you are actually comparing dissimilar things when you try to combine results from multiple studies.

Research design in an experimental study also involves selection of models, instruments, and techniques for measuring. Measuring involves assigning numerical values to the phenomena being studied, and it is vital to the experimental method because the experimental method is quantitative and compares numbers in aggregate. Once researchers have decided what they are going to measure, they still need to decide how to measure it. "Measurement involves making choices" (Best 2001, 104), as is shown by the example of researchers measuring library borrowing transactions. Even if they have already decided whether a library borrowing transaction involves a reader checking out a single volume or a single title, they still need to decide how to count these borrowing transactions. They could ask patrons to self-report on how many borrowing transactions they make in a week. They could position observers at the library exits to count how many titles/volumes people leave with. They could scan computer records and identify transactions. They could explore yet other options for determining how many/how much. Figure 6-7 lists the measurement models—or the plans for how to measure—for each study from Figure 6-1.

As you read this list, think of the assumptions behind each measurement model, and of how other measurement models could have been used to track the same thing. When picking a measurement model, researchers should keep in mind that some models are more rigorous than others; some are more justified in the experimental context than others; and the more complex the experimental situation, the more additional sources of error there are.

Measurement instruments are important components of measurement models because what is typically compared, in the final analysis, are mean scores linked to the study's dependent variables. The mean is one of three ways of calculating

Figure 6-7: Measurement Models Used in Selected Library Experiments

- The **number and content of results to searches** for a broad topic, its controversial subtopics, and its non-controversial subtopics were compared as a way of measuring to what degree controversial subtopics are visible among search engine results (Gerhart 2004).

- The **quality ratings given to 24 questions** answered by Google Answers were compared to the quality ratings given to those same 24 questions when answered by librarians as a way of measuring whether Google Answers or librarians gave better answers (Kenney et al. 2003).

- The **GPA, units completed, and persistence of enrollment** of students who took a library course were compared to those of a matched group of students who did not take the course as a way of measuring whether completion of the library course leads to improved student academic outcomes (Moore 2005).

- The **rankings of the top ten items** in three search engines and two metasearch engines were compared to the rankings given to those items by students as a way of measuring whether students' judgments of relevancy corresponded to the search engines, as well as whether particular search engines worked better or worse in meeting students' relevancy expectations (Nowicki 2003).

- The **factor loadings** on categories of questions relating to information literacy skills on a attitudinal survey of incoming first-year students were compared to those on categories of questions relating to computer literacy as a way of measuring whether information literacy is the same as computer literacy (Pask and Saunders 2004).

- **Midterm and final grades and class rank** for students in a college Information Research course who attended high school districts with school library media specialists were compared with those for students who did not as a way of measuring whether students who had high school library media specialists performed better in college (Smalley 2004).

- **Attitudinal surveys** were given before and after library instruction pre-sessions as way of measuring whether the pre-session contributed to a decrease in library anxiety among the experimental group (Vidmar 1998).

- The **number and types of results** found for 14 search topics on PsycINFO were compared to those found on Dissertation Abstracts as a way of measuring which database provided better access to psychology dissertations (Weston and Lauderdale 1988).

- The **ratings of bibliographies** of students who received a "traditional" version of library instruction were compared to those of students who got an experimental version as a way of measuring whether the experimental instruction led to improved student papers (Young and Ackerson 1995).

the average, or central tendency, among a group of numbers. It involves adding the value of each individual measurement and then dividing by the total number of measurements. In contrast, the median is the value where exactly half the values are above it and half below it and the mode is the most frequently occurring number in the set (see Figure 6-8). The mean is an important calculation in experimental methodology because, although any individual measure may vary considerably from what is typical, the average of a group of "measurements of some quantity should approach the true value of the quantity as the number of

Figure 6-8: Three Types of Averages Compared

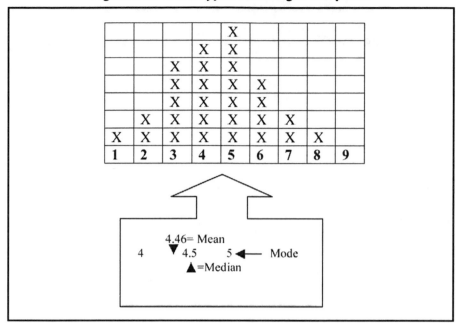

measurements increases" (Paulos 1988, 117). This is because of the central limit theorem, which holds that the average of a large group of measurements follows a normal, or bell-shaped curve even if the individual measurements themselves do not (Paulos 1988, 117). Figure 6-9 shows how this would work if several different scales, each of which measured a little bit differently, were used to measure an individual whose true weight is 120 lbs. Only one of the measurements came closer to the true value than the mean in this case, and only one came equally close. The other seven values were all more distant from the true value than the mean.

Possible instruments for obtaining measurements from subjects, and thus deriving means, include:

- frequency counts of the number of search results obtained for broad topics, controversial subtopics, and non-controversial subtopics (Gerhart 2004)
- rating sheets ranking the quality of answers to reference questions against established criteria (Kenney et al. 2003)
- registration data recording students' GPA, units completed, and enrollment status (Moore 2005)
- comparative rankings of the relevance of search engine results (Nowicki 2003)
- survey instruments measuring students' attitudes, comfort level, and self-reported skills in information and computer literacy (Pask and Saunders 2004)

Figure 6-9: "Correcting" Power of the Mean

True weight = 120		
Measurement Number	Value	Difference from the "True" Value
1	121.2	+1.2
2	122.0	+2.0
3	118.9	−1.1
4	119.7	−0.3
5	119.5	−0.5
6	120.3	+0.3
7	120.8	+0.8
8	121.0	+1
9	119.9	−0.1
	120.3	+0.3

- class rosters indicating students' midsemester and final grades in a library class, their rank in the class, and their high school and district (Smalley 2004)
- survey instruments with Likert scales for measuring library anxiety (Vidmar 1998)
- frequency counts of the number and types of results found on 14 topics in two different databases (Weston and Lauderdale 1988)
- ratings sheets scoring students' bibliographies against established criteria (Young and Ackerson 1995)

Some measurement instruments are fairly direct indicators of the attributes they are tracking, as when a researcher records the number of items retrieved with a given search. Other measurement instruments are more indirect indicators of the attributes they are tracking. While databases give the total number of results prominently at the top of results pages, people do not come with a number stamped on their foreheads telling how much library anxiety they have. Thus, instruments for indirect measures tend to be the most difficult to come by. Broadly speaking, indirect measurement instruments can be described as subjective, or self-assessment, instruments, where the individuals being investigated tell researchers how much of the investigated qualities they have; or objective instruments, which rely on external indicators of the degree to which subjects have given attributes. Instruments can also track subjects' attitude, aptitude, or achievement regardless of their actual use by the subjects. They can be criterion-referenced, comparing subjects' performance to established quality standards, or norm-referenced, comparing subjects' performance to other subjects. They can be paper-based or electronic, and they can display many other differences in their nature and use. There is not an absolute "best" from among the options here; there are simply "better" and "worse," more justified and less justified, approaches to measuring the phenomena of interest in a given situation.

For example, consider the case of whether your test, attitude survey, or other measurement instrument should be paper- or Web-based. Web-based instruments are currently popular because of their lower costs of production and distribution. Unfortunately, Web-based instruments also tend to have lower response rates, meaning that the people who do reply may differ from those who do not (Manfreda et al. 2002). You need to decide what is more important to your study (lower costs of measurement or higher response rates) and why. Be sure to justify your choices to your readers in any publications based on your research.

Researchers can do one of two things when it comes to getting indirect measurement instruments for their research; they can use preexisting instruments or create their own. If you use a preexisting instrument, it has been used before and something is known about how it works. Often, such instruments have been formally pilot tested, and their reliability and validity have been statistically proven. An instrument's validity is a measure of the degree which the instrument actually measures what it claims to measure, while its reliability is a measure of the degree to which the instrument measures consistently. Validity and reliability are both measures of degree (more or less), not absolutes, and they can be calculated in a number of ways (see Figure 6-10).

Figure 6-10: Common Types of Validity and Reliability

Validity
- *Content validity:* Measures the representativeness of the questions on the instrument in relation to the construct it claims to cover. Does the instrument cover the entire construct? Or does it focus too narrowly on part of it?
- *Predictive or criterion-related validity:* Measures the degree to which scores on the instrument compare to later performances in the construct's domain by people who passed or failed. Does the score subjects would get on one measure of a particular construct correspond to the score they would get on other measures of this construct?
- *Construct validity:* Based on the degree to which the instrument measures the construct it is designed to measure. Does using the instrument substitute for actually observing a person displaying the skill, attitude, and so forth, in everyday life?
- *Concurrent validity:* Asks whether data from the instrument agrees with the results of instruments administered at approximately the same time to measure the same construct.

Reliability
- *Test-retest reliability:* Measures the degree to which multiple administrations of the same instrument to the same subjects yield the same results.
- *Alternate-form reliability:* Measures the degree to which two essentially equivalent forms of the same instrument yield the same results for the same subjects.
- *Split-half reliability:* Treats two halves of the same instrument as separate instruments and administers them separately. Measures to what degree performance on part of the test corresponds to performance on the whole test.

Figure 6-11: Sources on Validity and Reliability

Sources for more information

Educational Testing Service. 2000. *ETS Standards for Quality and Fairness.* Princeton, NJ: ETS.

> *Has a chapter each on validity and reliability.*

Gustafson, Kent L., and Jane Bandy Smith. 1994. *Research for School Library Media Specialists.* Norwood, NJ: Ablex.

> *Chapter 5 covers reliability and validity.*

Litwin, Mark S. 1997. *How to Measure Survey Reliability and Validity.* Thousand Oaks, CA: Sage.

Westgaard, Odin. 1999. *Tests That Work: Designing and Delivering Fair and Practical Measurement Tools in the Workplace.* San Francisco, CA: Jossey-Bass.

> *Chapter on "Evaluating the Test" covers reliability and validity.*

With a preexisting instrument, the researchers save the time and effort they would have spent on instrument construction. Plus, they end up with data that is comparable with that from other studies using the same instrument. Young and Ackerson (1995) and Kenney at al. (2003) experience these benefits from using standardized instruments for rating student bibliographies and evaluating reference answers. (Figure 6-12 lists some standardized instruments commonly used in librarianship, as well as sources for identifying standardized instruments.)

However, preexisting instruments may not measure exactly what you want to measure, or they may take more time for subjects to complete than is available in your experimental situation. They also may not have proven reliability or validity for your population. As Gustafson and Smith (1994, 22) note, standardized

Figure 6-12: Standardized Instruments Commonly Used in Library Studies

- California Critical Thinking Disposition Inventory
- College Student Experiences Questionnaire
- Inquiry Mode Questionnaire
- Learning Organizations Practices Profile
- Library Anxiety Scale, recently updated as Multidimensional Library Anxiety Scale
- Myers-Briggs Type Indicator
- National Survey of Student Engagement
- Procrastination Assessment Scale—Students
- Wisconsin-Ohio Reference Evaluation Project

Sources for identifying additional instruments:
- ETS Test Collection Catalog
- Mental Measurements Yearbook
- Test Critiques
- Tests: A Comprehensive Reference for Assessment in Psychyology, Education, and Business
- Tests in Print

or "commercial tests are developed for a specific range of individuals and care must be taken not to use them with people outside those parameters." It is also imperative that researchers keep in mind that, if you modify a standardized instrument, you can no longer assume its psychometric properties; you need to re-establish its reliability and validity.

If you create your own instrument, it can measure exactly what you want to measure and can be designed to take as much or as little time as you want. However, you will need to prove the reliability and validity of your instrument in relation to your study's data. Your data might reveal that students displayed more information literacy skills after instruction via a tutorial than via a lecture, but how do we know that your test of information literacy knowledge was valid? Did it measure information literacy, or did it actually measure reading ability, or student knowledge? Or did guessing determine students' scores? Figures 6-10, 6-11, and 6-13 provide some guidance on the various types of validity and reliability and how you can prove them, as well as sources you can consult for help in writing your own measurement instruments.

Pre- and post-measurements are especially common in experimental studies, particularly studies of whether a treatment works and which treatment works better. If you only measured subjects at the end of the experimental treatment, you would have no way to know that their attitudes, knowledge, or skills were actually due to the treatment. The subjects may have had exactly the same attitudes, knowledge, or skills prior to and irrespective of the treatment. Because pre- and post-measurements are so common in experimental studies, researchers must be aware of some special considerations relating to pre- and post-measurements and take them into account in research design. The very act of measuring people's attitudes, knowledge, or skills prior to treatment can cause them to change in their responses, whether they are in the control or experimental groups.

Figure 6-13: Suggested Works on Question Writing

Fagan, Jody Condit. 2001. "Selecting Test Item Types to Evaluate Library Skills." *Research Strategies* 18: 121–132.

Gronlund, Norman E. 1993. *How to Make Achievement Tests and Assessments.* 5th ed. Boston: Allyn & Bacon.

Hopkins, Charles D., and Richard L. Antes. 1989. *Classroom Testing: Construction.* 2nd. ed. Itasca, IL: F. E. Peacock.

Janes, Joseph. 1999. "Survey Construction." *Library Hi Tech* 17 (3): 32.

Morris, Lynn Lyons, Carol Taylor Fitz-Gibbon, and Elaine Lindheim. 1987. *How to Measure Performance and Use Tests.* Newbury Park, CA: Sage.

Ory, John C., and Katherine E. Ryan. 1993. *Tips for Improving Testing and Grading.* Newbury Park, CA: Sage.

Westgaard, Odin. 1999. *Tests That Work: Designing and Delivering Fair and Practical Measurement Tools in the Workplace.* San Francisco, CA: Jossey-Bass.

Most people in the target population have probably not given all that much thought to the objects of your study, so simply by having subjects answer questions about these topics, you are prompting them to give more thought than they normally would, thereby skewing their results.

The effects of this phenomenon are especially acute in pre- and post-measurement designs because, by having the subjects complete a pre-measurement, you create the possibility that post-measurements will be improved not because of the treatment but because subjects have been prompted by the pre-measurement to give more thought and attention to the topics at hand. Researchers refer to this possibility as sensitization and plan strategies to overcome its operations in their research. There is a Catch-22 here, however: while allowing more time to pass between pre- and post-measurements lessens sensitization effects, maturation effects (or influences operating within the subjects due to the passage of time, such as growing older, becoming more mature), may skew results if too much time passes between pre- and post-measurements. Different researchers prefer intervals of 1–3 weeks, 8–10 weeks, or 12–15 weeks to balance the effects of sensitization and maturation effects on pre- and post-test findings. (See Asher [1976] for more discussion on this topic.) Others attempt to solve this problem by using equivalent but not identical instruments for pre- and post-measurements. Vidmar (1998, 85), for example, varied the order of the questions on his pre- and post-instruments in the hopes that "subjects would answer each question more carefully because they would not assume the two tests were the same." The complication here is that researchers need to demonstrate, not just claim, that the pre- and post-instruments are identical in reliability and validity. Question order is, unfortunately, a potential confound or source of bias, so care must be taken to ensure that the subjects' responses to the two versions with different question orders are identical.

GATHERING DATA

How the instrument is used matters as much as the quality of the instrument in obtaining accurate measures. Consider the simple case of a person whose experiment involves using a ruler to determine the length of 12 strings. Obviously, problems with the ruler—or the measurement instrument—could create error in the study. If it was an old plastic ruler and ¼ inch had worn off the left side where the 0 should be, any measurements obtained with it would be flawed in ways that would impact the experiment's findings. Even without this problem with the ruler, the person's technique in applying the ruler to the strings being measured could also impact the experiment's findings. Sometimes she pulls the string taut before measuring it, sometimes she does not. Sometimes she holds the string while measuring it, sometimes she has other people hold the string. Sometimes she leaves any knots tied in the string, sometimes she unties knots before measuring. By the time she is done, because she has not standardized the measurement procedures, the data will be full of errors and the eventual conclusions may be flawed because of these inaccurate measures. In an experiment, measurement values should reflect the item or quality being measured more than the method (instrument and techniques) of measurement.

There are numerous factors in experimental situations that can cause your measurements not to be "true" indicators of subjects' attitudes, knowledge, or performance. Researchers sometimes refer to these factors as confounds or sources of bias. Essentially, these include any "variables that may be operating in conjunction with the manipulated variable that make it impossible to determine whether observed changes or differences in the dependent variable are due to the manipulation, the confound, or the combination of the two" (Girden 1996, 2). Experimental studies aim at control, or negation or minimization, of such confounds or sources of bias within the experiment itself (Case 2002, 183). As Katzer (1981, 53) emphasizes, experimental research "methods are concerned with error. A researcher designs a study and employs certain methods to prevent and control potential error and to minimize and quantify whatever error remains." Researchers do this by anticipating potential sources of bias before starting their experiments. Then, they either turn potential sources of bias into constants within the study (e.g., by selecting only subjects of the same age) or they make potential sources of bias independent variables within the study (e.g., by investigating whether age as well as sex influences Internet use). Noise, or "haphazard distortion," which sometimes occurs in experimental situations, is not the same as confounds/bias. Noise involves nonsystematic error, which results in sometimes overestimating and sometimes underestimating the measured quality, while bias involves systematic error, which consistently overestimates or underestimates the measured quality (Katzer, Cook and Crouch 1997). Noise in different directions typically cancels out, so that "the net effect of noise is zero" (Katzer 1981, 54). Bias does not cancel out and so must be controlled for. While it can be difficult for researchers to predict in advance precisely what sources of bias are likely to arise in any given measurement situation (Katzer 1981), some sources of bias are so common to experimental situations that they even have their own names (see below). Broadly speaking, beyond the measurement instrument itself, there are three major sources of bias in most experiments: the experimenter, the experimental setting, and the subjects.

Even without intending to do so, experimenters can unconsciously cue the responses of their subjects. Perhaps the clearest example of this was a horse named Clever Hans, who seemed to be able to count. Hans' trainer would roll a die and ask the horse what number appeared on the die's face. Hans would paw the ground the right number of times and then stop, much to the amazement of observers.

> What was not so noticeable, however, was that the trainer stood stone-still until the horse pawed the correct number of times, and then, consciously or not, stirred slightly, which caused Hans to stop. The horse was not the source of the answer but merely a reflection of the trainer's knowledge of the answer. (Paulos 1988, 58)

Experimenters almost always have expectations of the overall results they will find (and sometimes even expectations of the performance of individual subjects), and they may indirectly signal these expectations to the subjects, influencing their performance. Experimenters are prone to the halo effect, whereby the global impact of a subject's likeable personality or some "desirable" trait irrelevant to the experimental situation (e.g., displaying good penmanship) leads to over-inflated and biased judgments of that person on rating instruments. Having multiple observers (as Young and Ackerson [1995] do) can sometimes help with this problem, since not every observer will recognize or value the same "halo" factors among subjects. Experimenters are also prone to experimenter effects, whereby differences in subjects' performance result from differences in the ways in which experimenters introduced the measurement situation to subjects. Do the experimenter or experimenters follow the same procedure in taking all measurements? Pask and Saunders (2004) ran into problems with experimenter effects because they asked first-year orientation team leaders to have students complete the questionnaire on team time. Not all team leaders did this. Team leaders also gave students different introductions to and instructions for the questionnaire, as well as different amounts of time to complete it.

Finally, there are all the forms of experimenter expectancy effects that arise whenever researchers' measurements are shaped by their hypotheses or expectations. More precisely, these are investigator effects, observer effects, and interpreter effects. Experimenter expectancy effects can be corrected for by creating, as Vidmar (1998) does, a double-blind experiment, where the ones making the measurements are not the primary researchers and are unaware of the hypothesized results.

The experimental situation is another source of possible errors in measurement. The day and time of the study can impact subjects' responses, so Vidmar controlled for this in his study by having each control and experimental pair attend library instruction on the same day. Historical effects can also influence results in certain experimental situations by opening the experiment to the effects of changes or events in the real world. Young and Ackerson note this possibility in relation to their findings because their study was conducted over five semesters at a time when student exposure to computers was greatly increasing because of factors outside of library instruction. Carryover effects appear in experimental situations when there have been multiple treatments and one experimental treatment continues to affect the subjects long after it was administered. The wording of questions on measurement instruments shapes responses, as does the order of questions, or the context effects. Gallup polls during the height of the Watergate controversy found that an overwhelming majority of respondents did not want Nixon to be "impeached," because they thought impeached meant "removed immediately from office." However, when Gallup eventually asked whether people favored trying Nixon before the Senate (the actual definition of impeachment), an overwhelming majority did favor this (Crossen 1996, 105). Similarly, question order plays a role in responses. Consider two different questions asked in different orders of subjects during the Cold War:

1. Do you think the U.S. should allow Soviet reporters to come here and send home whatever reports they wish?
2. Do you think the Soviet Union should allow U.S. reporters to go there and send home whatever reports they wish?

When Question 1 was asked first, only 36 percent of respondents thought the U.S. should let Soviet reporters come here and send home whatever reports they wished. In contrast, when Question 2 was asked first, 73 percent of respondents thought the U.S. should let Soviet reporters come here and send home whatever reports they wished. The key difference in the question ordering was that the 2/1 order had put the notion of "our" rights in subjects' minds and their sense of fairness then prompted them to support Soviet reporters in the U.S. The 1/2 order did not have the same effects (Crossen 1996, 25).

Finally, human subjects can introduce myriad confounds to experimental situations. Busha and Harter have noted that: "The fact that humans are frequently the subject of social science experimentation implies a basic difficulty in applying the experimental approach. . . . Humans cannot be manipulated as easily as white rats, for excellent moral, ethical, and legal reasons" (1980, 35–36). Humans are also infinitely more "clever" than Hans the horse, and they can introduce all kinds of confounds into experiments when they are aware that they are being observed (Goldhor 1972, 169). Simply experimenting on people can invoke the Hawthorne effect, whereby subjects produce better performances whatever the treatments. This phenomenon was first observed at the Western Electronic Company's Hawthorne plant in the 1920s and 1930s, when researchers investigating the impact of various conditions on workplace performance found that anything they did—even things that should not have worked—lead to higher productivity. Seemingly, the subjects "liked" being watched and did better simply because of this (Adair 2003, 452). Response bias can intrude whenever subjects use their responses to support certain representations of themselves. Response bias appears, for example, when subjects lie to make themselves seem more knowledgeable. Response bias was active in 1947 when some 70 percent of respondents voiced opinions about an entirely nonexistent Metallic Metals Act; it was similarly active when 30 percent of respondents managed to rate a nonexistent ethnic group, the Wisians, relative to other groups in social standing (Crossen 1996, 24). Response bias also appears when subjects respond with the socially acceptable responses instead of the "truth." This phenomenon can also be described as self-presentation bias or demand characteristics. As if all this were not enough, combine a human subject with a human experimenter and you get a range of interactional investigator effects—biosocial, psychosocial, situation, and modeling—whereby the subjects' responses are shaped by the sex or ethnicity of the experimenter; the personality or social status of the experimenter; situational factors such as prior experience with the experimenter; and the way in which the experimenter responds to the experimental situation. For all of these reasons, although research ethics say that subjects should be informed that they are subjects of study and of the study's topic (Case 2002, 171–72), most researchers do not disclose their specific hypotheses but only their general topic to subjects.

INTERPRETING THE EVIDENCE

Experimental methodology is, perhaps, known as much for its statistical treatments of data as for anything else. Descriptive statistics, or statistical methods for summarizing and presenting information, are common to many types of studies, and such ratios, proportions, percents, and so on, can also be used in experiments. Key to experimental studies, especially those investigating causation, though, are inferential statistics or statistical methods that "use[] probability theory to make predictions, to estimate important characteristics of a population, and to test the validity of hypotheses (Paulos 1988, 105). Researchers use inferential statistics to show the probability that their findings result from the effect of the independent variable, not chance or noise (Gerhan 2001, 362). The probability of two independent events (e.g., an experimental treatment and post-treatment means) occurring by chance is actually more likely than you may think: there is a human "tendency to dramatically underestimate the frequency of coincidences" (Paulos 1988, 27). How often would three flips of a coin obtain all tails? Many people intuitively think that this should almost never happen. Because there are three flips, and each flip has a one in two chance of getting a head, surely—they reason—the odds of getting three tails are quite small. Actually, though, there is a 1 in 8 chance of getting three tails in a row ($\frac{1}{2} \times \frac{1}{2} \times \frac{1}{2}$), meaning that one in every eight times you make three flips you should get all tails. Far from small odds!

Confidence intervals, which were discussed earlier in terms of sampling, actually provide good indicators of statistical significance without recourse to inferential calculations, as Figure 6-14 helps make clear. Suppose there was a study wherein the experimental and control groups each contained 100 subjects, and at the end of the study 42 percent of the experimental group and 30 percent

Figure 6-14: Confidence Intervals and Simple Tests for Statistical Significance

Example One

Sample size:	100, control group; 100, experimental group
Final mean measurements:	30%, control group; 42%, experimental group
Confidence interval:	+/– 10%
"Real" score ranges:	20–40%, control group; 32-52%, experimental group

20%   40%

         32%   50%

Example Two

Sample size:	500, control group; 500, experimental group
Final mean measurements:	30%, control group; 42%, experimental group
Confidence interval:	+/–4%
"Real" score ranges:	26–34%, control group; 38-46%, experimental group

 26%   34%

             38%   46%

of the control group tested "positive" for something. Forty-two percent minus 30 percent is 12 percent, which certainly seems a large enough number, no? Remember, though, that the confidence interval on a sample of 100 is ± 10 percent, which means that 42 percent really indicates 32–52 percent, while 30 percent really indicates 20–40 percent. Within these broader ranges, there is substantial overlap (the 32–40 percent area)—suggesting statistical insignificance for the 12 percent difference here. In contrast, if the sample had 500 subjects and obtained the same results (42 percent experimental group, 30 percent control group), the confidence interval of ± 4 percent would leave no overlap between the experimental range of 38–46 percent and the control range of 26–34 percent. Carey, the originator of this example, gives the following rules of thumb for thinking about statistical significance independent of more complex calculations:

- If there is no overlap in the intervals for the two, the difference is statistically significant.
- If there is some overlap in the intervals (less than one-third of values in common), the difference is probably statistically significant.
- If there is a good deal of overlap (more than one-third of values in common), the difference is probably not statistically significant (Carey 1998, 24).

The three most common inferential statistical calculations used in experimental studies are t-tests, analysis of variance (ANOVA) tests, and chi-square tests. Often these calculations are performed on per-question and aggregate scores, as Vidmar does. T-tests measure differences between pre- and post-measurements within a group or between two groups. A dependent t-test allows researchers to determine whether scores on a pre-measurement are statistically different from scores on a post-measurement when only one group of subjects is involved. Essentially, all a researcher needs to calculate the t-value are the pre-measurement scores as raw numbers, the post-measurement scores as raw numbers, the difference between pre- and post-measurement scores expressed as positive or negative raw numbers, and the value of the difference in measurement squared. The formula for combining these becomes more complex (see Rice 1981, 119), but once a t-value is obtained, researchers need only to compare the value to a standard table of t-values to determine its statistical significance. Independent t-tests, in contrast, are used when there are two groups of subjects. It uses post-measurements as raw numbers, calculations of deviations of these scores from the mean, and the square of these deviations. The formula for combining these numbers is also complex (see Rice 1981, 121), but once again, a researcher need only compare the t-value obtained to a table of t-values to determine significance.

ANOVAs (Analysis of Variance) come into play when there are more than two groups whose results are being examined for statistical significance. (ANOVAs also have some close relatives: MANOVAs [Multivariate Analysis of Variance] and MANCOVAs [Multiple Analysis of Covariance], which are used when several dependent variables are considered in a single analysis. MANOVAs work when all the variables are nominal, while MANCOVAs are used when some variables are quantitative and some are nominal. ANOVAs themselves come in three types, but those details are beyond the level of this book.) Both t-tests and ANOVAs can be one-way/one-tailed or two-way/two-tailed, depending upon the nature of the directional hypothesis. One-way versions test the significance of the findings only in the direction predicted, whereas two-way versions test the significance in both the direction predicted and its opposite. While some people have "suggested that the use of one-tail significance tests was perfectly OK if the [researcher] had no expectation that a [treatment] could have negative effects" (Gorman 2003, 8), two-tail tests are generally more desirable (Gustafson and Smith 1994, 158) because they are more conservative in their statistical assumptions than one-tailed tests. Chi-square tests, in contrast, are used in testing statistically for relationships between various characteristics of items or individuals. Researchers conducting a chi-square test use contingency tables to compare the values attained for those variables in the experiment with the values that would be expected were there no relationship between the variables. All of these tests actually rest on a number of complex assumptions and are quite detailed in their calculations. Researchers desiring to know about a particular test should consult one of the sources listed in Figure 6-15. Most researchers actually rely on software packages such as SPSS or GB-STAT to do their calculations, rather than doing them by hand.

Some researchers seem to revel in statistical oneupsmanship, spending much more time describing their statistical treatments than other aspects of their study. Inferential statistics are *not* the purpose of experiments, though; only a very unusual person would survey 500 subjects just for the privilege of conducting a chi-square test! Statistics are only a means to an end in experimental studies, not an end in themselves. As Best emphasizes, "Every statistic is a way of summarizing complex information into relatively simple numbers. Inevitably, some of the complexity is lost whenever we use statistics" (Best 2001, 166). The real end to an experimental study is to know more about the phenomena being investigated; statistics are simply a way to condense a great deal of information about those phenomena. For that reason, you should not feel a need for statistical virtuosity *before* conducting an experiment. It is perfectly acceptable to get help from experts in this part of your project. We agree with Katzer, Cook, and Crouch in saying: "Our major recommendation with regard to [statistical inference] is: IF IT'S IMPORTANT, GET EXPERT ADVICE" (1997, 124). Many librarians seem to rely on campus Office of Institutional Research (OIR) staff in their statistical analyses. This may work on some campuses, but on others, OIR staff may be too busy generating and analyzing data relating to the campus as a whole to help with librarians' studies. Where OIR staff is too busy, graduate or even undergraduate students in statistics or mathematics may be able to help.

Equally important as statistical treatments in data interpretation, though, is avoiding over-generalization, or drawing conclusions from the data or from the experiment that they do not actually support. Consider, for example, an infamous study that estimated that 2 percent of adult Americans—a total of 4 million people—had been abducted by UFOs. The study was based on a national

Figure 6-15: Suggested Works on Statistical Significance

Carr, Joseph J. 1992. *The Art of Science: A Practical Guide to Experiments, Observations, and Handling Data.* San Diego, CA: HighText.
  Chapter 10 includes t-tests.

Fink, Arlene. 1997. *How to Analyze Survey Data.* Thousand Oaks, CA: Sage.
  Covers t-tests, ANOVA tests, and chi-square tests.

Gustafson, Kent L., and Jane Bandy Smith. 1994. *Research for School Library Media Specialists.* Norwood, NJ: Ablex.
  Chapter 8 includes ANOVA and chi-square tests.

Lewis-Beck, Michael S., Alan Bryman, and Tim Futing Liao, eds. 2003. *The Sage Encyclopedia of Social Science Research Methods.* Thousand Oaks, CA: Sage.
  Individual entries on t-tests, ANOVA tests, and chi-square tests.

survey that presented respondents with five statements and asked them to indicate the strength of their feelings of agreement/disagreement with the statements. One statement noted that you had woken up paralyzed with "a sense of a strange person or presence or something else in the room." The researchers conclude that anyone agreeing with four out of these five statements had been abducted by UFOs (Best 2001, 48–49). The data and experiment here, however, do not support that broad conclusion. Other factors than abduction by UFOs could equally well explain people's waking with a vague feeling of someone or something having been in their room. People with certain sleep disorders, or who had experienced certain emotional or physical traumas, for example, might be equally likely as "UFO abductees" to have these sensations. The researchers, however, neither controlled for other causal factors in their research design nor considered these factors in their conclusions.

Always consider other factors beyond those in your hypothesis in explaining your conclusions, even if you have tried to control for them in the experimental situation. Beyond showing why your explanation works, you also need to show why other possible explanations do not work equally well. Kenney et al. (2003) do a thorough job of this in their study of reference answers given by librarians and by Google Answers. They note, of the ratings of reference answers in their study, that

> The evaluations, therefore, reflect a research library bias as to what constitutes a good response. The study did not focus on or measure user satisfaction, one of the three ways quality service is generally defined—the other two being accuracy and utility. For the purposes of the study, we assumed that users were satisfied with the responses they received. The evaluations implicitly reflect, then, reference librarians' notions of a quality answer, which includes accuracy and utility, but do not necessarily correspond to user satisfaction.

TELLING THE STORY

Experimental studies tend to take a highly predictable form when published: an introduction, which consists of a literature review and your hypothesis; a description of your experimental procedures (materials and methods); presentation and statistical treatments of your results; and discussion of your findings and their implications. Your publications based on experiments should take this model and should be sure to include the items listed in Figure 6-16.

Ideally, you want to include enough information about your experimental procedures so that other researchers could replicate your study to verify your results. Including in your publications any locally developed instruments used in your study is a major help to reproducibility, but be sure you include only locally developed ones to which you hold the copyright. Realistically, a very

Figure 6-16: Components of an Experimental Study

_____ Hypothesis
     _____ Clearly stated
     _____ Grounded in prior literature on the topic

_____ Population
     _____ Target population, and their relevance to the research problem
     _____ Sampling method
     _____ Way(s) in which the sample is representative of the target population
     _____ Confidence levels and intervals used in determining sample size
     _____ Sample size
     _____ Response rate, as well as any potential response bias

_____ Experimental and Control Groups
     _____ Their composition, way(s) in which they were matched
     _____ Procedures for randomization in assigning members to groups
     _____ Their treatment(s)

_____ Operational definition(s) of key term(s)

_____ Measurement model; description of how phenomena are to be measured and why this method was chosen

_____ Measurement instruments
     _____ Their type, construction, and relevance to the topic
     _____ Their reliability
     _____ Their validity
     _____ Any potential confounds in their use

_____ Measurement techniques
     _____ Control of confounds arising from the experimenter(s)
     _____ Control of confounds arising from the experimental situation
     _____ Control of confounds arising from human subjects

_____ Measurement data

_____ Inferential statistical treatment(s) of measurement data
     _____ Statistical test(s) used
     _____ Findings about statistical significance of data
     _____ Estimates of error

_____ Consideration of other possible explanations for the findings

_____ Suggestions for further research

detailed methods-and-materials section, along with reproduced instruments, can pose problems given the relatively limited page counts (typically ten to 30 pages) available for journal articles or conference proceedings. Balance the depth of your treatment of these various components with the particulars of your experiment and with the amount of space available to your publications. If your hypothesis is novel or non-intuitive, you may need to spend comparatively more time in the literature review and in grounding your hypothesis. If your methods and materials are innovative and detailed, they would get comparatively more attention. Similarly, if your data are voluminous or yield findings counter to the "conventional wisdom," they should get the bulk of your publication space. Sometimes as you review your data at the end of the project, you see that it can also be used to help describe relationships you did not originally address in your hypothesis. It is perfectly acceptable in such situations to include this analysis, along with a note about these findings being unplanned, in any subsequent write-up. Germain, Jacobson, and Kaczor (2000) do this, for example, when they note that their experimental exploration of whether Web-based or librarian-led instruction most improved student learning also yield data that helped to address the impact of prior knowledge on student performance and the impact of instructional format on learning specific content.

In presenting or writing up your experimental studies, be aware that experimental methodology assigns some very precise meanings to words that common usage treats more casually. The most important of these words is "significant." In everyday usage, "significant" often connotes "important," "of consequence," or "meaningful." Within the context of experimental studies, however, "significant" has only a much narrower connotation of "statistical significance." Do not refer to your findings as "significant" unless you have run the proper inferential statistical tests and have found them to be statistically significant. The same is true of the words "valid"/"validity" and "reliable"/"reliability." In everyday usage, we employ forms of "valid" to describe things that are "sound," "well-founded," or "effective," and forms of "reliable" to describe things that are "consistent" or "dependable." In experimental studies, though, these terms are only used to describe instruments that have statistically proven properties of actually measuring the phenomena in question (validity) and of doing so consistently (reliability). Also, on a semantic note, remember that "No hypothesis which states a general proposition can be demonstrated as absolutely true" (Cohen and Nagel 1983, 5). Experienced experimenters speak of hypotheses as being "tested," "verified," or "supported"—not as being "proved" (Goldhor 1972, 81). Moreover, experienced experimenters are always aware that "no one experiment . . . is likely to be conclusive, regardless of its results" (Goldhor 1972, 183). So, they do not speak of their experiment as being the "final word" on a topic, but rather invite other researchers to replicate their studies or develop them further by testing other hypotheses and independent variables. The "suggestions for further research" typically found at the end of write-ups of experiments thus represent not just a formal component of publications but also a vital aspect of the experimental ethos.

REFERENCES

Adair, John G. 2003. "Hawthorne Effect." In *The Sage Encyclopedia of Social Science Research Methods*, 452, edited by Michael Lewis-Beck, Alan Bryman and Tim Futing Liao. Thousand Oaks, CA: Sage.

Asher, J. William. 1976. *Educational Research and Evaluation Methods*. Boston: Little, Brown.

Best, Joel. 2001. *Damned Lies and Statistics: Untangling Numbers from the Media, Politicians, and Activists*. Berkeley, CA: University of California Press.

Bilal, Dania M. 1989. "International Students' Acquisition of Library Research Skills: Relationship with Their English Language Proficiency." In *Integrating Library Use Skills into the General Education Curriculum*, 129–145. New York: Haworth Press.

Brown, Ann Goebel, Sandra Weingart, Judith J. R. Johnson, and Betty Dance. 2004. "Librarians Don't Bite: Assessing Library Orientation for Freshmen." *Reference Services Review* 34 (4): 394–403.

Busha, Charles H. 1981. *A Library Science Research Reader and Bibliographic Guide*. Littleton, CO: Libraries Unlimited.

Busha, Charles H., and Stephen P. Harter. 1980. *Research Methods in Librarianship: Issues and Interpretation*. New York: Academic Press.

Carey, Stephen S. 1998. *A Beginner's Guide to Scientific Method*. 2nd ed. Belmont, CA: Wadsworth Publishing.

Case, Donald O. 2002. *Looking for Information: A Survey of Research on Information Seeking, Needs, and Behaviors*. San Diego, CA: Academic Press.

Cohen, Morris, and Ernest Nagel. 1983. "What is the Scientific Method?" In *Reader in Research Methods for Librarianship*, 3–9. Washington, DC: NRC Microcard Editions.

Crossen, Cynthia. 1996. *Tainted Truth: The Manipulation of Fact in America*. New York: Touchstone Books.

Fenske, Rachel. 1998. "Computer Literacy and the Library: A New Connection." *Reference Services Review* 26 (2): 67–78.

Fink, Arlene. 1995. *How to Sample in Surveys*. Thousand Oaks, CA: Sage.

Gerhan, David. 2001. "Statistical Significance: How It Signifies in Statistics Reference." *Reference and User Services Quarterly* 40 (4): 361–374.

Germain, Carol Anne, Trudi E. Jacobson, and Sue A. Kaczor. 2000. "A Comparison of the Effectiveness of Presentation Formats for Instruction: Teaching First-Year Students." *College & Research Libraries* 61 (1): 65–72.

Girden, Ellen R. 1996. *Evaluating Research Articles from Start to Finish*. Thousand Oaks, CA: Sage.

Goldhor, Herbert. 1972. *Introduction to Scientific Research in Librarianship*. Urbana, IL: University of Illinois.

Gorman, D. M. 2003. "Prevention Programs and Scientific Nonsense." *Policy Review* no. 117. Available: http://hoover.org/publications/policyreview/3449996.html (accessed May 16, 2007).

Green, Donald P. 2003. "Experimental Design." In *The Sage Encyclopedia of Social Science Research Methods*, 354–356, edited by Michael Lewis-Beck, Alan Bryman, and Tim Futing Liao. Thousand Oaks, CA: Sage.

Greer, Arlene, Lee Weston, and Mary Alm. 1991. "Assessment of Learning Outcomes: A Measure of Progress in Library Literacy." *College & Research Libraries* 52: 549–557.

Grotzinger, Laurel. 1981. "Methodology of Library Science Inquiry." In Busha *A Library Science Research Reader and Bibliographic Guide*, 38–50. Littleton, CO: Libraries Unlimited.

Gustafson, Kent L., and Jane Bandy Smith. 1994. *Research for School Library Media Specialists*. Norwood, NJ: Ablex.

Katzer, Jeffrey. 1981. "Understanding the Research Process: An Analysis of Error." In Busha *A Library Science Research Reader and Bibliographic Guide*, 51–71. Littleton, CO: Libraries Unlimited.

Katzer, Jeffrey, Kenneth H. Cook, and Wayne W. Crouch. 1997. *Evaluating Information: A Guide for Users of Social Science Research*. Reading, MA: Addison-Wesley.

Lewis-Beck, Michael, Alan Bryman, and Tim Futing Liao. 2004. *The Sage Encyclopedia of Social Science Research Methods*. Thousand Oaks, CA: Sage.

Manfreda, Katja Lozar, Zenel Batagelj, and Vasja Vehovar. 2002. "Design of Web Survey Questionnaires: Three Basic Experiments." *Journal of Computer-Mediated Communication* 7(3). Available: http://ascusc.org/jcmc/vol7/issue3/vehovar.html (accessed November 15, 2004).

Nichols, James, Barbara Shaffer, and Karen Shockey. 2003. "Changing the Face of Instruction: Is Online or In-class More Effective?" *College & Research Libraries* 64: 378–388.

Onwuegbuzie, Anthony J., and Qun G. Jiao. 2000. "I'll Go to the Library Later: The Relationship between Academic Procrastination and Library Literacy." *College & Research Libraries* 61: 45–54.

Paulos, John Allen. 1988. *Innumeracy: Mathematical Illiteracy and Its Consequences*. New York: Hill and Wang.

Peng, Chao-Ying Joanne. 2003. "Experiment." In *The Sage Encyclopedia of Social Science Research Methods*, 349–354, edited by Michael Lewis-Beck, Alan Bryman, and Tim Futing Liao. Thousand Oaks, CA: Sage.

Powell, Ronald R. 1999. *Basic Research Methods for Librarians*. 3rd ed. Greenwich, CT: Ablex.

Random House Webster's College Dictionary. 1991. McGraw-Hill edition. New York: Random House.

Rice, James. 1981. *Teaching Library Use: A Guide for Library Instruction*. Westport, CT: Greenwood Press.

Ware, Susan A., and Deena J. Morganti. 1986. "A Competency-Based Approach to Assessing Workbook Effectiveness." *Research Strategies* 4: 4–10.

Chapter 7

Bibliometrics

"**B**ibliometrics" comes from the Greek words for book (*biblios*) and measure (*metron*), suggesting its focus as a research methodology that "measures books." Bibliometrics, however, is not just any approach to quantification of publications. As Paisley (1989, 707) emphasizes, bibliometrics focuses on

> *extrinsic* facts about publications, broadcasts, and other forms of communication. For example, an article is coded by when and where it was published, by the identity and affiliation of the author, by the other articles it cites, and so on. *Intrinsic* content of the article is thought to be the domain of content analysis because of the need to develop coding categories based on a theory of the relationship of the text to intentions, effects, and the symbolic environment.

In other words, while other research methodologies are concerned with the content and interpretation of recorded information sources, bibliometrics concentrates upon those aspects of sources that do not require engagement with or interpretation of the sources' content—aspects such as

- author's affiliations, educational credentials, or geographic location
- number of circulations or re-shelvings of printed materials
- usage statistics on electronic resources
- which sources cite and are cited by other sources; or the number and types of linkages between Web pages

Essentially, if you can count something without too much debate over what it is—and it has something to do with any type of recorded information source—it could become the subject of a bibliometric study. Some people also use the terms "Webometrics," "cybermetrics," "scientometrics," or "infometrics" to refer to bibliometric studies. These different terms largely connote differences in the types of recorded information sources to which a common methodology is applied; Webometrics thus looks at Web pages, while scientometrics tends to focus on recorded information sources for scientific disciplines.

The relationship between bibliometrics and content analysis is complex. Some have equated bibliometrics and content analysis (Miller and Stebenne 1988), while others have made bibliometrics a type of content analysis (Bibliometrics 2005), and yet others have described the two as separate methodologies (Paisley 1989). This book obviously takes the latter view, largely because content analysis requires reading and often interpretation of sources' content, while bibliometrics does not.

Bibliometrics is one of the oldest research methodologies in library and information science. Histories of bibliometrics often trace its earliest use to 1913, when Felix Auerbach first articulated Zipf's law while formulating a relationship between the rank and size of German cities (Rousseau accessed 2007). It seems probable, however, that at least some studies prior to 1913 used counting of extrinsic facts about publications to test their hypotheses or support their arguments.

Despite its history, bibliometrics is not without its critics. Their objections tend to center upon what Borgman (1990, 11), herself a frequent user of bibliometrics, describes as the methodology's "application of mathematics and statistical methods to books and other media of communication." Some critics question the degree to which citations and other aspects of recorded communications actually and accurately reflect the intentions and behaviors of their human authors. Showing that a group of co-authors cited sources X, Y, and Z, for example, does not prove that they thought X, Y, and Z were the best sources on that topic. These co-authors might have preferred A and B as their sources, but they could not find their personal copy of A while they were writing, and they waited until the last minute to do their work—just to find out that B could only be gotten by interlibrary loan.

Other critics claim that bibliometrics obscures individual experiences and differences within numerical averages (Edge 1977, 15–16). While one author might have cited source X in the belief that it was the "best" source on a topic, another author might have cited it simply because a coworker wrote it, and yet another author might have cited it because a peer reviewer noted its absence from his bibliography. Emphasizing that all three authors used the same source hides their very different reasons for doing so. Still other critics object to the typical focuses of bibliometric studies on formal scholarly publications, as well as the tendency of bibliometrics to view scholarly communication as predictably patterned. Edge (1979, 113) claims that "in emphasizing formal communication through the published literature, quantitative methods [such as bibliometrics] perpetuate a 'rationalized' view of the nature of [scholarship]."

Most bibliometricians do not fundamentally dispute these claims. Rather, they reiterate one of bibliometrics' key assumptions: "A scientific paper, article, or book is a rich resource of data on . . . communication patterns and cognitive processes" (Parker and Paisley 1966, 1067). Note that Parker and Paisley claim only that bibliometrics is "a rich source of data," not that it should be the only source of data. Indeed, it is not uncommon for researchers to use bibliometrics in conjunction with other methodologies better suited to gauging individual perspectives and differences.

Provided that beginning researchers do not assume they have learned everything there is to know about a topic from a single bibliometric study (for reasons that will become clearer later), bibliometrics can be a particularly good methodology for a first research project. Several characteristics of bibliometrics make it easier for beginning researchers to get started with bibliometrics than with some other methodologies. First, bibliometrics is unobtrusive; its focus is upon the products of human activity (books, articles, Web pages, and so on), not upon humans themselves. This means that there is no need to control for experimenter, interactional investigator, or other similar effects arising from the influences of researchers and human subjects upon each other. Institutional review board approval is also typically not required for bibliometric projects, removing another hurdle to getting started. Second, bibliometricians' data sources preexist the study, and they are usually readily accessible. Third, sampling is generally only of the simple random or systematic sort, not stratified. Fourth, bibliometricians work from a number of shared operational definitions, research designs, and measurement instruments, freeing novice researchers from the complexities of constructing these from scratch. Fifth, data tends to be numerical, meaning that it is less enmeshed in interpretive ambiguities. However, although the data is numerical, knowledge of inferential statistical techniques is not required for interpreting or presenting it. All of these factors make bibliometrics one of the more straightforward ways to get started in research.

FINDING A TOPIC

As one of the oldest and most commonly used methodologies in library and information science research, bibliometrics displays a wide range of topical applications. Broadly speaking, bibliometric studies can be categorized into the following four groups:

- *Studies that seek to learn about information sources*, such as the contents and functionality of different databases or the time frames within which scientific research results in different types of publications (conference papers, preprints, journal articles, review articles, and so on). When focused upon the value of individual journals or other publications to specific disciplines and fields, such studies are often used in institutional decision making about what to acquire, keep, discontinue, or weed. The study by Fosmire and Yu (2000) listed in Figure 7-1 is an example of a bibliometric research project that seeks to learn more about information sources per se, while the study by Smith (1981) describes bibliometric studies of information sources in support of local decision making.

- *Studies that seek to learn about institutional trends*, such as the impact of decreased library spending for print monographs upon patrons' use of library resources over time. These studies often factor in institutional decision making, particularly collection development, and in outcomes assessment projects. Smith's study (listed in Figure 7-1) of whether the usefulness of the University of Georgia Library's collection has changed over the past ten years because of the introduction of electronic resources and increases in the periodical budget is an example of such a study, as are the studies by Edwards (1999) and Walcott (1994).

- *Studies that seek to learn about people's behavior*, such as what sources undergraduate students, laboratory scientists, or other researchers use in their work, or to what degree researchers from different fields, institutions, countries, professional ranks, or sexes co-author publications. Especially when focused on the products of undergraduate researchers, some such studies are conducted for assessment purposes (e.g., seeing how the sources cited relate to changes in assignments, instructional methods, or materials). Bahr and Zemon's (2000) study listed in Figure 7-1 examines the extent of co-authorship within academic librarianship, especially the number, gender, and institutional settings of co-authors.

- *Studies that seek to learn about socio-intellectual phenomena*, such as the formation of disciplines or of interdisciplinary research fronts, the spread of ideas between disciplines or geographic regions, or the impact of print, electronic-by-subscription, and open access publishing models on scholarly communication. Youngen's study (1998), listed in Figure 7-1, for example, tracks the increasing acceptance of electronic preprints in the physical sciences.

Fosmire and Yu's article, "Free Scholarly Electronic Journals: How Good Are They?" published in *Issues in Science and Technology Librarianship* in 2000, illustrates many typical aspects of bibliometric research. Fosmire and Yu conducted their research as a follow-up to a study by Harter five years earlier on the impact of open access journals on various scholarly fields. Like Fosmire and Yu's study, most bibliometric studies draw heavily upon prior studies in finding their research topics (and in interpreting their data, as will be seen below). The reason for this is simple: a single, self-contained bibliometric study is no more widely interesting or generally informative than a photograph of particular people at a particular time in a particular place.

Suppose you found a photograph from the 1960s of your parents' college roommates at Ohio University. You would probably be somewhat interested in the photograph because it showed people connected to your parents; others who graduated from the same institution or lived through the 1960s might also have some interest. Most people, though, would have no interest in the photograph based simply on its content. Its meaning would interest more people, but it is hard to supply this meaning without knowledge of the time, place, and people in question. Had people always dressed like that? Do we dress differently now? Did students in the U.S. do their hair in the same way as students in France or China? Was roommate Bob's hairstyle a relic of the 1950s and completely atypical for 1960s' hairstyles? Knowing more about the context of your photograph helps make it more interesting and understandable to others. Similarly, situating bibliometric research projects within the context of prior studies helps give meaning to the data—and to see what is researchable. Bibliometric studies tend to be particularly concerned with addressing whether what was true then holds true now, as well as whether this category of authors resembles that category of authors in the materials they cite and produce. Fosmire and Yu ultimately found that now, unlike five years ago, there "are several free scholarly journals that have a significant impact on their respective fields."

Fosmire and Yu (2000) are also typical of other bibliometricians in their operationalization of research terms by using established definitions for topics of interest. They take their definition of "impact factor" from the Institute for Scientific Information® (ISI), whose definition of impact factor (as the number of citations to articles published in a particular journal in a two-year period divided by the total number of articles published in that journal in the same period) is widely used by other bibliometricians. They also used standard directories of information sources to select their research population. By focusing on science, technology, and mathematics journals listed in the *Directory of Electronic Journals; Newsletters; and Academic Discussion Lists* (7th ed.), they protected themselves against skewing their study's findings through a personal and idiosyncratic population selection. Because there were only 85 such journals, they studied the entire population, not just a sample. If they had been forced to sample, they—like most bibliometricians—would likely have chosen a simple random or systematic sample. Because "impact" was defined in terms of the number of citations to a journal, Fosmire and Yu searched Web of Science® to determine the number of citations to each journal. Citations, or references by one work to other, earlier works, are a particularly common source of data in bibliometric projects. Fosmire and Yu were well acquainted with how Web of Science® works (e.g., it "searches citations based on a 20 character code"), and they described their searching or data gathering mechanisms in detail ("for example, *Emerging Infectious Diseases* was searched as 'eme* inf* dis*'"). Such knowledge of data-gathering tools and detail about data-gathering procedures is essential to ensure the validity and reliability of results. If the database's workings skew data gathering, then the validity of the study is questionable; if insufficient details are provided about how the data were gathered, the study's reliability is questionable. Fosmire and Yu present their data in seven tables that give the impact factor, immediacy index, and total number of current articles for each journal. This data underlies the study's conclusion that "overall, it appears that several high-quality, productive, free scholarly electronic journals exist currently. These journals scored very well in impact factor and immediacy index, and they have reasonable numbers of articles published."

Figure 7-1 lists some other exemplary bibliometric studies by practicing librarians and information scientists.

Figure 7-1: Studies Using Bibliometrics

Bahr, Alice Harrison, and Mickey Zemon. 2000. "Collaborative Authorship in the Journal Literature: Perspectives for Academic Librarians Who Wish to Publish." *College and Research Libraries* 61 (5): 410–419.

> *Researchers used articles published in* College & Research Libraries *and the* Journal of Academic Librarianship *between 1986 and 1996 to track co-authorship among academic librarians. Tracked number and percentage of co-authored articles in each journal per year, also tracked the number, gender, and institutional setting of co-authors. Included a lot of information about prior studies of co-authorship in librarianship and other fields.*

Davis, Philip M. 2005. "The Ethics of Republishing: A Case Study of Emerald/MCB University Press Journals." *Library Resources and Technical Services* 49 (2): 72–88.

> *Researcher examined degree to which Emerald (formerly MCB University Press) engaged in republication without notification, as well as whether articles were republished in journals with the same or similar subjects. Identified a number of republished articles via keyword searches, then examined them for notices about republication and tracked the journals in which they appeared. Also included some data about the library holdings of the journals republishing articles.*

Fosmire, Michael, and Song Yu. 2000. "Free Scholarly Electronic Journals: How Good Are They?" *Issues in Science and Technology Librarianship.* Available: http://library.ucsb.edu/istl/00-summer/refereed.html (accessed May 18, 2007).

> *Researchers calculated the impact factor and immediacy index of 85 science, technology, and medicine journals listed in the* Directory of Electronic Journals, Newsletters, and Academic Discussion Lists *(7th ed.) as a way of determining whether free scholarly electronic journals have more impact than they were found to have in a study by Stephen Harter five years earlier. Impact factor and immediacy index were based on standard calculations of these constructs.*

Germain, Carol Anne. 2000. "URLs: Uniform Resource Locators or Unreliable Resource Locators?" *College & Research Libraries* 61 (4): 359–365.

> *Researcher randomly selected 31 journal articles published in journals in various fields (library and information science, science, computer science, humanities, and social sciences) between 1995 and 1997. All citations with URLs (N=64) in these articles were checked as to the persistence of the URL cited every three months for a three-year period (1997-1999). Tracked number and percent of articles with inaccessible citations by year.*

Rhodes, Jo Ann. 1997. "Sentimentality? An Exercise in Weeding in the Small College Library." *The Christian Librarian* 40 (1): 16–17 and 20.

> *Researcher tracked number of circulations by call number range for one year after a project to reclassify some 50,000 items left as a separate collection when the library joined OCLC in the mid-1970s. Data on the age of the items as well as their eventual circulations underlie conclusion that some of reclassified materials might better have been withdrawn.*

(Cont'd.)

Figure 7-1: Studies Using Bibliometrics *(Continued)*

Smith, Erin T. 2003. "Assessing Collection Usefulness: An Investigation of Library Ownership of the Resources Graduate Students Use." *College & Research Libraries* 64 (5): 344–355.

Researcher examined up to 75 citations from 30 dissertations in four subject fields (education, social sciences, sciences, and humanities) from 1991 and from 2001 to see the types of materials cited (e.g., book, newspaper, etc.), as well as the percentage of cited materials that were locally owned. Study intended to help in evaluating the "fit" of the University of Georgia Library's collections with the needs of its patrons.

Youngen, Gregory K. 1998. "Citation Patterns to Traditional Electronic Preprints in the Published Literature." *College & Research Libraries* 59 (5): 448–456.

Researcher used ISI's SciSearch® database to track the number of journals publishing articles with citations to preprints and e-prints, as well as the overall number of citations to preprints and e-prints over the past ten years. Trendlines from the data show increasing citations to and acceptance of e-prints.

FORMULATING QUESTIONS

In part because the total number of publications in recorded history is so vast, bibliometric research projects involve quite narrow research questions. For example, instead of studying the frequency of citations to various types of Web and print resources by all researchers, a bibliometric research project may limit its focus to the frequency of citations to various types of Web and print resources by first-year students, undergraduate history majors, or practicing chemists. As Figure 7-2 suggests, there is simply too much recorded information to look at all examples of anything unless that "anything" is something quite small. (For example, when Fosmire and Yu [2000] did their study, there were only 85 free scholarly electronic journals in the fields of science, technology, and mathematics. Eighty-five is, in itself, a researchable number, but the number would not have been so researchable had they looked at all open access journals.) Bibliometricians also use such narrow research questions because publication and citation patterns generally hold true for only limited times, places, and populations. While there is an overall phenomenon consisting of the frequency

Figure 7-2: Estimates of the Total Amount of Recorded Information

Source Type	Yearly Quantity of Information
Books	39 terabytes
Newspapers	138.4 terabytes
Mass market periodicals	52 terabytes
Journals	6 terabytes
Newsletters	0.9 terabytes

This figure is based on information from Lyman and Varian (2003).

of citations to various types of Web and print resources by all researchers, this overall phenomenon is composed of smaller phenomena—the frequency of citations to various types of Web and print sources by specific types of researchers—that comprise but are not identical to the overall phenomenon. Figure 7-3 illustrates this in more detail.

While chemists might have something in common with physicists or biologists in terms of the frequency with which they cite various types of Web and print sources, they do not have everything in common with physicists or biologists, and they have little in common with historians or mathematicians. Even within chemistry, there may be sizeable differences between biochemists and physical chemists in the frequency with which they cite various types of Web and print sources. Failure to treat different communities as distinct in gathering and interpreting data would yield conclusions that, while purporting to include everyone, actually represent no one.

Many bibliometric studies are purely descriptive. They seek to do no more than provide numbers (such as frequency counts or percentages) that help to illuminate the topics they are discussing. All of the studies from Figure 7-1 are of this type.

Figure 7-3: Bibliometrics' Focus on Small Questions

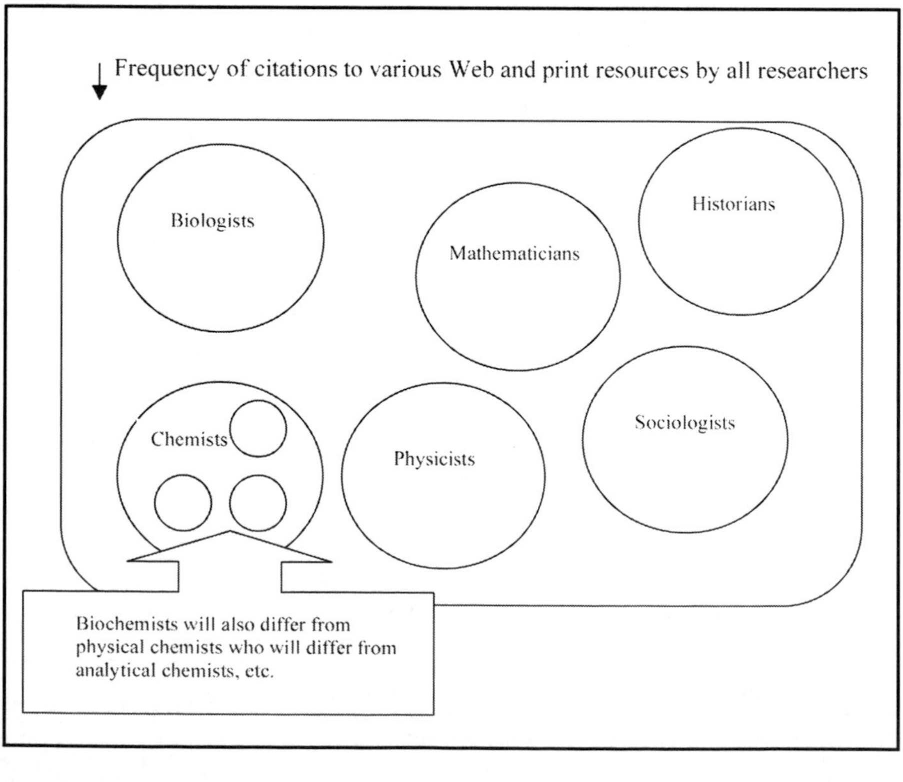

- Bahr and Zemon (2000) provide raw numbers and percentages of co-authored articles in two journals, as well as raw numbers and percentages of co-authors by sex and institutional status.
- Davis (2005) provides frequency counts and title lists of Emerald journals that have republished articles without notification.
- Fosmire and Yu (2000) give the impact factors, immediacy index, and total number of articles published over a two-year period by open access journals in science, technology, and medicine.
- Germain (2000) tracks the total number and percentage of articles citing to inoperative URLs over a three-year period.
- Rhodes (1997) provides total numbers and percentages of reclassified volumes by age and circulation count.
- Smith (2003) gives the number and percentage of source types cited in dissertations, as well as the number and percentage of cited items locally owned.
- Youngen (1998) gives the number of citations to preprints and e-prints in journals included in ISI's (Institute of Scientific Information®) SciSearch.

These studies use their data in drawing conclusions about the topics studied, but they generally do not have formal hypotheses, nor do they subject their data to tests of statistical significance. Some bibliometric studies do have formal hypotheses (e.g., circulation percentages of books selected by faculty will be higher than those selected by librarians, or open access will lead to higher impact factors for articles). Bibliometric studies can also use tests of statistical significance, such as chi-square or Analysis of Variance tests, on their data. However, it is precisely because bibliometricians work so often without formal hypotheses or tests of statistical significance that they spend so much time replicating studies. Another researcher taking and interpreting a different "picture"—or set of data—will necessarily reach different conclusions, a fact which makes the taking of multiple "pictures" important. The more "pictures" that show the same thing, the more sure researchers can be of their interpretations.

DEFINING THE POPULATION

The immense number of publications and the differences in publications over time, space, and socio-intellectual groups also helps to explain why bibliometricians focus on specific populations. Some populations studied by bibliometric researchers in library and information science include:

- articles published in *College & Research Libraries* and the *Journal of Academic Librarianship* between 1986 and 1996 (Bahr and Zemon 2000)
- electronic-by-subscription journals published by Emerald/MCB University Press (Davis 2005)

- sixty-four URL-including citations from 31 randomly selected journal articles in 13 different fields (Germain 2000)
- open access journals in science, technology, and mathematics (Fosmire and Yu 2000)
- 50,000 items not reclassified when Columbia International University shifted from Dewey to Library of Congress classification (Rhodes 1997)
- dissertations written in 1991 and 2001 by students at the University of Georgia (Smith 2003)
- journals indexed in ISI's SciSearch® database over ten years (Youngen 1998)

Figure 7-4 lists other possible subjects used by bibliometricians.

It is not uncommon for bibliometricians to use all members of a narrowly drawn target population rather than a sample. Bahr and Zemon, Davis, Fosmire and Yu, Rhodes, and Youngen all do this. When bibliometricians do sample, however, they tend to focus more on simple random rather than stratified samples. Bibliometricians do this in large part because they often do not know enough about the items being studied to determine what the proper population subgroups and ratios of population subgroups should be for stratified sampling. Bibliometricians also use systematic samples, selecting every n^{th} item from directories of resources; cluster samples, randomly selecting naturally occurring units

Figure 7-4: Some Subjects Used by Bibliometrics Researchers

- Articles from particular journals over given time periods.
- Articles published by faculty at a particular institution.
- Articles published in a given time period and indexed in particular databases.
- Authors in a particular field and geographic region.
- Bibliographies of student research papers (first-year students, undergraduates, history majors, etc.).
- Circulation counts of materials (with differing selectors, classification systems, etc.).
- Citations to e-prints in specific journals.
- Database vendors.
- Databases.
- Journal publishers.
- Journals in a particular field or format.
- Library holdings of best sellers.
- Links on Web pages in a specific field, from specific types of institutions, etc.
- Open access journals in a specific field.
- Search engines.
- Usage statistics on electronic resources.
- Web pages listed in particular review sources.

(e.g., dissertations, articles), and then studying all members (e.g., citations) within those units; and multistage sampling, randomly selecting naturally occurring units (e.g., dissertations, articles) and then randomly selecting members (e.g., citations) from these.*

Bibliometricians often display more care in showing that their sample is not unrepresentative (because of "cherry picking" of subjects on the researchers' part) than in showing that it is actually representative of some larger population. They often do this by showing that their population was taken from some standard directory of resources: *Ulrich's Periodicals Directory, Magazines for Libraries*, the *Directory of Electronic Journals, Newsletters, and Academic Discussion Lists*, core lists of periodicals in given disciplines, or even complete title lists from comprehensive periodical indexes. An example should make it clearer why they do this.

If Youngen (1998) had selected his population of journals citing preprints and e-prints from a list of journals that he himself had brainstormed—rather than relying upon the journals indexed in ISI's SciSearch®—his list might well have over-represented journals whose articles cited preprints and e-prints. Such journals would, after all, have been prominently in his mind as he brainstormed his list. By relying upon ISI's selection of journals for SciSearch®, however, he lessened the chances that the phenomenon he observed was simply due to his initial biased selection of subjects.

When bibliometricians sample from non-standard lists of items, they should explain who selected the items for the list and how the items were selected. Thus, for example, if you work from a list of journal titles selected by faculty experts in various disciplines, you must explain to your readers what made these people experts and how they made their selections. You should also tell your readers why their selections comprise the appropriate population for study. In fact, all bibliometricians should explain why the population they have selected should be expected to reveal something about the topic at hand. Art historians, for example, have no tradition of using preprints to communicate their research, so a researcher should not be too surprised to find that art historians do not use e-prints extensively. As a population, art historians should not be expected to reveal anything significant about academics' increasing acceptance of e-prints.

Some bibliometricians have used convenience samples, such as the research papers of student volunteers. Local lists of holdings are a type of convenience

---

* Although Germain (2000) and Smith (2003) describe their samples as simply "random," both actually engage in cluster sampling: Smith randomly selected 60 dissertations and then used all, or the first 75, citations in these dissertations as her sample, while Germain randomly selected 31 different articles and then used all citations, including URLs from these articles, as her sample.

sample, so if you want to check citations by physics faculty to Web pages in their publications, using the journal titles to which your library subscribes might not be a good idea. Those subscriptions represent particular choices, choices which could skew the titles included to make them unrepresentative in all but the most comprehensive collections.

Finally, bibliometricians must always remember that their actual subjects are the products of humans' recorded communication, not the humans themselves. Bibliometricians are, to be sure, often concerned with the people behind these recorded communications. A citation analysis of first-year students' research papers would, after all, not be of much interest to anyone were it not for the fact that students' choices are presumed to reveal at least some aspects of their thinking about the research and writing processes. Bibliometricians must, however, constantly remain aware of the gap between the products of humans' recorded communication (their actual subjects) and the real desires and intentions of human beings (their ultimate objects of interest). It is far from uncommon, for example, for people to cite a source because it was convenient, because they want to use it as a "negative example" and are citing it to disagree with it, or for other reasons that do not necessarily reflect positively on the quality of the work. Researchers who ignore this fact can end up drawing negative conclusions about their subjects simply because they assume that the sources cited in people's bibliographies represent the best sources these people could find. For example, not a few librarian-researchers have determined that first-year college and university students do not know how to find or evaluate information because they cite Web pages in their bibliographies. This is a problematic conclusion, however, since it presumes that first-year students cite in their research papers the same sources they would otherwise cite if they had a great deal of time to research, great investment in their topics, and great interest in the outcome of their product.

SELECTING A RESEARCH DESIGN

Bibliometrics research design involves identifying the units of analysis (e.g., citations, hyperlinks, authors' names) and the methods of retrieving the units of analysis. Bibliometricians tend to draw upon a narrow range of units of analysis, or data sources, in implementing their studies, and these data sources have widely agreed upon definitions and interpretations. The shared interpretations of these units of analysis are particularly important. Bibliometricians are well aware that while these interpretations will not hold in 100 percent of cases, they will hold in a large enough percentage of cases to support thinking about the units of analyses in those ways. Common units of analysis or data sources include:

- *Citations*, or references made by one source to other sources. Citations are "formal, explicit linkages between papers that have particular points in common;" authors make citations to documents that support, provide precedent for, illustrate, or elaborate on what the authors have to say (Garfield 1979, 1). As has been widely noted, "[c]itation analysis is the best-known bibliometric technique" (Borgman 1990, 13).
- *Impact factor*, or the number of citations to articles published in a particular journal in a two-year period divided by the total number of articles published in that journal in the same two-year period. The impact factor is a measure of the relative importance of journals; journals with a higher impact factor are presumed to have greater relevance within a discipline than those with a lower impact factor.
- *Immediacy index*, or the number of citations to articles published in a particular journal in a given time period divided by the total number of articles published in that journal in the same time period. The immediacy index measures how quickly the average article in a particular journal is discovered by other researchers and cited. Journals that are more prestigious within a field often have higher immediacy indexes than less prestigious journals because most researchers are reading them on a regular basis.
- *Hyperlinks*, or references made from one electronic resource to other electronic resources. The meaning of hyperlinks within bibliometrics is more contested than that of other data sources listed here. Some argue that a hyperlink is equivalent to a citation. Others disagree, noting that hyperlinks do not display the same relationship of earlier (cited) and later (citing) sources that citations do; an earlier Web page can be updated to link to a later page that had previously linked to it. Moreover, with hyperlinks, "[t]he citing/cited symmetry itself [is] challenged by the frequent practice of reciprocal links" (Prime, Bassecoulard and Zitt 2002, 304). Some researchers view search engine algorithms that rank results based on the number and quality of other pages that link to a page, such as the Google PageRank, as the Web equivalent of impact factors. Others are more skeptical because pages with high in-link counts tend not to be direct providers of content, as cited articles or books are (cf. Prime, Bassecoulard and Zitt 2002).
- *Library holdings*, or institutional ownership of specific items. Library holdings are presumed to be completely physically available to researchers at any time. Library holdings are also presumed to reflect libraries' conscious materials selection and retention decisions.
- *Circulation counts*, or records of the number of times patrons have officially taken particular items out of the library with them. A circulation is presumed to equal a personal use by the person who checked the book out, not people taking things home for family or friends or taking them home and returning them without use.

Classifications of periodicals by type (refereed or non-refereed); classifications of materials by subject content (business, music, etc.); classifications of materials by publication type (newspaper, book, Web page, etc.); classifications of material by format (print or electronic); and classifications of authors by factors such as academic rank, disciplinary field, and geographic location are also commonly used data sources. If you are using a personal definition or interpretation of any of these units of analysis, or if you are using some other less commonly used unit of analysis, you should make this clear to your readers.

Whenever possible, bibliometricians rely upon standard and shared sources for gathering data. ISI's *Journal Citation Reports* provides impact factors and immediacy indexes for the journals indexed in ISI databases, and researchers use these numbers in preference to calculating their own impact factors. Similarly, researchers may rely on *Ulrich's Periodicals Directory*, *Magazines for Libraries*, or a similar source for classifying periodicals by type instead of relying on their own classifications. The titles of best sellers are taken from *The New York Times* best-seller lists.

Researchers do this in order to increase the validity and reliability of their data. By drawing upon standard and shared resources for gathering data whenever possible, researchers help to ensure that their findings are not skewed by selection of non-representative items and that other researchers can more easily replicate their results.

Sometimes, however, researchers work on subjects for which standard and shared sources of data are not possible. Classifications of materials by subject content or by publication type are usually done locally, especially when researchers are identifying the materials to be classified from student bibliographies. Then coding of the sort discussed in Chapter 3 becomes an issue. Would another researcher looking at a citation to an online newspaper article in a student bibliography classify it as a newspaper or a Web page? Would the same researcher coming across multiple citations to online newspaper articles always class them in the same way? In such situations, you should establish a code list, which spells out what counts as an occurrence of or evidence for the items being coded (publication type, URL connectivity, completeness of citations, authors' institutional status, etc.). See Figure 7-5 for a sample code list.

You should then address the operationalizations that underlie your code list in any publications about this research project. Whenever possible, you should also have multiple researchers involved in coding the data and provide your readers with information on inter-rater reliability. That way your readers know that your findings do not reflect just the possibly biased perceptions of a single individual.

Products of the Institute for Scientific Information® (ISI) occupy a special place among the sources used by bibliometricians. *Science Citation Index®*, *Social Science Citation Index®*, *Arts and Humanities Citation Index®*, and *Web*

Figure 7-5. Sample Code List

Code Name, or Code Number	Description
LIBLIB	All co-authors have the professional degrees or titles of librarians.
LIBFAC	At least one co-author has the professional degree or title of librarian, AND at least one co-author has the professional title of higher education faculty member (non-library and information science faculty only).
LIBADMIN	At least one co-author has the professional degree or title of librarian, AND at least one co-author has the professional title of higher education administrator (non-library administrators only).
LIBSTAFF	At least one co-author has the professional degree or title of librarian, AND at least one co-author has the professional title of college or university library staff.
LIBINSTSTAFF	At least one co-author has the professional degree or title of librarian, AND at least one co-author has the professional title of college or university staff (non-library staff only).
LIBOTHRRES	At least one co-author has the professional degree or title of librarian, AND at least one co-author has the professional title of researcher at some non-college or university institution.
LIBLISFAC	At least one co-author has the professional degree or title of librarian, AND at least one co-author has the professional title of library school faculty member.
LIBOTHER	At least one co-author has the professional degree or title of librarian, AND at least one co-author has a non-librarian degree or title not covered above.

of Science® are commonly used for determining which articles cite and are cited by each other. *Journal Citation Reports*® provides impact factors and immediacy indexes. *Web Citation Index*® debuted in 2005 and tracks both citations to Web publications by traditional scholarly works and citations to traditional scholarly works by Web publications. All of these are subscription-only products, but ISI does make *ISIHighlyCited.com*SM available for free. This database allows researchers to identify—and thus study—the 250 researchers in 21 subject fields who were most highly cited between 1981 and 1999. Of course, ISI's SciSearch® does not itself provide a representative listing of all journals in existence. Rather, ISI is selective; it selects only approximately 10 percent of the 2,000 journals it reviews each month for inclusion in its databases. ISI also includes a disproportionately high percentage of English-language journals. Still, this lack of representativeness is a problem shared by all bibliometricians who use SciSearch® for their research, not one that the researchers introduced into the project by their own potentially biased choices of subjects.

Other non-subscription products available for tracking citations include: *CiteSeer.IST* (http://citeseer.ist.psu.edu), which provides impact ratings and most cited documents and authors for computer science; *ParaCite* (http://paracite.eprints.org), which tracks citations to open-archives publications; and *The Annotated New York Times* (http://annotatedtimes.blogrunner.com), which tracks references by bloggers to *New York Times* stories. Google's Advanced Search screen offers a Page-Specific Search option which finds links to a particular Web page by other pages (the command "link": followed directly by a URL also works). Other search engines also provide "link" searching, although you may have to explore the help or advanced search pages of these engines to find out how to search. AlltheWeb (http://alltheweb.com) is commonly used for this purpose. Its search command is "link": followed directly by the URL. Some researchers actually prefer AlltheWeb to Google because AlltheWeb allows researchers to limit or focus "link" searches by adding additional search terms, something not possible with Google. AlltheWeb also will often produce larger results lists for "link" searches than Google. Web transaction logs as well as some Web sites also provide information on the number of downloads, which could be used for tracking frequency of usage.

In using such tools to gather data, researchers must keep two important factors in mind. First, data gathered from different tools is not directly comparable (Brody 2004): a citing reference in an ISI database does not mean the same as a citing reference (an in-link) on Google. These databases index different types of publications (selected scholarly journals versus a wide range of Web pages); they display differing levels of selectivity in choosing materials for inclusion (ISI including only some 10 percent of new submissions, Google being more inclusive); and they index pages that have different methods and purposes for citing (non-Web publications can generally only cite earlier sources and cannot make reciprocal citations, while Web pages can be updated to cite sources created after the page was originally written, and reciprocal citations are common). Researchers should be careful not to combine data from different sources and not to draw overly strong conclusions based on data from different sources. While it is certainly possible to track both the traditional and the Web citations to given publications, these numbers should be kept separate and not submerged in a total (traditional + Web) citations category. Second, the way in which the tool works, or is used by particular researchers, can greatly influence the data gathered. ISI's databases, for example, often include several variants of the same author's name, as well as several variants of institutional abbreviations. Susan E. Beck, for example, can be listed as Beck, S. or Beck, S. E., while New Mexico State University can be listed as NMSU, or New Mex. St. U. A researcher needs to be aware of this and control for it by searching all possible variants. This means that researchers need to know a great deal about the tools they use to gather data. They also need to share information about how they used various tools to gather data with the readers of their research-based publications.

GATHERING DATA

The time frame within which data is gathered becomes a particular concern for bibliometricians. Suppose you want to count the number of citations to a sample of 260 journals. You have no research assistance available and you can only do your research in small increments while accomplishing your regular job. You decide to look at 10 journals a week over 26 weeks. Each week you search a database and note the total number of citations to 10 of your 260 journals. But as Figure 7-6 shows, each week you search, the database adds 250 new records, each one of which includes citations to journals.

By the time you finish in week 26, the database includes 6,250 more records than it did when you started in week 1. Given this, it would not be surprising if you found that the journals you searched toward the end of the project had more citations than the journals you searched at the beginning of the project. There were 6,250 more records with possible citations at the end than at the beginning. Additionally, consider how seriously your findings would be skewed if you searched social science journals in weeks 1–4, education journals in weeks 6–12, humanities journals in weeks 18–20, and science journals in weeks 20 26. Were the science journals really more cited than social science journals, or did they simply have 6,250 more opportunities in which to be cited than the social science journals?

It is advisable to do your searching and data-gathering in as condensed a time period as possible, preferably within a single update cycle (daily, weekly, biweekly, monthly) of the database you are using, or to include consistent date limits in all searches (all citations to X publications between 1/1/2003 and 12/31/2004). However, it is also advisable to have multiple data gathering periods and use the average of the number of results obtained in each of these periods, particularly for Web link studies. Web search engines are notoriously prone to time-outs, excessive user demands which slow searching, and other glitches which can influence the number of items retrieved. Searching one day might yield a much lower number of results than searching the next day. Thus, conducting two searches several days apart and using the average of the number of results obtained each day can minimize these difficulties.

Bibliometric studies can certainly be longitudinal, or track phenomena over time. Germain's study is an excellent example of a longitudinal bibliometric study. She checked the workability of 64 URLs every three months for three years in order to understand better how many URLs cited in scholarly articles become "dead ends" and over what time frames this happens. Other longitudinal studies have checked the online availability of titles received in print over six

Figure 7-6: Effects of Time in Bibliometric Studies

Week Number	Number of Journals You Search	Total Number of Journals You've Searched	Number of New Records Added to Database Weekly	Total Number of Records in Database
1	10	10	250	X+250
2	10	20	250	X+500
3	10	30	250	X+750
4	10	40	250	X+1000
5	10	50	250	X+1250
6	10	60	250	X+1500
7	10	70	250	X+1750
8	10	80	250	X+2000
9	10	90	250	X+2250
10	10	100	250	X+2500
11	10	110	250	X+2750
12	10	120	250	X+3000
13	10	130	250	X+3250
14	10	140	250	X+3500
15	10	150	250	X+3750
16	10	160	250	X+4000
17	10	170	250	X+4250
18	10	180	250	X+4500
19	10	190	250	X+4750
20	10	200	250	X+5000
21	10	210	250	X+5250
22	10	220	250	X+5500
23	10	230	250	X+5750
24	10	240	250	X+6000
25	10	250	250	X+6250

weeks and differences in student bibliographies between 1996 and 2000. Even in such longitudinal studies, however, data gathering at each time interval should still be in as condensed a period of time as possible. For example, the study of online availability of titles received in print checked the online availability on the same day that each title was received in print.

One final solution to the "time problem" for bibliometricians is to explicitly include time as a variable within the study. For example, if you were looking at something only produced sequentially over time, such as the monthly "Internet Resources" column from *College and Research Libraries News*, it would be impossible to compare multiple items from the same date. Some columns would obviously be older than others, and age could become a factor if, for example, you were tracking how many of the URLs cited in these columns disappeared over time. An older column would have had longer for its URLs to go bad, so including the number of months since the column's publication as an explicit unit of analysis along with the column's topic would be an excellent stategy (cf. Taylor and Hudson 2000).

INTERPRETING THE EVIDENCE

Bibliometric researchers take the raw data they have compiled in tables, spreadsheets, or databases and aggregate them before interpreting them. Frequency counts and percentages are common. Researchers might note, as Bahr and Zemon did, that 29–40 percent of the articles published in particular journals in particular time periods were co-authored.

Frequency counts and percentages are quite straightforward. A frequency count is simply a count of the total number of occurrences of something, with each occurrence counting as one. If you are counting a factor that appears in some but not all members of the population, you can arrive at a percentage indicating how common that factor is within the population by dividing the number of occurrences of the factor by the total size of the population and then multiplying by 100.

The third type of aggregate number commonly used in bibliometric studies is more problematic to determine and interpret. This third type is the average, which is used when a researcher says, for example, that the average age of the sources cited in science dissertations is 1.3 years old, that in social sciences dissertations is 4.5 years old, and that in humanities journals is 9.8 years old. What the average indicates is that the researcher had a large number of measurement values (e.g., ages of publications) in a given class (e.g., science publications) and arrived at a single number that represents the central tendency among this group of numerical values. However, there are actually three different ways of calculating an average, and the researchers' choice of which "average" to use can substantially skew their interpretation of the data.

These three types of average are the mean, the median, and the mode. The mean results from adding the value of each individual measurement and then dividing by the total number of measurements. The median is the value where exactly half the values are above it and half below it. The mode is the most frequently occurring number in the set. It is certainly possible that the mean, median, and mode might be so close to one another as to render moot your choice of which one to use as the basis for your "averages." Figure 7-7, for example, illustrates both the differences between these three types of "averages" and a situation in which all three calculations are close to one another.

The example goes back to the hypothetical age of the sources cited in different disciplines and focuses on the social sciences. Here, there is one source that is one year old, two sources that are two years old, five sources that are three years old, and so on. Five years of age is obviously the mode; it is the number that appears most often in the table. The mean, or the sum of all these values divided by the total number of values, is 4.5. The median, or the value with half the numbers below it and half above it, is 4.46—calculated by putting the numbers in order from the lowest to the highest and then taking the number that corresponds to the $(n+1) \div 2$th number in the list, with n representing the number of numbers in the set. If the value of $(n+1) \div 2$ does not correspond to a whole number, use the value of the mean of the number below and the number above where $(n+1) \div 2$ would fall in the list of numbers.

At other times, though, your data might be distributed in such a way that the mean is very different from the median and the median from the mode. Suppose you had many low numbers and some high numbers among your measurement values, as Figure 7-8 shows.

**Figure 7-7: Mean, Median, and Mode: A Case Where All Three
Are Closely Clustered**

			X				
		X	X				
	X	X	X				
	X	X	X	X			
	X	X	X	X			
X	X	X	X	X	X		
X	X	X	X	X	X	X	X
1	**2**	**3**	**4**	**5**	**6**	**7**	**8**	**9**

4.46 = Mean
4.50 = Median
5.00 = Mode

Figure 7-8: Mean, Median, and Mode: A Case Where the Three Differ Widely

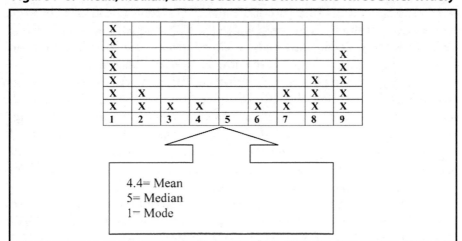

Here your mode would be 1, your mean 4.4, and your median 5. In this case, the mean or median is clearly a better indicator of the central tendency among the group of numbers than the mode. In other cases, however, a mean can totally obscure the real central tendency among a group of numbers. Suppose you were calculating the "average" salary of a group of 12 workers at a company. Ten of the 12 made very low salaries of $30,000; one had a larger salary of $60,000, and one had a very much larger salary of $300,000. Here the mean would be $55,000, while the mode would be $30,000—and a much better indicator of the true central tendency among workers' pay. When researchers have in their data a few very high or very low values, they should be aware of the potential effects of these values in calculating means.

One of the authors of this book had an atypical data distribution in a research project on e-prints. She was tracking, among other things, the number of co-authors per e-print. One of the e-prints in her randomly selected sample, however, had an atypically high number (101) of co-authors. No other e-print in the sample had remotely that high a number of co-authors. If the average number of co-authors per e-print had been calculated, the mean without this e-print would have been 5.29, but that with it would have been 30.45.

Some researchers will exclude such obviously atypical and skewing items from the sample as it is gathered. Others, recognizing their uniqueness only later, will exclude them from their final calculations. Because researchers get to select which measure of the "average" best reflects their data's distribution, they should calculate and consider all three and be as honest as possible with themselves and their readers about the differences between the three types of averages.

Once the numbers are aggregated, bibliometricians then attempt to draw conclusions from them—often by considering these aggregated numbers in light of the findings of prior studies. Bibliometrics differs from other research methodologies in that a large part of the interpretive context is supplied by prior studies, not just the study at hand. Consider, for example, how comparatively self-contained an experimental study is. Experimental researchers might refer to other studies in formulating their hypothesis, in operationalizing key terms, in selecting and designing measurement instruments, and even in understanding the findings. Nevertheless, the ultimate interpretive focus of experimental studies is internal: do the data gathered reveal statistically significant differences between pre- and post-measures of the populations or between control and experimental groups? If your findings are statistically significant, they are significant for the purposes of your experimental situation, even if every other study on the same topic has had different findings.

Most bibliometric studies, in contrast, must confront the so-called "baseline problem" in any attempt to interpret—rather than simply report—their data. The "baseline problem" arises from the fact that a number, by itself, in and of itself, has no real meaning. Suppose you find that that the new fiction books in your collection circulated 72 times in the past two years, while the new computer books circulated 48 times, the new history books 27 times, and the new cookbooks 112 times. Are your numbers high? Higher than they used to be? Do you have a success story to report? Are your numbers low? Have these numbers stayed the same over time? Unless you have numbers from other places or times—baseline numbers—to compare to your numbers, your numbers actually reveal very little.

The "baseline problem" thus requires bibliometricians to filter their data through other findings in order to really interpret them. Suppose, for example, you did a study which found that Ph.D. candidates in computer science cited open access articles seven to ten times more frequently than non-open access articles. Not knowing anything else about the citation patterns of computer scientists, of open access articles, or even of non-open access articles, the most that you would be able to report is that Ph.D. candidates in computer science cited open access articles seven to ten times more frequently than non-open access articles. In contrast, knowing that computer science researchers, as a group, cite open access articles three to five times more frequently than non-open access articles (as found by Brody 2004), you could safely say that computer science Ph.D. candidates are particularly heavy users of open access articles.

Remember that not every "pattern" that emerges from researchers' data is indicative of a real or significant phenomenon. Perhaps the best example of this comes from a quasi-bibliometric study of data from the National Center for Science Education's Project Steve, "an effort to compile a list of scientists who both support the theory of evolution and happened to be named Steve. 'The original idea was to mock these lists you see from creationists of scientists doubting Darwinism'" (Engber 2004). People can order Project Steve t-shirts, and as a parody, some researchers took the t-shirt sales data—which included sizes and shipping addresses—and used them to find a "mid-continental Steve deficit" within the U.S., with more Steves on the East and West Coasts than in the Midwest; sexual dimorphism, with Stephanies having larger body sizes than Steves; and insular dwarfism, with the "island Steves" of Australia and the U.K. being smaller than those in the U.S.

As Prime, Bassecoulard and Zitt (2002, 303) note, when no prior studies of a topic have been conducted, getting baseline data is impossible and the "technical obstacles can be serious." Comparing your data to that on the most closely related topics, as well as noting possible differences based on the different topical areas, is the only possibility here.

Bibliometrics has certain laws that are commonly considered in interpreting data. These include:

- *The Matthew Effect*, whereby authors and sources that are already well known get more credit than comparatively unknown authors and sources even if their work is similar. The Matthew Effect happens in part because individual authors tend to reproduce the citing practices of their colleagues, so that sources that are already frequently cited, become even more highly cited. Because of the Matthew Effect, all sources in a topic area will not be equally cited, even if they were otherwise equally accessible to researchers.

- *Publication Bias*, or the joint tendencies of authors, peer reviewers, and journal editors to write up and publish studies whose findings are dramatic or support the original hypothesis more often than studies with "negative findings," or findings that are not statistically significant or supportive of the original hypothesis (Dickersin 1990). Because of publication bias, you cannot presume that the universe of published works on a topic represents the universe of research projects in a topical area. Many research projects go unpublished because of publication bias.

- *Lotka's Law*, which describes the frequency of publication by authors in a given field. It specifies that "the number [of authors] making n contributions is about $1/n^2$; and the proportion of all contributors, that make a single contribution, is about 60 percent" (Lotka 1926, quoted in Potter 1988). This means that 60 percent of the authors in a field will have authored just one publication; 15 percent (or $1/2^2$) will have authored two publications; 7 percent (or $1/2^3$), three publications, and so on. Lotka's Law reminds bibliometricians that all researchers in a field are not equally likely to author/cite or to have produced many works/have many opportunities to be cited. Lotka's Law is also a good reminder that recorded publications do not capture all of the members or activity of a given field.

- *Bradford's Law*, which holds that journals in a particular field can be divided into three groups, each containing approximately the same number of articles: (1) a small, core group of journals that produces about one-third of all articles; (2) a larger group of journals that produces about one-third of all articles; and (3) an even larger group of journals that also produces about one-third of all articles. What Bradford's Law means is that researchers working in a field must look at substantially more journals (calculated by a formula of 1:n:n²) in the second and third groups to obtain the same number of relevant articles as was obtained in the first group. If five journals in the core had to be scanned to find 12 relevant articles; 10 journals in group 2 would need to be scanned; and 100 journals in group 3. Because of these diminishing returns, researchers' citations and libraries' holdings tend to focus most on journals in the central core.

Figure 7-9 gives references to some key texts on bibliometrics that novice researchers should consult in order to become more familiar with such laws.

Even when aggregated data is examined within the context of prior studies and bibliometric "laws," researchers' interpretations can still go astray. In fact, bibliometric research projects are, arguably, most prone to falter in their interpretations. Sometimes this is because of the assumptions that researchers made in selecting their populations, or in selecting or implementing their research designs. For example, suppose a bibliometrician had chosen to code researchers' citations to newspapers on the Web as citations to Web sites, rather than including them into the "newspaper" category, which included only print newspapers. This bibliometricians's coding choice makes her conclusion that researchers relied

Figure 7-9: Suggested Works on Bibliometric Laws

Borgman, Christine, and Jonathan Furner. 2002. "Scholarly Communication and Bibliometrics." *Annual Review of Information Science and Technology* 36: 3–72.

Diodato, Virgil. 1994. *Dictionary of Bibliometrics*. New York: Haworth Press.
> *Includes definitions of over 200 key terms. Also gives numerous citations to articles and books using these terms.*

Egghe, Leo. 2005. *Power Laws in the Information Production Process: Lotkian Infometrics*. New York: Academic Press.

Hertzel, Dorothy Hoffstetter. 1987. "Bibliometrics, History of the Development of Ideas in." In *Encyclopedia of Library and Information Science* (Vol. 42, Supplement 7, pp. 144–211). New York: M. Dekker.

Narin, Francis, and Joy K. Moll. 1977. "Bibliometrics." *Annual Review of Information Science and Technology* 12: 35–58.

Thelwall, Mike. 2004. *Link Analysis: An Information Science Approach*. New York: Academic Press.

White, Howard D., and Katherine W. McCain. 1989. "Bibliometrics." *Annual Review of Information Science and Technology* 24: 119–186.

more on Web sites than on newspapers questionable. She has, after all, chosen to class certain newspapers as non-newspapers because of their format. At other times, researchers bring assumptions to their interpretations that are not necessarily true; often these are assumptions that equate people's actual behavior (e.g., the sources they cite) with their preferred or intended behavior (i.e., the sources they would have cited in an ideal world). Such researchers might conclude that, because none of the student "works cited" they examined included references to sources on a research guide that librarians provided to students, the students did not use the research guide. This conclusion confuses one artifact of student behavior (their "works cited") with the totality of student behavior (their use of the guide). Students might have used sources on the resource guide in identifying topics or gathering background information, but because of the conventions of a works-cited list, they do not appear to have "used" it. Unlike a bibliography, a works cited lists only those resources the author cited in the paper, not those she/he consulted in formulating or researching the topic but did not cite.

Other examples of problematic conclusions are illustrated in Figure 7-10, along with notes on why they are problematic.

Because numbers rarely lead everyone to the same conclusions, researchers should be quite clear in spelling out the assumptions underlying the conclusions that they draw from the data. Smith's (2003) study of the types and local holdings of sources cited in dissertations at the University of Georgia does a good job of this by stating that, due to a systems migration which precluded obtaining information about dates of purchase for items purchased prior to 1999, she assumed that the materials the library owned in 2002 (when the study was done) had also been owned and available to students in 1991. This assumption seems somewhat safe, since the University of Georgia had not engaged in retrospective

Figure 7-10: Problematic Interpretations in Bibliometric Studies

Interpretation	Its Grounds for Being Problematic
Student bibliographies revealed that even after library instruction students still cited a high percentage of "low quality" information sources, suggesting that the instruction is ineffective.	This interpretation presumes that if researchers cite a resource they must presume it is the "best" or most "high quality" one possible. However, researchers often cite known "low quality" resources simply because they are accessible. At other times, they cite "bad" sources to discuss why they disagree with them, meaning that a citation to them is not an endorsement of their content.
Materials selected by librarians in particular subject areas have higher circulation percentages than materials selected by faculty, suggesting that librarians need to introduce faculty selectors to additional sources of book reviews.	This interpretation presumes that faculty and librarian selectors have the same user communities in mind when selecting materials. For example, faculty selectors might be selecting for history faculty and students, while librarians might be buying more interdisciplinary sources that would thus display higher circulation percentages.

purchases for its collection, but might have resulted in over-estimating the materials locally available to students in 1991. Because Smith spelled out this assumption, readers at least know about it; they are free to question it to the degree they wish. Similarly, in a study of the electronic availability of items received in print, researchers distinguished between publishers from whom they received more than ten print issues during the study and those from whom they received fewer than ten print issues. They did this because, "A longer survey period with receipt of more print issues would give a better picture of the publishers from whom we received ten or less issues during the six-week study period" (Shaffer et al. 1999). Here, the assumption seems solid: the fewer the print issues received, the more likely researchers' data on concurrent availability of electronic issues could reflect the working of chance. Others are, however, free to disagree with this decision and interpretation because the researchers have made their assumption, as well as the rationale for this assumption, public.

TELLING THE STORY

The numerical nature of the data underlying bibliometric studies can make writing up such studies easier than writing up content analyses or interviews. Instead of numerous, different, verbal accounts relevant to the subject of the investigation—accounts which must somehow be summarized while still preserving individual differences—bibliometric studies have only aggregated numbers: frequency counts, percentages, averages. These numbers are commonly presented in charts, graphs, and tables. Researcher-writers should take care in constructing such images. Just as numbers do not "mean" anything, in and of themselves, so, too, do numbers not "naturally" lead themselves to certain visual presentations. In fact, guides such as Darrell Huff's *How to Lie with Statistics* (1993) devote substantial attention to the ways in which the graphs used by otherwise well-intentioned researchers can mislead their audiences. Figure 7-11 shows how the same data can give readers very different impressions based upon how researchers label the X and Y axes of graphs.

Examples 1 and 2 are both graphs showing an increase of approximately 1 percent, from $20 billion to $22 billion over 12 months. However, this 1 percent increase seems much larger in Example 1 than in Example 2. That is simply because the units chosen to label the Y (or vertical) axis are smaller and do not start at zero. Depending upon the journal or other publication venue, authors may either explicitly address the data from the figures in the text, or they may expect the figures to stand on their own without walking readers through a textual summary of the pictorial information. Otherwise, a bibliometric study should include the components listed in Figure 7-12.

One final caution in writing up bibliometric studies deserves special mention here—the potential complications arising from the fact that the authors and

Figure 7-11: Two Ways of Displaying the Same Information

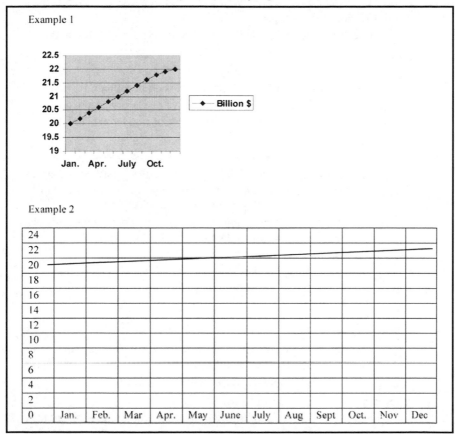

publishers whose works bibliometricians study have vested interests in their works and may object to certain characterizations of these products in biblio-metric research projects. Perhaps the most famous example of this is the series of ultimately unsuccessful lawsuits filed by publisher Gordon and Breach, in part against researcher Henry Barschall. Barschall, a physicist, wrote articles for *Physics Today* and the *Bulletin of the American Physical Society* in which he com-pared physics journals on the basis of their "cost-effectiveness" (Barschall 1988; Barschall and Arrington 1988). Barschall's operational definition of "cost-effec-tiveness" specified that it was the cost per printed character divided by the fre-quency with which articles were cited. Since researchers are allowed to set their own operational definitions, and since cost per printed character and frequency of citation are independently verifiable, mathematical measures, it might seem that Barschall was on perfectly solid ground. Gordon and Breach, however, did not like the suggestion, implicit in the research data, that since their journals came out near the bottom in rankings based on Barschall's calculations, these

Figure 7-12: Components of a Bibliometric Study

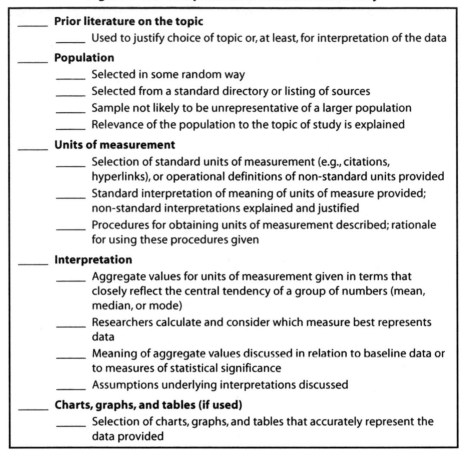

_____ **Prior literature on the topic**
    _____ Used to justify choice of topic or, at least, for interpretation of the data

_____ **Population**
    _____ Selected in some random way
    _____ Selected from a standard directory or listing of sources
    _____ Sample not likely to be unrepresentative of a larger population
    _____ Relevance of the population to the topic of study is explained

_____ **Units of measurement**
    _____ Selection of standard units of measurement (e.g., citations, hyperlinks), or operational definitions of non-standard units provided
    _____ Standard interpretation of meaning of units of measure provided; non-standard interpretations explained and justified
    _____ Procedures for obtaining units of measurement described; rationale for using these procedures given

_____ **Interpretation**
    _____ Aggregate values for units of measurement given in terms that closely reflect the central tendency of a group of numbers (mean, median, or mode)
    _____ Researchers calculate and consider which measure best represents data
    _____ Meaning of aggregate values discussed in relation to baseline data or to measures of statistical significance
    _____ Assumptions underlying interpretations discussed

_____ **Charts, graphs, and tables (if used)**
    _____ Selection of charts, graphs, and tables that accurately represent the data provided

journals were not "cost-effective." In 1993, Gordon and Breach sued Barshall and the American Institute of Physics and the American Physical Society, publishers in whose journals Barschall's works appeared, claiming that Barschall's studies were commercial speech and so "constitute[d] a literally false advertisement" in violation of the Lanham Act (ARL, 1998). The U.S. District Court for the Southern District of New York eventually found in Barschall's favor, stating in 1997 that "scholarly speech related to academic endeavors, such as the Barschall articles, is <u>not</u> commercial speech, and <u>is</u> entitled to unqualified First Amendment protection, whether or not it reflects unflatteringly on products produced by the competitors of the publisher of the speech" (973 F. Supp. 414, 420 [S.D.N.Y. 1997]). While the Barschall decision is a confirmation of the rights of researchers, researchers should keep in mind that this decision took four years, during which time Barschall and his publishers had to live with the anxiety generated by these lawsuits. Moreover, the decision of a U.S. District

Court is only a persuasive authority for courts in other districts; courts in other districts are not bound by it. Nor are courts in foreign countries, which can have very different laws about commercial speech, false advertisements, and free speech, a factor that came into play when Gordon and Breach sued Barschall and his publishers in various European countries as well as in the U.S.

Bibliometricians should, therefore, be careful in their research to rely upon standard definitions in operationalizing their terms, to describe clearly their methodologies, to document and retain their data, and to have objective evidence for any potentially judgmental-sounding conclusions. Certainly, do not be afraid to undertake a bibliometric research project because of situations such as Barschall's, but do take care that your characterizations of other people's works or products can stand careful scrutiny. Selecting "problematic" publications from standard lists or basing your calculations on standard formulas helps here. Eugene Garfield and Alfred Welljams-Dorof (1990) thus once wrote up a bibliographic study whose very title ("The Impact of Fraudulent Research on the Scientific Literature: The Stephen E. Breuning Case") equated Breuning's work with fraudulence, a potentially libelous statement were it not for the facts that (1) scores of newspapers had carried stories about Breuning's fraudulent work and (2) Breuning had been found guilty of scientific fraud in federal court. Picking an author you personally suspect but whose work has never been publicly questioned and calling it "fraudulent," on the other hand, could potentially lead to some nasty legal consequences.

REFERENCES

Association of Research Libraries (ARL). 1998, April 13. *Gordon and Breach Decision.* Available: www.arl.org/scomm/gb (accessed November 15, 2004).

Barschall, Henry H. 1988. "The Cost-Effectiveness of Physics Journals." *Physics Today* 41 (7): 56–59.

Barschall, Henry H., and J. R. Arrington. 1988. "Cost of Physics Journals: A Survey." *Bulletin of the American Physical Society* 33: 1437–1447.

Bibliometrics. 2005. April 26. *Wikipedia.* Available: http://en.wikipedia.org/wiki/Bibliometrics (accessed May 18, 2007).

Borgman, Christine L. 1990. Editor's introduction. In *Scholarly Communication and Bibliometrics*, 10–27. Newbury Park, CA: Sage.

Brody, Tim. 2004. "Citation Analysis in the Open Access World." Available: www.ecs.soton.ac.uk/~harnad/Temp/timOA.doc (accessed May 18, 2007).

Dickersin, Kay. 1990. "The Existence of Publication Bias and Risk Factors for its Occurrence." *Journal of the American Medical Association* 263 (10): 1385–1389.

Edge, David. 1979. "Quantitative Measures of Communication in Science: A Critical Review." *History of Science* 17: 102–134.

_____. 1977. "Why I Am Not a Co-citationist". In *4S: Society for the Social Studies of Science*, 13–19. Bloomington, IN: Society for the Social Studies of Science.

Edwards, Sherri. 1999. "Citation Analysis as a Collection Development Tool: A Biblio-metric Study of Polymer Science Theses and Dissertations." *Serials Review* 25: 11–21.

Engber, Daniel. 2004. "Major Breakthrough in Steve Research." *Chronicle of Higher Education* 51 (5): A6.

Garfield, Eugene. 1979. *Citation Indexing: Its Theory and Application in Science, Technology, and Humanities.* New York: Wiley and Sons.

Garfield, Eugene, and Alfred Welljams-Dorof. 1990. "The Impact of Fraudulent Research on the Scientific Literature: The Stephen E. Breuning Case." *Journal of the American Medical Association* 263 (1): 1424–1426.

Huff, Darrell. 1993. *How to Lie with Statistics.* New York: W.W. Norton.

Lyman, Peter, and Hal R. Varian. 2003. "How Much Information 2003?" Available: www.sims.berkeley.edu/research/projects/how-much-info-2003 (accessed May 18, 2007).

Miller, T., and D. Stebenne. 1988. "The Bibliometrics of Politics." *Gannett Center Journal* 2 (4): 24–30.

Paisley, William. 1989. "Bibliometrics, Scholarly Communication, and Communication Research." *Communication Research* 16 (5): 701–717.

Parker, E., and W. Paisley. 1966. "Research for Psychologists at the Interface of the Scientist and His Information System." *American Psychologist* 21 (11): 1061–1072.

Potter, William Gray. 1988. "'Of Making Many Books There Is No End': Bibliometrics and Libraries." *Journal of Academic Librarianship* 14: 238a–238c (insert between 238 and 239).

Prime, Camille, Elise Bassecoulard, and Michel Zitt. 2002. "Co-citations and Co-situations: A Cautionary View on an Analogy." *Scientometrics* 54 (2): 291–308.

Rousseau, Ronald. "Timeline of Bibliometrics." Available: http://users.pandora.be/ronald.rousseau/html/timeline_of_bibliometrics.html (accessed May 18, 2007).

Shaffer, Shelley, Susan S. Berteaux, Brandon Oswald, and Peter Breuggeman. 1999. "Going Electronic? Receipt of Print Journal Issues and Their Electronic Availability." Available: http://sclib.ucsd.edu/sio/guide/prices/z-iamslic.html (accessed June 17, 2000).

Smith, Linda. 1981. "Citation Analysis." *Library Trends* 30: 83–106.

Sullivan, Danny et al. 2004. June 18. "Fox News and the Danger of Citing Search Counts." *SearchEngineWatch.* Available: http://forums.searchenginewatch.com/showthread.php?t=299 (accessed May 18, 2007).

Taylor, Mary K., and Diane Hudson. 2000. "'Linkrot' and the Usefulness of Web Site Bibliographies." *Reference and User Services Quarterly* 39 (3): 273–277.

Walcott, Rosalind. 1994. "Local Citation Studies: A Shortcut to Local Knowledge." *Science and Technology Libraries* 14: 1–14.

Chapter 8

Action Research

Action research is a methodology focused upon practitioners solving problems at the local level. Action research has its philosophical roots in John Dewey's work with progressive and experimental education and the Science-in-Education movement, both of which applied the inductive scientific method to the field of education, a field that has embraced action research methodology. Dewey's main desire was to provide teachers with empirical methods to improve their teaching.

The Group Dynamics movement in social psychology and human relations in the mid-twentieth century also contributed to the development of action research. Kurt Lewin, a noted social scientist, was a major figure in this movement and is frequently cited as action research's originator. His model of action research—that of analysis, finding, conceptualization, planning, implementation, and evaluation—forms the basic structure of the action research methodology that is currently employed. Lewin believed that those most affected by a problem in the workplace should take action in seeking its resolution and thus pointed out the need for a different type of research aimed at empowering practitioners. He envisioned a type of research that investigated local problems; was conducted by all relevant stakeholders as researchers; and led to social action in the form of solutions to local problems.

Similar to Mahatma Gandhi's adage that "you must be the change you wish to see in the world," action research focuses on reflective problem-solving that leads to service or program improvements. Because of its practical nature, action research has four overarching goals:

- social change
- empowerment of individual stakeholders
- collaboration
- knowledge acquisition

The focus on problem-solving is one way in which action research differs from classroom research, and is one reason why we have addressed these two related methodologies in separate chapters. Action research rests upon a problem to be solved; classroom research, in contrast, does not require a problem to be solved and can be conducted simply to heighten practitioners' understanding of classroom phenomena. For example, if 95 percent of students are mastering the content sufficiently using the current instructional materials and methods, no action research project is likely to be undertaken, since there is no "problem" to be solved here. Even with 95 percent mastery, though, a classroom research project still might be undertaken, especially if the mechanisms whereby the instructional materials and methods that lead to this mastery are not understood.

Over the past 60 years, action research has spawned several offspring methodologies, including:

- *Action science:* A methodology that encourages researchers to study themselves in action with others with the intent of influencing social science research practices (Argyris, Putnam and Smith 1985).
- *Cooperative group inquiry:* This methodology seeks to involve peers (nurses, managerial teams, social workers, and so on) in self-study groups to affect improved group processes in the workplace (Heron and Reason 2001).
- *Participatory action research:* A methodology that is focused on social justice and societal change as it seeks to empower the poor and semi-literate (Freire 1970).

Despite the differences in names and focus, the basic tenets of action research are interwoven into all three of these methodologies. Thus, researchers comfortable with action research in its original sense are well suited to expand their methodological repertoire to these off-shoots.

Action researchers' focus upon solving local problems with input from stakeholders is precisely what troubles critics, who sometimes characterize action research projects as "how I done it good in my library" studies. They are concerned that because action research studies focus on specific local settings—which may not be "typical"—their findings are not representative or generalizable. They also worry that because stakeholders have the opportunity to shape the course of an action research project as it progresses, data gathering instruments may not be rigorously designed or implemented. Were that the case, research findings might be neither valid nor reliable. While there is some truth to these criticisms, they miss the point of action research and too narrowly construe what can be learned from an action research project. While not claiming that its results are completely representative or generalizable, action research does include a number of methodological steps to ensure that it is rigorous in obtaining its results, and these steps help to ensure that results are at least somewhat representative or generalizable.

Such criticisms overstate the importance of findings by making them the only thing that readers can learn from a study. Action research studies can be a major source of information about processes of conducting research and seeking change locally, even for readers who are in settings so different that the studies' findings are inapplicable. Still, would-be action researchers need to be aware of such criticisms, not only in order to take steps in their research projects to mitigate them but also to make an informed choice whether to use action research as their methodology. Action research is less universally accepted than, for example, experimental methodology.

Other potential drawbacks include the fact that action researchers only work with solvable problems. It is not a methodology appropriate for *all* on-the-job problems because not all on-the-job problems are solvable. Consider the situation at Suburban Library System, where everyone but the systems librarian, Ned Nolte, agrees that the library's Web page needs revision because most users cannot find what they are looking for. Because the systems librarian has sole authority over the Web page, no amount of research is going to change the fact that Ned alone is in control of the Web page. And because Ned does not see the library's Web site as a problem, any research findings presented to him will most likely increase his intractability. The systems librarian is a major stakeholder in any project involving the library's Web site, and a Web-site-design action research project is a non-starter if it does not involve all the stakeholders.

Another potential drawback is that action research requires that the researchers have the capacity for reflective thought and critical self-evaluation. If researchers are not the sort that can step back from a very personal situation (i.e., reflecting on one's practice and philosophy) and attempt to be unbiased, then action research is not a good choice. Action research will not suit everyone's cognitive comfort zone because it demands that the researcher allow others to help determine the goals of the research project, its methods, and its outcomes. It also reveals who the researcher is and what that person values, and for many, this self-revelation and public display of one's philosophy can be uncomfortable. Action research can also be difficult for those just starting out in the profession because one typically needs a background of practice and a significant level of experience to take on an action research project.

However, the benefits of action research can outweigh these potential drawbacks. First and foremost, action research is possible wherever researchers have a work-related problem that is solvable. This can make finding a topic much easier because almost every workplace has an abundance of solvable problems that are obvious to most workers. With an action research project, researchers do not need to spend a great deal of time reviewing the literature or thinking about how to situate their study in relation to prior studies. They simply need to look closely at their workplace to identify a solvable problem that they wish to work on. For example, if your library has not revised its collection development plan for the past 25 years, you might select creating an up-to-date collection development plan for a library as your action research project. Additionally, because of this focus on workplace problems, action research projects are an excellent way to achieve synergies between your job responsibilities and your research activities. Rather than having a research project that is "in addition" to your job responsibilities, action research transforms components of your job responsibilities into your research activities—so that you are, in effect, doing two things at once. Finally, action research tends to fit well with the values of libraries and the characteristics of librarians because it continuously seeks improvement. Libraries, too, continuously seek improvements in library services and processes, and most librarians pride themselves on being practical, problem-solving people who offer the best services and programs at the local level.

We think these benefits more than outweigh the drawbacks of action research, especially when you consider that the action research process can be approached as a simplified version of the traditional seven-step research process. While we introduce you to action research using all seven steps of the research process in this chapter, you will want to keep in mind that experienced action researchers tend to approach their research as a recursive application of three main steps. As shown in Figure 8-1, action research has three main phases that include several subordinate activities.

1. Plan: Pose the problem, identify stakeholders, define the project, determine what data to collect, how to collect it, and how often.
2. Act: Implement the project, collect and analyze the data, critically reflect on action taken.
3. Reflect: Evaluate results, describe in what ways findings can be used, share results with stakeholders.

In the planning phase, researchers look at a known problem and decide where to start and how to seek a resolution. Next, they take action by collecting data as outlined in their implementation plan. In the third stage, action researchers look at their research findings, prepare the subsequent plan of action based on the results of their findings, and share their findings and action plans with primary stakeholders as well as the wider community. At this point, the action research cycle moves on to a new cycle of planning and then taking action to implement changes in the workplace (see Figure 8-1).

Action researchers know that most solutions to workplace problems are temporary and give rise to other problems. A revised collection development plan, for example, is not an eternal solution to the old out-of-date plan. Eventually, the current plan will also need to be revised. Alternatively, attempting to implement the revised collection development plan might prompt researchers to realize that there are problems in how the acquisitions budget is allocated.

Figure 8-1: The Action Research Cycle

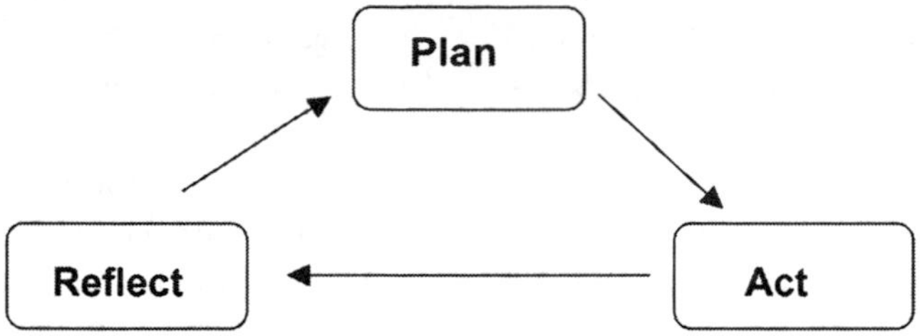

FINDING A TOPIC

Many profession-oriented research fields such as education, nursing, social work and, to some extent, librarianship have embraced action research because it focuses on the practitioner taking charge of solving workplace problems through research. Several useful texts that provide an overview of action research are shown in Figure 8-2.

These texts both outline the research process from the action research point of view and also offer helpful analyses of action research projects. However, only Howard and Eckhardt focus specifically on library science—in particular, school librarians. It is not surprising that school librarians have embraced action research

Figure 8-2: Suggested Works on Action Research

Howard, Jody K., and Su A. Eckhardt. 2005. *Action Research: A Guide for Library Media Specialists.* Worthington, OH: Linworth.

> *The authors provide step-by-step guidance in carrying out an action research project by means of a sample middle school project. Each chapter leads the reader in topic selection, assessing the environment, collecting and interpreting data and sharing the results.*

Johnson, Andrew. 2004. *A Short Guide to Action Research.* 2nd ed. Boston: Allyn and Bacon.

> *Writing for K–12 educators, Johnson offers a helpful guide to conducting research in the classroom. Other than providing direction on how to go about conducting action research projects, the work also includes chapters on quantitative methodologies as well as effective ways to present the final project.*

Stringer, Andrew. 2007. *Action Research.* 3rd. ed. Thousand Oaks, CA: Sage.

> *The author gives readers a series of tools to assist them as they work through the research process. Stringer's text is a simple but highly effective model for approaching action research that comprises three basic stages: look, think, and act.*

Whyte, William Foote. 1991. *Participatory Action Research.* Newbury Park, CA: Sage.

> *Leads reader through the process, from the initial design of a project, through data gathering and analysis, to final conclusions and actions arising out of the research. The theory and methods governing participatory action research are outlined and several case studies from organizational and agricultural settings are examined.*

since K–12 educators also commonly use action research. As we shall see later in this chapter through our examination of model research studies, action research is also used in both academic and school librarianship outside of the United States. However, it has yet to make its mark within academic and public library research in the United States.

That said, action research is an excellent candidate for adoption in these environments because there is a good fit between (1) its goals and applications and (2) the types of projects normally carried out in academic and public libraries. Many library problems and projects are appropriate for action research. Among these, for example, are projects that increase productivity in a library unit or department; those that analyze, plan for and reallocate space based on changing needs and functions; and those that emphasize new directions in public relations or personnel allocations. Action research is also appropriate for projects emphasizing new directions or programs within the library as a whole.

Although many of the studies listed in Figure 8-3 are centered upon school libraries or teaching, action research can embrace a variety of library specializations such as cataloging, collection development, acquisitions, or interlibrary loans.

Improved practice is a major component of any action research project, and this is evident in several of the studies described in Figure 8-3. For example, Kendall sought to improve students' comprehension of citation style and their ability to correctly apply that style in their research papers. She also wished to improve the way this unit was taught within the university's first-year program. Swan and Rosenquist-Buhler (1995) similarly wanted to create a new approach to collection development and cataloging, as well as improve scholarly communication outreach to faculty. Their action research project was to launch an Internet research gopher, and this project specifically concentrated upon garnering widespread staff involvement. Their project became a success story since it both informed library administration about the possibilities for enhanced staff involvement and strengthened the library's relationship with the campus computing center. Although this particular project may now seem outdated, at the time it offered outreach and partnership opportunities not heretofore available both within and outside of the library. Another improvement project was the effort by Harada and Yoshima (1997) (a librarian/teacher team) to improve student performance in information search processes through several intervention and assessment strategies.

Action research is suitable for many problems in the workplace. For example, it can be applied to studying a new method for collecting reference statistics in comparison with a previous method. Or it can be used to study different ways to allocate acquisitions fund lines so that book, serial, and electronic resource purchases reflect current community and institutional needs. However, although it has this wide range of topical applications, action research is not a panacea for solving all workplace problems. It is not an appropriate method to

Figure 8-3: Studies Using Action Research

Brin, Beth, and Elissa Cochran. 1994. "Access and Ownership in the Academic Environment: One Library's Progress Report." *Journal of Academic Librarianship* 20 (4): 207–212.

Describes a task force project to analyze and recommend achievable options that guided the University of Arizona library in providing their users with most appropriate means to research materials. The task force employed focus groups for feedback regarding users' information needs, analyzed interlibrary loan statistics, and conducted a citation study of theses and dissertations to determine research patterns.

Greenan, Elizabeth. 2002. "Walking the Talk: A Collaborative Collection Development Project." *School Libraries in Canada* 21 (4): 12–14.

The author conducted a two-year action research project on establishing a collection development plan while involving the school community in the process to ensure a sense of shared ownership. Employed both qualitative and quantitative data collection measures.

Harada, Violet H., and Joan Yoshima. 1997. "Improving Information Search Process Instruction and Assessment through Collaborative Action Research." *School Libraries Worldwide* 3 (2): 41–55.

The authors, a teacher-librarian team, employed action research as a way to improve student performance in the information search processes. Authors used pre- and post-tests, analyzed students' research logs and process portfolios, kept reflective journals to document their research activities, and used field notes taken by an external observer to assess student performance.

Kendall, Margaret. 2005. "Tackling Student Referencing Errors through an Online Tutorial." *Aslib Proceedings* 57 (2): 131–145.

Describes a multi-year project to teach students the basics of citation style. The author analyzed error type as a starting point for development and implementation of an online tutorial, then used pre- and post-test methodology to track student learning from the online tutorial and also monitored the online tutorial's use and understanding through WebCT tracking facilities and usability tests.

Swann, Julie, and Carla Rosenquist-Buhler. 1995. "Developing an Internet Research Gopher: Innovation and Staff Involvement." *Journal of Academic Librarianship* 21 (5): 371–375.

Describes staff initiated project to implement a research gopher that served the needs of the entire campus. Professional and classified staff explored, employed, and evaluated a number of new workflows associated with the gopher project.

use to study a failing program where one or more of the key players are hostile to any type of inquiry or to the planned change. Action research is also inappropriate in situations involving complex political issues or problems centered upon unhappy staff members. Some workplace problems are so fraught with emotional, psychological, or political snares that they require more than an action research study to bring about change.

In figuring out which types of research problems to target with action research, librarian-researchers ought to follow two general principles as outlined by Kuhne and Quigley (1997). First, researchers need to focus their study on what can be managed and completed, resisting taking on too much at once.

Second, researchers should start with a small part of the problem and, as they take action to improve the first part, they should plan on resolving other aspects of the larger problem in future interventions.

In other words, "how to make your library better," or even "how to make reference better" are subjects too broad for an action research project. However, a series of action research projects could, in the aggregate, tend toward the same effect: for example, how to change the design of the reference desk so as to improve its approachability; how to change the configuration of the reference stacks so as to increase the ease with which patrons can find materials; and how to make the electronic reference collection better known to users. Kuhne and Quigley's two principles apply to all research projects, generally, but are especially important in action research projects because they help to ensure the success of such a project. Keep them in mind when selecting your own topics for action research projects.

DEFINING THE POPULATION

We have reversed the second and third steps of the traditional research process in this chapter because the population in an action research study does not play its traditional role. The research population does not serve primarily as a pool of subjects from whom the researchers obtain information once the researchers have formulated their research questions. Rather, the population in an action research study collaborates with the researcher to formulate the research questions. For this reason, the researcher must identify the research population before attempting to formulate research questions. This population is commonly known as the "stakeholder group" to indicate its active involvement in shaping the goals and procedures of the research project.

Identifying the stakeholders for an action research project is the key to the success of the project. Within a library, researchers encounter many different stakeholder groups that range from a variety of user groups (children, adults, the elderly, students, faculty) to library administrators and staff. Before launching any action research project, the researcher needs to conduct an analysis of the work environment to ascertain which relevant groups need to be included in the research process. This inclusion is especially important in "whole workplace" projects because members of groups that have no voice in the research process may not buy into the project and could well undermine any resulting actions taken.

Action researchers commonly identify relevant stakeholders by engaging in a process called social mapping, which brainstorms and charts the connections between the various groups of people whose interests are implicated by the research topic (Stringer 2007). In performing social mapping, researchers need to do more than simply list groups with interests in the problem. They must also think critically about the nature and relationships of those groups. See Figure 8-4 for a checklist to help identify stakeholders.

Figure 8-4: Identifying Stakeholders

1. Who is involved?
   _____ Staff
         List departments   _____
                                    _____
                                    _____

   _____ Students
         Grade levels/Degrees   _____
         Majors   _____

   _____ Teachers/Faculty
         Departments/Subjects   _____
                                    _____

   _____ Community and/or user groups (describe characteristics such as age,
         interest areas)   _____
                                    _____

   _____ Other groups   _____
                                    _____

2. How are these groups related?

3. Who are the influential groups? Who are the key people in each group?

4. Describe your view of the problem or the situation.

5. Describe the problem or the situation through the viewpoint of each group
   involved.

Researchers must also examine the relationships among groups and within individual groups. They must consider the power structure of the different groups, and how each group perceives the problem under investigation.

For example, if a research topic dealt with design of the reference collection area in a public library, the stakeholder group might be comprised of reference librarians, library shelvers, and library users. You might also recognize that the reference librarians and the shelvers have a history of reflexively opposing each other and that the long-term head of access services, who supervises the shelvers, has more power than the new head of reference. The community of library users, however, merely wants to maintain free access to the collection and has an interest in the collection maintaining its integrity. While some parts of this scenario might seem unpleasant, it provides an important caution that action research requires substantial honesty on the part of the researcher. To be an effective action researcher, you must be able to recognize the hard truths about yourself and others. Because this particular scenario is emotionally charged, it probably would not be a good choice for an action research project.

The researchers and their stakeholders also form a population that is the main focus of the study in action research projects. This is partly because action research emphasizes both practice improvement and stakeholder involvement and partly because researchers and stakeholders are considered components of the research project whole. In this more traditional sense of population as an object of study, library collections, processes, or programs can also comprise the population for an action research study. Such was the case in Greenan's (2002) two-year collection development action research project (described in Figure 8-3), in which the elementary school's collection formed the population under investigation. In another study, Brin and Cochran (see Figure 8-3) examined the library's mission of disseminating scholarly communication. Through the work of a task force, the researchers set out to determine the best policies and procedures for the library to adopt regarding whether to purchase scholarly items or to obtain access for a fee.

Whether viewed as the creators of the research questions or the subjects about whom data is gathered, populations in action research projects always include the researchers. Researchers must recognize and situate themselves as members of the research population. This is one of the things that particularly distinguishes action research from most other positivist methodologies, in which researchers strive to position themselves as objective observers outside the research process. Action researchers, in contrast, actively work to incorporate themselves within the research project and the target population. Doing so involves more self-examination, requiring researchers to ask:

- Why did they identify the particular work place problem that forms the research topic?
- How might their views on the existence and nature of this problem be incorrect?
- What do they stand to gain from the resolution of this problem?
- What do the other stakeholders with interests in the problem think about the researchers?
- What do these stakeholders have to gain or lose from the resolution of this problem?

Particularly when viewed in their traditional role as subjects from whom data is gathered, the population in action research studies is non-representative, at least in the sense that it (1) is not intended to provide information about a larger group for whom its members are surrogates, and (2) is not selected by sampling from a larger target population. This is acceptable as long as the action research project includes all stakeholder groups within its population. Thus, if an action research project centered in a school library media center includes only students, teachers, librarians, administrators, and staff within that school among its stakeholders, as Harada and Yoshina's project did, then the fact that these stakeholders were not selected by sampling from a larger population is only important to someone judging action research by the standards of another methodology. Representativeness is not important in action research. This is another factor that makes action research unique.

FORMULATING QUESTIONS

Action research projects take pragmatic and solvable research questions as their focus. These questions are frequently locally based because they typically concern workplace issues. That is not to say that action research questions are not of interest to the profession. Nor is it true that action research questions are so narrowly focused that they cannot be replicated in other library environments. The studies shown in Figure 8-3, as well as many other library science action research studies, are both relevant to the profession and replicable. For example, as described in Figure 8-3, Greenan's (2002) two-year project that explored and evaluated a collection development process at her elementary school library illustrates an approach to problem-solving that other school librarians can employ in their libraries. Likewise, Kendall's (2005) study of improving students' knowledge of and ability to correctly apply citation style through the use of an interactive online tutorial gives both instructors and school librarians ideas for improving students' learning about citation styles and for using technologies in teaching.

Because action research projects focus on empowering the practitioner and concentrate on "solving" researcher-defined problems, action research studies have investigated issues such as the following:

- What are the most effective strategies in increasing high school students' information literacy competencies? (Farmer 2001)
- What aspects of traditional library service delivery systems hinder effective delivery to social workers? (Blake, Morkham and Skinner 1980)
- What elements in a teaching unit help high school students to learn how to critically evaluate Internet sites? (Heil 2005)
- What types of interventions can an elementary school employ to improve student performance in their comprehension and ability to apply the steps found in the information search process? (Harada and Yoshima 1997, described in Figure 8-3)
- Which are the most appropriate practices and philosophical approaches for a library task force to recommend in future policy development related to access and ownership issues? (Brin and Cochrane 1994, described in Figure 8-3)

- What are effective ways to create an elementary school library collection development plan that is relevant, current, and reflects institutional needs? (Greenan 2002, described in Figure 8-3)
- Which are the most frequent citation errors that university students commit and what is the impact of student use of a specifically designed online tutorial aimed at improving citation errors? (Kendall 2005, described in Figure 8-3).

In constructing a research question for an action research project, a librarian-researcher needs to take stock pragmatically and systematically of the situation, asking such questions as those shown in Figure 8-5. By considering this set of questions, as well as a host of others associated with specific projects, researchers and their wider stakeholder groups establish the project's boundaries. It is also important to note that the answers to these questions can and most likely will change somewhat over the course of the project. For example, after the first year of her collection development project, Greenan (described in Figure 8-3) realized she needed to include many of the elementary school staff in her second-year phase of developing the collection. As a result, she formed a committee to analyze the collection and its use, and to recommend appropriate changes.

Action research questions in library science practitioner studies are frequently locally focused ones, like Greenan's. Because of their narrow focus, they are achievable. Action research does not attempt to discover universals or make generalizable conclusions regarding the problems it studies; instead, it concentrates on actively resolving the problems at hand. For example, Heil (2005) focuses only on a specific teaching unit in her study of how to best teach middle school students to critically evaluate the Internet. Farmer (2001) takes a similar narrow approach in her analysis of ways to teach information literacy skills that produce

Figure 8-5: Defining the Project

1. How can I implement a new approach to see if it makes a difference?
2. When and how should I start?
3. Who is affected by this project?
4. How will they be involved?
5. How will I communicate with the stakeholders in the project?
6. Will I need to obtain internal and/or institutional approval for the project?
7. If so, from whom and how do I go about getting that approval?
8. What types of resources do I need to help me with my project?
9. Where can I acquire these resources and who can help me get them?
10. What types of measures should I implement? And when and how and with whom?

effective outcomes, and Harada and Yoshina (see Figure 8-3) echo that narrow focus in their efforts to improve students' comprehension and successful completion of an information search.

Finally, it should be noted that including the stakeholder community or research population in the process of formulating the final research question can pose some dilemmas for the action researcher. What happens if the stakeholder group does not see the same problem as the librarian-researcher? In such a case, researchers need to return to step one and define a different problem. They might also want to reflect on why they felt that the problem was due to one thing but those in the stakeholder group believed that it was due to something completely different.

SELECTING A RESEARCH DESIGN

The next step is to design a research plan that targets the main components of the problem to be solved. General questions such as those outlined in Figure 8-5 are the natural starting point when designing a plan to solve a practice-based problem. Answering these questions will provide the appropriate structure for the implementation of an action research project. Another major consideration when outlining the research plan is figuring out a timeline. How long should researchers spend on collecting the data? What is a fair period of time?

In our everyday lives, many of us use the trial-and-error method to figure out if a new approach works. Since there is no fixed end to the trial-and-error process, it will not work for an action research project. Having a timeline both prompts you to gather certain kinds of data and provides a fixed end for projects focused on improvement, which is itself an endless process.

Action research requires that researchers document (1) the preexisting state of affairs that represents the problem researchers are attempting to solve; (2) the nature of researchers' interventions in attempting to solve the problem; and (3) the results of these interventions. If researchers intend to determine whether something is better as the result of their action research plan and if they wish to make an objective comparison and be taken seriously in their research, they ought to know where they started so as to avoid biased value judgments when intervening to solve the problem and recording the results of their interventions.

For example, you might feel very strongly that the previous periodical shelving configuration was not working, but what hard evidence do you have that would convince others of your belief? You need baseline data regarding the workings of the current periodicals shelving arrangement. Having such baseline data, you then intervene in the problem situation by attempting to solve it. In the periodicals shelving example, you might implement a new shelving arrangement and then gather hard evidence of the effectiveness of this new arrangement, which you can then compare to the baseline data about the earlier plan.

Alternately, you could create several different shelving arrangements and test them out in an experimental fashion to see which is better.

Greenan's collection development project (described in Figure 8-3) is an excellent example of how action researchers use both timelines and baselines. She constructed a deliberate timeline, spanning two years, for her project. Her first year was spent weeding the collection under the guidance of a regional consultant and conducting small and informal assessments of the collection's usage. She spent the subsequent year creating a new collection development plan with the help of her school library committee. As a group, they conducted both qualitative and quantitative assessments to measure the strengths and weaknesses of the collection. Greenan (2002) and her group conducted a curriculum survey with the teachers to garner their input regarding specific uses and importance of collection areas, and this group also conducted a companion student survey. Quantitative measures consisted of relative use factor studies of the collection as well as collection statistical analyses showing where the collection was best developed and most current. Greenan's timeline told her what to do when, and the qualitative and quantitative data she gathered established baselines by which she could compare the effectiveness of library operations before the collection development plan was created with the effectiveness of library operations after the collection development plan was created.

Greenan's study is also a good example of triangulation. In analyzing her elementary school library collection, she looked at many different data sets to arrive at an action plan for collection improvement. She analyzed circulation data and collection statistics by subject area and currency. She surveyed both teachers and students to find out the ways each group valued the collection, and she methodically chronicled her work through a two-year journal. All of these "mixed methods" approaches served to strengthen her study because each provided a different view of the library's collection, pointing out areas that needed to be improved and other areas that were already an asset to the school.

Action researchers must be especially careful to avoid personal bias. Action research seeks to foster individual and group empowerment, but because of this focus, action research can be prone to unsuccessful projects stunted by short-sightedness. Many proponents of action research (Howard and Eckhardt 2005; Schmuck 1997; Stringer 2007) advocate keeping a research log or journal to alleviate this problem. Throughout the research process, researchers are encouraged to reflect on the topic being researched, note any personal ideas, and list any concerns with the research process as well as the outcomes they hope will result from new practices. As researchers keep track of their hopes and desires for the research project, they also become more aware of any personal viewpoints that could skew their analyses. Keeping a research journal is part of the larger framework of reflective decision making that sets action research apart from more traditional methodologies.

Action research does not specify particular data collection methods. What is important, however, is that data collection methods match the goals of the project as a whole, as well as those of practice improvement and knowledge acquisition. Many of the standard ways to collect data consist of making note of and then comparing earlier results and later results. Keeping a log to carefully track outcomes is one recommended data collection method for action research projects. Other types of record keeping can be equally useful, such as noting how many times a phenomenon occurs or recording participants' viewpoints and observations. Other major data collection methods include:

- *Performance/achievement tests:* Pre- and post-tests can be invaluable means to determine if change has occurred.

- *Questionnaires/surveys:* To collect specific information, use closed surveys with fixed choice selections that do not allow for respondent interpretation. To gather opinions or to gather data in respondents' own words, use open surveys that ask open-ended questions.

- *Interviews:* These are helpful in delicate or emotionally charged situations and gather more detailed information than questionnaires.

- *Document/content analysis:* Examining institutional records, written reports, letters, memos, and other documents can help to establish baselines as far as past or present practices or even future plans and can also help to compare new approaches with those in the past.

- *Statistical data:* Libraries keep many different types of statistics that are easily mined: circulation records, items purchased or withdrawn, reference queries, items cataloged, and instruction statistics. All of these data sets are potentially useful in making comparisons.

- *Focus groups:* Similar to interviews, focus groups can be employed to gather impressions, opinions, and viewpoints from specific groups. Focus groups can also be used to gather information from specific stakeholder groups.

- *Field notes:* These written observations of the researcher's interpretations and impressions of an event as it occurs can be used to see patterns over time.

- *Video/audio taping:* Video tapes can be exceptionally valuable if researchers need an exact record of participants' viewpoints that reveal non-verbal information such as pauses, gestures, facial expressions and other body language. They can also be useful if researchers are studying actions and/or decisions that participants make in situations like Web searching. Audio tapes provide an accurate record of the participants' exact words and can also provide other linguistic information such as pauses, use of idioms or regionalisms, which could prove valuable to researchers.

- *Research logs/journals:* Although it is entirely up to the researcher to decide what to include, his/her research log or journal should—at minimum—provide a carefully recorded listing of events and activities occurring over the course of the research project. They can also include a combination of field notes, observations, sketches, plans, diagrams, thoughts, impressions, coworker or student comments or even feelings and impressions. Researchers might prefer to keep a computer log or an ordinary paper notebook. Whatever type of information that is kept, notwithstanding its format, researchers are cautioned to be consistent and always make back-ups.

GATHERING DATA

Once the research design and the data collection methods have been determined, researchers can begin to gather information that will inform their subsequent action plan. Depending on the method of data collection, researchers may need to ensure participant anonymity, as well as follow any institutional guidelines that address research involving human subjects. As discussed previously, care should be taken with responses to interviews, focus groups, or surveys to ensure anonymity. If classroom data is used, researchers need to obtain student permission to use them as subjects, as well as ask them to fill out consent forms if seeking to use students' work in any work that will later be published. These ethical issues are covered in depth in Chapters 9 and 10.

Researchers also need to prepare for and be ready to act on any problems that arise in the data collection. Accurate record keeping can help to ensure that all data, no matter how seemingly insignificant at the time, are collected. For example, Kendall (described in Figure 8-3) kept meticulous records in her documentation of the type and frequency of citation errors students committed in three different pieces of work even after they had received a face-to-face instruction session and an online instruction booklet. Her tracking of these errors through an elaborate checklist helped to shape the next phase of the research project, which was to develop an online tutorial aimed at improving student performance based on the most frequently occurring errors. The resulting tutorial was implemented on WebCT, a Web-based course management system that allowed for online quizzes. The checklist of errors was used to design the WebCT quizzes and also provided pre-intervention baselines for comparison with the subsequent quiz results. Kendall then used WebCT to survey students' reactions to the tutorial, and this data set also helped inform her and her advisory team on whether their tutorial had been a success. What she and her team could not control for, however, was that the guidelines for the particular citation style they were teaching changed during the second phase of the study, skewing the post-test results. Fortunately, Kendall had maintained a solid research log detailing all of the error types and their frequencies in students' pre-tests, so she was able to present this data in the final report. Librarian-researchers can attend to the problems that arise during data collection by maintaining good records, keeping a level head, and honestly addressing the issue in their research report—as Kendall did.

INTERPRETING THE EVIDENCE

Since the ultimate goal of action research is to use the research findings to bring about effective change, researchers need to be particularly careful to ensure that their data collection and analysis is both accurate and credible. Within the realm of action research, accuracy means that the data collected gives a relatively factual and authentic picture of the problem under investigation. Accuracy helps researchers or research teams make decisions for future directions that best fit their situation.

Credibility means that the research conducted is trustworthy and that it is believable to colleagues, other researchers, or others interested in the topic. The following tips are taken from Johnson (described in Figure 8-2) and provide librarian-researchers with solid guidance in ensuring their action research projects are accurate and credible.

1. Carefully and accurately document all observations in a research log or journal.
2. Thoroughly explain all data collection and analysis phases.
3. Ensure that everything of importance is documented.
4. Strive for objectivity in all documentation.
5. Apply triangulation in data collection.
6. Be sure to collect data that clearly measures what it is supposed to measure.
7. Allow enough time in the data collection phase to provide an accurate picture of the research problem.

Many of the items listed above speak to three essential components in ensuring accuracy and credibility: triangulation, validity, and reliability.

TELLING THE STORY

Action researchers use data analysis to inform them and their stakeholders as to the most appropriate action to take based on the research project. In some instances, researchers find that there is no need for change. In other cases, the data collected through the project indicate that a change is needed. In the workplace, the planned action often takes the form of a series of recommendations that can be accompanied by a presentation to the administration, to the library board or even to the entire staff. But how can researchers best shape that presentation?

Figure 8-6: Matrix for Organizing an Action Research Plan

Summarize research findings	Recommended action	Who is responsible?	Who needs to be consulted?	Who will monitor the activity?	Time period

Mills (2003) suggests using a matrix as a visual organizer and a way to sort out both the research findings and a plan of action. This matrix is shown in Figure 8-6 and is particularly useful because it charts out duties for who is responsible for ensuring that the recommended action be undertaken, that stakeholders are kept informed, that data are collected and monitored, and that all this activity adheres to a timeline. The matrix can also form the basis for local presentations to staff and regional presentations at library conferences. Presenting a research project to the staff helps to promote positive conversations among colleagues about ways to improve problems in the workplace. Such presentations can help to empower staff, instilling feelings of inclusion. The presentation should be short, focused, and relate as much as possible to staff members' workplace knowledge and experience. It also helps to have visual aids to illustrate particular points. Researchers might want to consider creating a handout, a poster, a Web page, or a PowerPoint presentation to help explain the project. Specific items to address in a staff presentation should include:

- *Purpose of the project:* What particular problem, question or point of interest led to this research? Summarize the research questions.
- *Research plan:* Describe how data was collected, from whom, when, why, and how.
- *Findings:* Explain discoveries and key learning points. Visuals can be helpful tools in explaining findings.
- *Conclusions:* Tell what these findings mean or imply. Describe how conclusions were reached.
- *Plan of action:* Describe subsequent plans based on the findings and analyses. Ask for staff input for their ideas of improvement.
- *Question/discussion period.*

Conference presentations to peers are also a valuable way to share the results of an action research project. These are obviously more formal than staff presentations and require a higher emphasis on research design, data collection methods and findings. Typically, attendees are in the audience to pick up tips they can take back to their library, so an added emphasis on the practical aspects of the project is always important. Although action research is not usually generalizable in the common sense of research studies, sharing one's research project helps to further the knowledge of the profession about the topic at hand.

REFERENCES

Argyris, Chris, Robert Putnam, and Diana McLain Smith. 1985. *Action Science: Concepts, Methods and Skills for Research and Intervention*. San Francisco, CA: Jossey-Bass.

Blake, Bill, Trevor Morkham, and Alison Skinner. 1980. "The Two Cultures: An Examination of the Factors Inhibiting the Provision of Effective, Library-based Information Services to Social Welfare Practitioners." *Aslib Proceedings* 32 (4): 170–178.

Farmer, Lesley. 2001. *Information Literacy: A Whole School Reform Approach*. Boston, MA: 67th IFLA Council and General Conference, text-fiche ED 459 716.

Freire, Paulo. 1970. *The Pedagogy of the Oppressed*. New York: Herder and Herder.

Heil, Delilah. 2005. "The Internet and Student Research: Teaching Critical Evaluation Skills." *Teacher Librarian* 33 (2): 26–29.

Heron, John, and Peter Reason. 2001. "The Practice of Co-operative Inquiry: Research 'With' Rather Than 'On' People." *Handbook of Action Research: Participative Inquiry and Practice*, 179–188. Thousand Oaks, CA: Sage.

Howard, Jody K., and Su A. Eckhardt. 2005. *Action Research: A Guide for Library Media Specialists*. Worthington, OH: Linworth.

Kuhne, Gary W., and B. Allan Quigley. 1997. "Understanding and Using Action Research in Practice Settings." In *Creating Practical Knowledge through Action Research: Posing Problems, Solving Problems, and Improving Daily Practice*, 23–40. San Francisco, CA: Jossey-Bass.

Lewin, Kurt. 1946. "Action Research and Minority Problems." *Journal of Social Issues* 2 (4): 34–46.

McNiff, Jean, Pamela Lomax, and Jack Whitehead. 1996. *You and Your Action Research Project*. London: Routledge.

Mills, Geoffrey E. 2003. *Action Research: A Guide for the Teacher Researcher*. 2nd ed. Upper Saddle River, NJ: Merrill/Prentice Hall.

Schmuck, Richard A. 1997. *Practical Action Research for Change*. Arlington Heights, IL: Skylight Professional Development.

Stringer, Ernest T. 2007. *Action Research*. 3rd ed. Thousand Oaks, CA: Sage.

Chapter 9

Classroom Research

Classroom research is cumulative research conducted by practitioners in educational settings. Practitioners undertake classroom research to improve their work by documenting relationships between student learning outcomes and instructional materials and methods. Because it is cumulative, looking at phenomena over time, classroom research explores cause and effect in ways typically impossible with case studies or other descriptions of events at single points in time. The research aspect of classroom research also sets it apart from case studies. In investigating causal relationships between teaching strategies and learning outcomes, classroom research analyzes—not just reports—classroom phenomena. It draws upon other research methodologies, including those discussed in the prior six chapters, in doing this, but it implements these methodologies in a specific setting.

Classroom researchers are typically instructors working in their own classrooms with their own students. Improving student learning is a primary goal of classroom research, and classroom researchers seek to do this by empirical investigation of classroom phenomena. In gathering concrete evidence to improve their students' performance, however, they also generate findings with potential applicability to others. Classroom research is sometimes known as practitioner research, or teacher research. It is sometimes classified as a type of action research. We treat action research and classroom research separately, however, because of the different levels of cooperation required to initiate such projects. Action research invariably requires cooperation from the researcher's peers, as well as other stakeholders, to initiate a project. Classroom research does not; researchers can unilaterally implement projects in their own classrooms. For this reason, new librarians—especially those not in charge of programs—often have more opportunities for classroom research than for action research. They often will have sole control over teaching situations where they could initiate research. They will not generally have sole control over other aspects of their professional settings, and—especially for a new librarian—implementing a research project focused on another's programmatic responsibilities (as in an action research project) can be daunting.

Those who believe all research projects must be constructed on "scientific" models, with formal hypotheses tested experimentally and statistically, sometimes scoff at classroom research for being insufficiently rigorous. Classroom research has, however, developed an extensive body of techniques to deal with its own recognized methodological limitations. These techniques are presented in more detail later in this chapter, but brief mention of one of them now should help persuade readers still skeptical of classroom research methodologies. Classroom research recognizes, for example, that a large, representative, randomly selected sample population is impossible in classroom settings. Traditionally, scientific studies use random selection techniques to gather sample populations that are also large enough to be representative of the total target population. If there are 10,000 people in a target population, a scientific study might use a table of random numbers to select 1,000 (or 1/10) of these people, knowing that if a sufficiently large number of people are randomly selected, they will likely be representative of the broader population in their demographic distribution. With this randomly selected, representative population, scientific studies such as polls can predict outcomes fairly accurately by using a single instrument a single time to ask questions of the sample.

Classroom research, in contrast, recognizes that it operates with small, unrepresentative populations that were not randomly selected. In fact, many classroom groupings are deliberately non-random, as when special classes for honors students or senior citizens single out those who performed better than average on tests or who are over 65 years of age. Because of this, classroom research does not rely on a single instrument, or a single use of an instrument, in order to gather data. Rather, it seeks to increase its predictive ability, or its ability to say that a particular teaching method leads to increases in student learning, through triangulation.

Classroom research is one of the most user-friendly research methodologies. It does not require sophisticated research apparatus, knowledge of statistical calculations, research grant funding, or the recruitment of large random or weighted sample populations. Any professional who teaches in any setting can use classroom research because it simply involves formalizing, as researchers, what they already do, as teachers. With this having been said, one caveat must be kept in mind. Implementing a classroom research project requires a certain view of teaching. Successful classroom researchers see teaching as a process of continual development and improvement. They do not see teaching as something one either can or cannot do, or as something that is mastered once for all time. They are also reflective about teaching, exploring the causes of successes and failures in a data-driven way, rather than reducing teaching to a series of unrelated techniques.

FINDING A TOPIC

Educators have long used classroom research methodologies. Chaudron's study of classroom research articles published in *The Modern Language Journal* goes back to 1916, but classroom research has probably occurred as long as there have been teachers. In beginning a classroom research project, educators start with a mental model of classroom interactions similar to that in Figure 9-1.

This model assumes that all classroom interactions involve three interrelated components: (1) the inputs of the educational process, such as instructional goals and student demographic characteristics; (2) the instructional methods and materials, including everything used by the teacher to help students meet instructional goals; and (3) student learning outcomes, providing evidence of the degree to which instructional materials and methods help to meet instructional goals. All three components are interconnected, and each can be studied in relation to the others. Most commonly, though, instructional methods and materials form the locus of classroom research projects, with researchers investigating whether particular methods or materials maximize student learning outcomes and how they do so. Classroom researchers within education have explored whether active learning strategies improve the quantity or quality of student learning, as well as how the introduction of instructional technologies impacts teacher goals, teaching materials and methods, and strategies for assessing student learning (cf. McNiff 1993).

Librarians have recently begun using classroom research methodologies, although often without explicitly describing them as such. Common uses of these methodologies include investigating to what degree particular instructional methods or materials are effective, determining which of two or more instructional methods or materials are more effective, and establishing how instructional methods and materials can be modified to increase their effectiveness. Although somewhat atypical in that the researcher in this investigation was not

Figure 9-1: Components of Instructional Settings

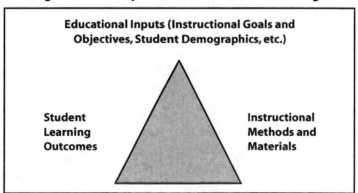

also the teacher, Kai Halttunen's "Students' Conceptions of Information Retrieval: Implications for the Design of Learning Environments" is otherwise an excellent representative of the classroom research studies in the library literature. Halttunen was interested in whether constructive instructional design is effective in teaching information retrieval. Students in a first-year Introduction to Information Retrieval course were the subjects upon whom this method was tested, and there is no claim that the 57 students who took this course in Fall 2000 are representative. Perhaps most striking about this study is the range of evidence that Halttunen gathered and considered in answering the research question. Data included:

- comments students made in short essays describing their conceptions of information retrieval at the beginning of the course
- results of a questionnaire asking students about these conceptions
- results of students completing a learning-style inventory
- logs of student computer searches during course exercises
- comments students made in short essays describing their conceptions of information retrieval at the end of the course
- student comments in empathy-based stories describing their learning experiences
- student feedback at the end of the course

Not every classroom research project uses seven data sets, but many projects resemble this one in that they gather data from students before and after instruction in the hopes of attributing changes in student knowledge or attitudes to the intervening instruction. Also noteworthy about Halttunen's study is the way in which other research methodologies are used in classroom research: for example, content analysis is performed on student essays and transaction log analysis is performed on their searches. Figure 9-2 provides an annotated listing of other library studies using classroom research methodologies.

As the examples in Figure 9-2 suggest, the study of anything classroom-related that connects teaching methods and materials to student learning outcomes can qualify as classroom research. What specifically makes a study a classroom research project, though, is its ethos. Classroom research is not interested in studying relationships between educational inputs, teaching materials and methods, and student learning outcomes in the abstract. Rather, it examines these relationships in order to attain a better, closer fit between instructional goals and their realization, to improve instructional methods and materials, and to increase student learning. Classroom research presumes that "Without data, instruction becomes a series of well-intentioned but essentially 'random acts of teaching'" (Fox 2001, 14). Without data, teachers have nothing beyond their personal beliefs and feelings to rely upon in determining what works in the classroom. They have no evidence that would persuade someone unconvinced

Figure 9-2: Studies Using Classroom Research

Ardis, Susan B. 2003. "A Tale of Two Classes: Teaching Science and Technology Reference Sources Both Traditionally and through Distance Education." *Issues in Science and Technology Librarianship*. Available: www.istl.org/03-spring/article7.html (accessed May 19, 2007).

> *Compared effectiveness of two different methods of teaching the same course: in-person and online. Looked at student demographics and outcomes before and after the change. Learning performance remained the same regardless of format, but students in the online class displayed more problems in the affective domain.*

Arnold, Julie, Robert Kackley, and Stephen Fortune. 2003. "Hands-on Learning for Freshman Engineering Students." *Issues in Science and Technology Librarianship*. Available: www.istl.org/03-spring/article3.html (accessed May 19, 2007).

> *Examined library component of Introduction to Engineering Design over 7 years. Approximately 800 students per year. Changed teaching methods to hands-on components instead of just lecture. Compared data from students before and after change. Found that "students are learning more through 'hands on' instruction."*

Brown, Cecelia, Teri J. Murphy, and Mark Nanny. 2003. "Turning Techno-Savvy into Info-Savvy: Authentically Integrating Information Literacy into the College Curriculum." *The Journal of Academic Librarianship* 29 (6): 386–398.

> *Looked at effectiveness of a "series of hands-on/minds-on information literacy activities that dissolve students' misconception that 'techno-savvy' is synonymous with information literate" (386). 15 students. Used interviews and surveys. Found [i]t is possible to bridge the gap between techno-savvy and information literacy through the provision of information literacy instruction that is of relevance to college and university students' lives, learning styles, and information requirements" (396).*

Halttunen, Kai. 2003. "Students' Conceptions of Information Retrieval: Implications for the Design of Learning Environments." *Library and Information Science Research* 25: 307–332.

> *Focus on constructive instructional design as method to teach information retrieval. Used 7 different measures of students' attitudes and learning. 57 participants. Author/researcher not course instructor. Found that constructive instructional design was an effective teaching method for this topic.*

Hinchliffe, Joseph. 2000. "Faculty-Directed Library Use Instruction: A Single Class, Retrospective Study." *Research Strategies* 17: 281–289.

> *Addressed whether "structur[ing] a term paper assignment in a way that afforded students opportunities for feedback on both the final product of their efforts and, more importantly here, the intermediate steps of their research" (281) would lead to better papers. Looked at student research logs, bibliographies, term papers, grades. Used 26 students. Found that restructuring improved students' results.*

Orians, Colin, and Laurie Sabol. 1999. "Using the Web to Teach Library Research Skills in Introductory Biology: A Collaboration between Faculty and Librarians." *Issues in Science and Technology Librarianship*. Available: www.library.ucsb.edu/istl/99-summer/article2.html (accessed May 19, 2007).

> *Looked at effectiveness of Web-based instruction in teaching students in an introductory biology class at Tufts University to use library resources. Described evolution of site over time in response to students' evaluations. Compared student evaluations from 1996 to 1997/1998, the first 2 years of Web-based instruction. Found that the evaluations were more positive after the shift. Also looked at open-ended comments on evaluations.*

(Cont'd.)

Figure 9-2: Studies Using Classroom Research *(Continued)*

Paglia, Alison, and Annie Donahue. 2003. "Collaboration Works: Integrating Information Competencies into the Psychology Curricula." *Reference Services Review* 31 (4): 320–328.

> *Focus on a pilot offering of a "super-size bibliographic instruction" (SSBI) session for an upper-level research methods course in Psychology. Used four measures of student learning. Class consisted of 14 students. "The results of this pilot study indicate that the SSBI approach was a successful method of library instruction . . ." (325).*

Scholz-Crane, Ann. 1998. "Evaluating the Future: A Preliminary Study of the Process of How Undergraduate Students Evaluate Web Sources." *Reference Services Review* 26 (3/4): 53–60.

> *Investigation of which method of introducing students to criteria for evaluating Web pages is most effective: giving students pre-established checklists of criteria or having them generate their own criteria. There were 28 students in one group and 21 in the other. Found that students did not evaluate particularly well with either method.*

---

of the truth of their beliefs and feelings. They have no basis for establishing how and why particular methods or materials work in the classroom. In contrast, with data, the possibility and predictability of improvements in education increases, as does the ability of educators to share their experiences with each other.

This focus on data does not mean that classroom research presents its findings as universal truths independent of the classroom settings involved. Classroom research does assume that it is possible to learn about what constitutes effective teaching materials and methods from the findings of other studies. However, classroom research also respects the autonomy and uniqueness of each instructional situation by maintaining that the "way to improvement is not through trying to copy what other people do, but by critical understanding of one's own practice" (McNiff 1993, 13). In other words, classroom research does not ask readers to implement uncritically the findings of other studies but rather to take these findings and verify them in their own classroom practices. Because this orientation toward the research process and research findings is a key part of classroom research, studies in the spirit of classroom research—with small sample sizes but multiple data sets, done for the sake of improving local practices but also helping to inform the practices of others—are possible in non-instructional settings. Figure 9-3 lists some studies from librarianship which resemble classroom research, though this may not be intentional in all cases.

FORMULATING QUESTIONS

Because it works with unrepresentative populations and generates sizable quantities of data, classroom research limits itself to comparatively small and focused research questions. The practical concerns limiting classroom research to "small," focused questions also reflect the complex model of instructional

Figure 9-3: Other Studies That Display Characteristics of Classroom Research

Cardwell, Catherine, Katherine Furlong, and Julie O'Keeffe. 2001. "My Librarian: Personalized Research Clinics and the Academic Library. *Research Strategies* 18: 97–111.

Includes statistical data on research clinics, surveys of users, surveys of librarians.

Eysenbach, Gunther, and Christian Kohler. 2002. "How Do Consumers Search for and Appraise Health Information on the World Wide Web?" *British Medical Journal* 324 (7337): 573–577.

Twenty-one subjects. Uses focus groups, usability tests, in-depth interviews.

Foley, Marianne. 2002. "Instant Messaging Reference in an Academic Library: A Case Study." *College and Research Libraries* 63 (1): 36–45.

Uses patron survey, librarian reports, usage statistics. Lots of details on implementation of IM services.

Norlin, Elaina. 2000. "Reference Evaluation: A Three-Step Approach—Surveys, Unobtrusive Observations, and Focus Groups." *College and Research Libraries* 61 (6): 546–553.

Use of surveys, unobtrusive observations, and focus groups.

Phillips, Lori, and Jamie Kearley. 2003. "TIP: Tutorial for Information Power and Campus-wide Information Literacy." *Reference Services Review* 31 (4): 351–358.

Includes usage statistics, student quizzes, student comments.

Reeb, Brenda, and Susan Gibbons. 2004. "Students, Librarians, and Subject Guides: Improving a Poor Rate of Return." *portal: Libraries and the Academy* 4 (1): 123–130.

Use of surveys, usability tests, usage statistics.

settings within which classroom research operates. When researchers must factor educational inputs, teaching materials and methods, and student learning outcomes into their studies, it is hard to cover large, general topics such as the most effective teaching method for all students in all subjects at all times. Figure 9-4 shows an example of how researchers can work from "larger" to "smaller" research questions.

Because smaller questions work better in classroom research, classroom research-type studies in librarianship have explored issues such as the following:

- Is in-person or online instruction a better way to teach a particular course? (Ardis 2003)
- Does the addition of a hands-on component to library instruction for an Introduction to Engineering Design course increase student learning in comparison to a lecture-only component? (Arnold, Kackley and Fortune 2003)
- How effective is a particular "series of hands-on/minds-on information literacy activities" in "dissolv[ing] students' misconception that 'techno-savvy' is synonymous with 'information literate'?" (Brown, Murphy and Nanny 2003, 386)

Figure 9-4: "Small" Focused Questions

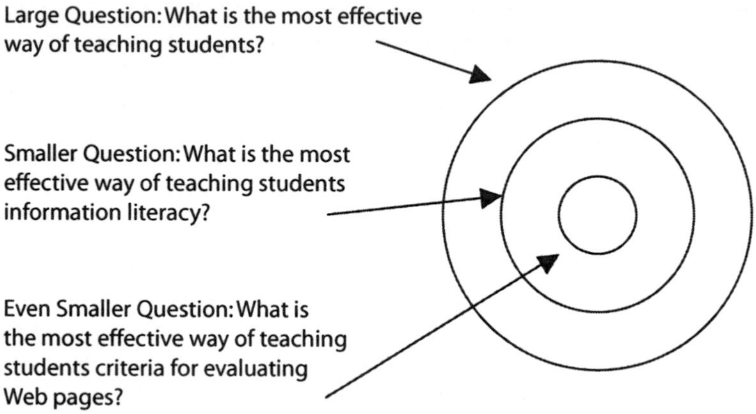

Large Question: What is the most effective way of teaching students?

Smaller Question: What is the most effective way of teaching students information literacy?

Even Smaller Question: What is the most effective way of teaching students criteria for evaluating Web pages?

- How effective is constructive instructional design in teaching information retrieval? (Halttunen 2003)
- Does "structur[ing] a term paper assignment in a way that afforded students opportunities for feedback on both the final product of their efforts and, more importantly here, the intermediate steps of their research" lead to better papers? (Hinchliffe 2000, 281)
- How have changes in a Web site teaching information research skills to introductory Biology students impacted student learning and student attitudes toward the Web site? (Orians and Sabol 1999)
- Is a "super-size bibliographic instruction session" an effective method of library instruction for students in an upper-level research methods course in Psychology? (Paglia and Donahue 2003)
- Will students evaluate Web pages more effectively if given a checklist with pre-determined criteria or asked to write essays in which they introduce and apply their own evaluative criteria? (Scholz-Crane 1998)

How small should a classroom research question be? There are no absolute rules, as the above examples show. Still, almost all classroom research studies limit themselves to a single variable within the instructional setting. Arnold, Kackley and Fortune (2003), for example, focus on the difference between hands-on and lecture-only instruction in their study. They do not simultaneously investigate differences between hands-on and lecture-only instruction for students with different learning styles studying different subject content. Keeping the research question small helps to explicitly link the question to specific aspects of the instructional situation that are not under investigation—for example, how effective is X in teaching what to whom under which circumstances? Classroom research seeks not universal truths, but classroom-specific data on outcomes.

DEFINING THE POPULATION

Classroom research almost always works with preexisting instructional groups or classes. This is one of the factors that makes classroom research easy to implement. Researchers need not identify and recruit subjects for their studies. They just need to have a class with which they work. The fact that classroom research relies on preexisting instructional groups also means that researchers must be cautious in interpreting and reporting their findings. The members of any particular class may not be representative of the target population, or all students who normally take the class, major in that subject, attend a specific university, or are at the same educational level nationally. Figure 9-5 illustrates more clearly how any one class could differ from what is "typical."

As will be discussed later, classroom research controls for the fact that any particular group of students is not representative by triangulating, or by using multiple data sets, investigators, research methods, or theoretical perspectives.

Classroom researchers must also struggle with difficulties in obtaining control groups when defining their research populations. Although most commonly associated with experimental studies, control groups are also important for classroom research, especially for those studies that compare different methods or materials for teaching the same content. If a study is designed to determine, as Scholz-Crane did, whether giving students a checklist with pre-determined criteria or having them write an essay in which they introduce and apply their own criteria is a more effective way to get students to evaluate Web pages, the researcher should create two groups of students: one group uses the checklist and the other group writes essays. Once the two groups have done their work, the researcher compares their work, looking for differences that can be attributed to the different methods of instruction they received. However, any major differences characterizing the two groups other than the different instructional methods could obviously also account for differences in results, so researchers attempt to match experimental and control groups as closely as possible in terms of their demographics and the conditions under which they work (e.g., time and place).

Figure 9-5: Example of the Problem of Population Representativeness in Classroom Research

Students in your class	Students who normally take the class	Students in a particular major	Students at a particular university	All students at the same educational level nationally
78% male	65% male	59% male	42% male	45% male
average age = 20.2	average age = 18.7	average age = 19.7	average age = 28.4	average age = 24.5

Classroom research projects have three ways of dealing with the need for experimental and control groups in studies. Each way has its own advantages and disadvantages.

1. *Study two groups of students in the same course*
   The researcher could "split" a single class into two or more parts and use these parts as control and experimental groups. Researchers who only have access to a single class at any given time may take this approach, but it can lead to tiny control and experimental groups that do not resemble each other in their demographics. Suppose a class had eleven students: one male and ten females, including one Hispanic, one Native American, and one African American. Splitting this class into two for control and experimental groups would yield groups of five or six members, and only one group could have a male, a Hispanic, a Native American, or an African American member.

2. *Study two simultaneous sections of the same course*
   Alternately, a classroom researcher could work with two or more sections of a course simultaneously. Here, though, it is difficult to ensure that the groups do not have demographic differences that could impact the findings, and different sections may work under conditions so different (e.g., classroom location, time of day) that these could impact the findings.

3. *Study two consecutive sections of the same course*
   Finally, a researcher could work with different sections of the same class at different times. Researchers often do this when they lack access to multiple sections simultaneously. But when an experimental group in one year is compared to a control group from three years earlier, groups are particularly likely to differ in the conditions of their instruction.

There is no right answer when it comes to the problem of control and experimental groups; most researchers simply select the best among the options available to them. Hinchliffe (2000) split a single class into two groups; Scholz-Crane (1998) worked with multiple sections of the same course simultaneously; and Arnold, Kackley and Fortune (2003) used asynchronous sections of the same course. When writing up a research report, the researcher should explain his or her reasons for selecting that approach, note the strengths and drawbacks of the approach, and explain how any differences between the control and experimental groups may have impacted the findings.

SELECTING A RESEARCH DESIGN

With a classroom research project, research design involves: (1) determining the types of data that will be needed to answer the research question(s); (2) identifying or developing instruments for collecting that data; and (3) establishing procedures for employing these instruments to gather data. Steps two and three are among the easier parts of classroom research projects because classroom research prefers to use actual classroom products obtained through normal classroom procedures as its instruments. For instance, in his study of the effectiveness of a particular approach to teaching the research paper, Hinchliffe gathered data from the texts of student research papers, student bibliographies, and final grades in the course. All these sources of data would have been created without Hinchliffe's (2000) research project, and procedures for their production (what completed papers were to look like, when grades were due, and so forth) existed independent of the research project. He simply turned existing classroom products into data-collection instruments and used established procedures for the gathering of these products/instruments. Classroom research uses actual classroom products as its research instruments because it believes that data sources more authentic and natural to classroom settings more accurately measure classroom phenomena. Similarly, relying on standard classroom procedures for the production and collection of course products/research instruments helps to minimize self-presentation effects among the subjects. Because their behavior is what it normally would be in the classroom setting, subjects are less conscious of being researched and are thus more likely to produce authentic behaviors and products. Classroom researchers are, however, free to create data collection instruments or procedures specific to a classroom research project. Hinchliffe also did this when he required students to keep logs during research and writing.

When considering potential instruments for collecting data, think in terms of demographic, process, and outcome data (cf. Fox 2001), and plan instruments to collect all three types. Demographic data establish the population for whom the classroom research findings are valid and include things such as students' age, sex, and major. A student demographic survey at the start of class is a good instrument for gathering demographic data. Process data document the nature and use of the instructional materials and methods. Potential instruments for capturing process data include lesson plans or audio or video recordings of classroom interactions. Process data can be the hardest data to gather, but they are necessary so that others can reproduce and test the instructional materials and methods that lead to the researcher's findings. By showing how instructional materials and methods relate to student learning, outcome data help to prove cause-and-effect relationships in classroom settings. Instruments for gathering outcome data are the most numerous instruments in most classroom settings; they include student work samples, test results, final grades, and teacher or course evaluations. Figure 9-6 lists additional sources of demographic, process, and outcome data.

In addition to identifying instruments for gathering demographic, process, and outcome data, classroom researchers must also plan to use multiple instruments for obtaining each kind of data. Triangulation is vital in classroom research

**Figure 9-6: Sources of Demographic, Process, and Outcome Data
for Classroom Research**

Demographic data	Process data	Outcome data
• Student personal characteristics (age, sex, socioeconomic background, grade level, academic major, language proficiency, primary language, prior school experiences, attendance patterns, etc.) • Student grade point averages • Student scores on standardized tests (SAT, ACT, other tests) • Student attitudes prior to the instruction • Student scores on pre-tests specific to the course • Teacher responses to questionnaires (e.g., attitudes, expectations)	• Measures of student behavior in relation to the topic of interest (how much time they spend in laboratories or studying outside of class) • Contents of student notebooks or journals • Teacher lesson plans or daily journals on classroom events • Content of instructional handouts or activity sheets • Photographs of classroom interactions • Audio or video recordings of classroom interactions • Records of third-party observations of classroom interactions • Teacher's recorded observations of student behavior, e.g., during group work	• Student completed assignments (contents and scores) • Student tests (contents and scores) • Student portfolios • Public student exhibitions or performances • Student grades in the course • Student course completion rate • Student performance on standardized tests • Questionnaires given to students after instruction (e.g., teacher-course evaluation forms, post-tests, post-instruction attitudinal surveys) • Interviews with students after instruction

as a way to increase the validity and reliability of its findings. Triangulation is a term taken from geometry and surveying; it suggests, as Figure 9-7 shows, the benefits of viewing an object from more than one angle.

When an object is viewed from one angle, a limited amount of information is available about its positions and nature, since entire sides of the object are not visible. When an object is viewed from two different angles, its position is more precise and more aspects of it can be seen. Classroom research uses triangulation to obtain a fuller view of the phenomena under study. It does this by using several different kinds of triangulation in obtaining and interpreting data.

In gathering data, classroom researchers use data, investigator, and methodological triangulation. Data triangulation involves the use of multiple data sets as evidence for a finding. These data sets may be obtained by using the same data-gathering instrument at different times or with different subjects, or by using different data-gathering instruments. Researchers using data triangulation would thus have a group of subjects complete a data collection instrument multiple times, or have two groups of subjects complete the instrument, or have two different instruments (e.g., Form A and Form B) for subjects to complete. Use of multiple observers in recording classroom phenomena is known as investigator triangulation. Investigator triangulation serves to ensure that phenomena

Figure 9-7: Single Perspective View versus Triangulated View

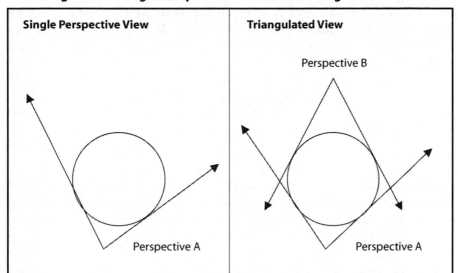

that a single researcher notes in the classroom would also be noted and interpreted similarly by others. Different observers may see very different things in the same situation, and they can interpret the same thing very differently. One researcher might notice a student looking at a cell phone during class and decide that the student is not paying attention. Other researchers might not notice this student looking at the cell phone, or they might note that the student used the cell phone only to check the time and is paying attention.

Methodological triangulation uses at least two different kinds of instruments, reflecting two different research methodologies, to gather data on a topic. Researchers using methodological triangulation might use data gathered from student pre- and post-test scores (experimental), their comments in interviews, and their course journals (content analysis) in concluding that a particular instructional method was effective in improving student learning. As this example suggests, there is definite value in triangulating using both quantitative and qualitative methodologies. What is not apparent with one often becomes apparent with another.

Some data collection instruments (e.g., teacher-course evaluations) may be available only to instructors of for-credit courses, but many data collection instruments are available to librarians teaching "drop in" workshops or course-related instructional sessions. In fact, powerful evidence for student learning can be quickly attained by librarians who make use of Classroom Assessment Techniques (CATs) as their data collection instruments. CATs were created by Thomas Angelo and Patricia Cross as components of a "learner-centered, teacher-directed, mutually beneficial, formative, context-specific, ongoing" approach to assessment (1993, 4–6). CATs also give faculty members frameworks for quickly obtaining demographic, process, and outcome data from students in a short time. Figure 9-8 lists several CAT instruments and suggests possibilities for their use by librarians as data-gathering tools in classroom research.

GATHERING DATA

When gathering data, classroom researchers must ensure that standard classroom procedures or specified research protocols are, in fact, followed. Lapses can occur more easily in classroom than in experimental settings, especially if researchers do not keep careful track of data and how they are gathered. Suppose, for example, that student learning outcomes in a course are measured, in part, by a pre-test students take during the first class. Some students will not add the course until after the first class. Do late additions skip the pre-test? Do they take their pre-tests by appointment? Do they take their pre-tests home, with all the advantages in extra time and consulting external sources that go with take-home

Figure 9-8: CATs for Gathering Data for Classroom Research

- **Misconception/Preconception Check:** Use for demographic data.

  Get students at the start of class to write their answers to 3 (or so) questions that get at key course content but whose answers are often subject to misunderstandings. Takes 5 minutes. Responses can be anonymous or with names.

- **Teaching Goals Inventory:** Use for demographic data.

  Instructors complete before the start of class to get an idea of what their real goals and aims with the course are. 5 minutes.

- **Empty Outlines:** Use for process data.

  Students given an empty or partially completed outline of an in-class presentation or homework assignment after the presentation or assignment. They have a limited time (10–15 minutes) to fill in the blank spaces. Responses can be anonymous or with names. Good way to link short-term student recall to lecture or other teaching methods.

- **Muddiest Point:** Use for process data.

  Students asked to answer question: "What was the muddiest point in _____?" 1–3 minutes. Responses can be anonymous or with names. Can help to establish that particular content was taught in a certain way, as well as how effective this way was.

- **Minute Paper:** Use for process or outcome data.

  Students respond to some variation on two questions: "What was the most important thing you learned during this class?" and "What important thing remains unanswered." 2–3 minutes. Responses can be anonymous or with names.

- **Analytic Memos:** Use for outcome data.

  Students write a one- or two-page analysis of a specific problem or issue. Memos typically addressed to an employer, client, or stakeholder who will be using the memo to make a decision. Responses can be anonymous or with names. Can perform content analysis on students' responses.

tests? Do they complete the pre-test under conditions as close as possible to the in-class group, with their results nevertheless not being factored into the final analysis in the same way? The last question, of course, hints at the best answer to this conundrum, but it is very important in classroom research to make sure that "standard" classroom procedures for gathering student work products are actually standard. The pressures of the academic term can also pose threats to data gathering in long-term classroom research projects. If one data collection instrument is the teacher's daily journal, the teacher must set aside time to write in the journal every day, even during busy periods in the term.

When gathering data, researchers must also consider carefully the ethical and legal issues that arise when their subjects are themselves, their students, and their professional colleagues. For example, if particular knowledge and skills covered in a course will be tested on an exit examination that students must pass to earn their degrees, how much creativity should a researcher employ in the testing of possible instructional methods for teaching this content? If 70 percent of students master this content sufficiently to pass the test with current instructional methods, should a researcher test a method that might lead to a 50 percent pass rate, even if he or she is testing this method in the hopes of ultimately increasing the pass rate to 90 percent? How do personal interests as a researcher relate to professional responsibilities as a teacher? There are few easy answers here, and there are also legal considerations. If a researcher uses student works as instruments in classroom investigations, he or she must remember that the students own the copyrights to those works. This can become a problem if one wants to reproduce the entirety, or even a sizeable amount, of a student work in publications describing the research findings. There is a similar problem relating to any classroom materials that might result from the project. Some institutions and bodies of case law view instructors' course materials as "works made for hire," or works whose copyright belongs to their employing institution. Many institutions and many bodies of case law also view the copyright to instructors' published articles and books as belonging to the instructor (Twigg 2000). When it comes to reproducing classroom research-inspired course materials in a journal article or other publication, these two views are obviously contradictory.

To prevent such problems, always obtain students' consent in writing before publishing their work and clarify the ownership of any materials resulting from classroom research projects with your employer. Also remember that any research project using people as subjects must comply with human subjects review and approval processes before they are undertaken. For more on this see Chapter 10.

INTERPRETING THE EVIDENCE

Classroom research operates on the belief that analysis of research data should be no more complicated than is necessary to turn data into information that can be used to improve learning. Simple frequency counts and percentages often suffice. Ardis (2003) used both raw numbers (N students) and percentages in comparing in-person and online approaches to teaching the same course; Orians and Sabol (1999) similarly used raw numbers and a bar graph in tracing student learning from and responses to a Web site over time. Other approaches to analyzing data are certainly possible, depending upon the instruments used by the researcher and the researcher's knowledge of more advanced statistical procedures. For example, if students keep journals and the researcher uses comments from these journals as data, she is likely to draw upon content analysis in doing so.

The only common instance in which a classroom researcher needs knowledge of advanced statistical procedures is when the research question concerns differences in student knowledge or attitudes before and after the use of particular instructional methods or materials. Answering the question of whether the instruction caused the change from students' state before to their state after might entail comparing student pre-test scores to their post-test scores within a class, or it might involve comparing the mean final grade for this year's class to that of last year's class. This line of research is based on the premise that if the only—or a primary—factor different between the before and the after scores is the educational intervention (or the use of particular teaching methods or materials), then the educational intervention is the most likely cause of the change. (See Figure 9-9.)

Unfortunately, some amount of change in students' scores is inevitable due to the effects of chance and other factors outside the research setting. To rule out the effects of chance, t-tests and other tests of statistical significance are commonly applied to before and after measures of student learning and attitudes. Such comparisons are typically the only time that classroom researchers need have recourse to statistical methods, and even here researchers can avoid this—should they be so inclined—by framing their findings in terms of correlation rather than causation. (For more on t-tests and other tests of statistical significance, see Chapter 6).

Figure 9-9: Model for "Before" and "After" Comparisons of Student Work

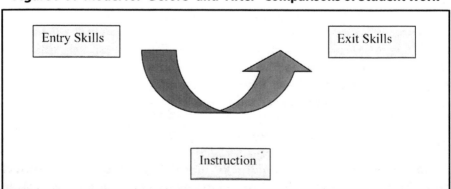

Entry Skills

Exit Skills

Instruction

Once the data have been analyzed, the researcher then draws conclusions from them. Here, classroom research returns to triangulation techniques similar to those described in the section on selecting a research design. Investigator triangulation, which has already been mentioned, can mean not only the involvement of multiple researchers in gathering data but also the involvement of multiple researchers in interpreting data. The latter could happen, for example, if a classroom researcher were performing a content analysis of the comments in students' journals. Only a single researcher would be needed to collect student journals, but more than one researcher should review the journal contents to ensure that comments one researcher codes as having a particular meaning/significance would be similarly coded by others.

Theoretical triangulation can also be used in interpreting data. Theoretical triangulation uses different conceptual perspectives to analyze the same data. Theoretical triangulation can be challenging for novice researchers, but it is important because looking at data from different perspectives often changes the way they are interpreted. Suppose a study found, as Scholz-Crane (1998) did, that students fail to really evaluate Web resources. Is this finding to be interpreted in terms of demographics (e.g., generational differences involving Generation Y); pedagogy (e.g., active learning versus lecture); psychology (e.g., the influence of prior knowledge on learning); or in some other way?

In any classroom research study, some form of triangulation should be used within the processes of gathering or interpreting data. A classroom research study that relies on a single one of anything—a single data set, observer, data-gathering method, or theoretical framework—is more vulnerable to errors than one that is triangulated (McGroarty and Zhu 1997).

Triangulation is the basis upon which classroom research projects establish their reliability and validity. Many scientific research projects establish their reliability and validity through statistical calculations. Classroom research, in contrast, has its own criteria for determining the reliability and validity of projects, and these typically involve triangulation. These include:

- Internal reliability: or, would an independent researcher, on re-analyzing the data, come to the same conclusion?
- External reliability: or, would an independent researcher, on replicating the study, come to the same conclusion?
- Internal validity: or, is the research design such that it can be confidently claimed that the outcomes are the result of particular teaching methods or materials?
- External validity: or, is the research design such that generalizations can be made from the subjects under investigation to a wider population?

Investigator triangulation ensures internal reliability by using independent researchers to check the researcher's observations of trends in the data and conclusions about these trends. Data, methodological, and theoretical triangulation increase the chances of external reliability by making it more likely that one's findings have a basis and that other researchers would interpret them similarly. Data, methodological, and investigator triangulation are important for establishing internal reliability. Multiple sets of data, multiple ways of gathering data, and multiple interpreters of data make it more likely that the research outcomes really relate to the instructional treatments. For similar reasons, all types of triangulation serve to promote external validity.

The more sets of data that support the conclusion, the more independent observers drawing the same conclusions, and the more theoretical frameworks that have been used in thinking about conclusions, the more sound the generalizations from the subject population to larger populations.

It is good form—as well as good strategy—to allow the subjects of classroom research projects to see and respond to one's interpretation of the data. Checking the interpretation of the data with the research subjects is sometimes called "member checking" (cf. Rice-Lively 1997), and it reflects classroom research's concern with empowerment. It would be ironic if a methodology that sought to empower teachers by encouraging them to provide documentary evidence of the efficacy of their teaching methods and materials were to disempower the subjects of this research by denying them their voices in the process. One way to empower the subjects of classroom research is for researchers to check their interpretations of the data with the subjects. The subjects are free to accept the researchers' interpretations as valid representations of themselves, or to dispute these interpretations. Consulting subjects on one's interpretation of the data is one way to establish the reasonableness of this interpretation. [Asking one's peers as educators to confirm the validity of one's interpretation of the data is another possibility, although a less desirable one from the perspective of empowering the research subjects.] Publishing the data without input from research subjects could lead, in a worst-case scenario, to subjects publicly disputing the findings of the research. This happened recently when Native American students at Fort Lewis College objected to an article by professor Andrew J. Gulliford. Beyond claiming that Gulliford "appropriated 'confidential statements by... students,' exhibiting a 'callous disregard' of their privacy rights" (Fogg 2004), students disputed Gulliford's interpretation of their classroom behaviors as "passive," "quiet," and "typically" Native American. Gulliford had, of course, not checked his conclusions with his subjects prior to publishing. This is an extreme example, but remains a worthwhile caution for classroom researchers.

TELLING THE STORY

In classroom research, writing up the results can be one of the more challenging steps. There are two interconnected reasons for this. First, classroom research conceptualizes all instructional interactions in terms of three variables: educational inputs, classroom materials and methods, and student learning outcomes. This means that all three variables need to be explicitly addressed in analyses of classroom situations. Add to this the fact that classroom research operates with "multiples"—multiple data sets, multiple interpreters, multiple data-gathering instruments, multiple theoretical perspectives. Each one of these multiples must be presented in sufficient detail so that readers understand it. These two factors mean that written reports of classroom research projects tend to be lengthy, but most journal articles are quite short. This means that for classroom researchers, as for other qualitative researchers, when it comes to publishing, "The greatest challenge . . . is 'not to get data, but to get rid of it!'" (Rice-Lively 1997, 198). Researchers must include enough data that their conclusions are meaningful and replicable, but not so much that their studies are unpublishable. The Web helps here because researchers can set up Web sites providing additional documentation to support their published findings.

Beyond finding ways to "reduce" but still fully present their voluminous data, classroom researchers have other unique concerns in writing up their research projects. First, be sure that the report captures the research aspects of the project. "Research is not merely the reporting of events"; rather, "the context, description, process and participant perspective must be analysed in a meaningful and coherent manner" (Gorman and Clayton 1997, 26). The purpose of classroom research is not simply to describe what happens in a particular classroom and the outcomes connected to it. Instead, classroom research seeks to prove something about the relationship between classroom events and outcomes. Providing such proof typically involves keeping theoretical explanations for possible relationships in the foreground. Instead of formulating the research question in a simplistic, nominal fashion ("I'm going to investigate the difference between methods X and Y"), ground the research question in the pedagogical, psychological, or sociological principles that underlie the investigation and the conclusions (cf. Chaudron 2001). Brown, Murphy and Nanny (2003) do this quite well in contextualizing their findings about the effectiveness of a particular instructional approach with broader discussions of the learning styles of Generation Y.

Also be sure to provide process data, or describe the nature of the instructional materials and methods, as Brown, Murphy and Nanny do. Many classroom research studies are strong in their presentation of demographic and outcome data, but they omit all meaningful details about the instructional intervention, severely reducing others' ability to interpret or replicate the results.

Finally, ensure that there is hard data behind your study. You need more than your word or anecdotal evidence that particular classroom methodologies and materials were employed or that particular outcomes were seen. You need evidence that could prove these happenings to others. With this evidence, classroom research studies become persuasive and valuable contributions to the literature.

Figure 9-10: Components of a Classroom Research Study

_____ **Focused research question**

 _____ Grounded, where possible, in the prior literature on the topic

_____ **Detailed description of the classroom setting**

 _____ Listing of the goals and objectives that the instruction supported

 _____ Student demographics

 _____ Identity of participants sufficiently confidential

 _____ Triangulation used where possible

_____ **Detailed description of instructional materials and methods**

 _____ Key materials reproduced in the text, if possible

 _____ All materials made available somehow, perhaps on a supporting Web page

 _____ Evidence of instructional methods

 _____ Triangulation used where possible

_____ **Detailed description of student learning outcomes**

 _____ Triangulation used where possible

 _____ All materials made available somehow, perhaps on a supporting Web page

_____ **Explicit recognition of the limitations the classroom setting imposed on the research project**

_____ **Interpretation**

 _____ Findings presented in such a way that other researchers can both learn from them and attempt to replicate them in their own classrooms

 _____ Use of "member checking"

REFERENCES

Angelo, Thomas A., and K. Patricia Cross. 1993. *Classroom Assessment Techniques: A Handbook for College Teachers.* 2nd ed. San Francisco, CA: Jossey-Bass.

Chaudron, Craig. 2001. "Progress in Language Classroom Research: Evidence from *The Modern Language Journal,* 1916–2000." *The Modern Language Journal* 85 (1): 57–76.

Fogg, Piper. 2004. "Professor's Article Called Offensive." *Chronicle of Higher Education* 51 (15): A15.

Fox, Dennis. 2001. "No More Random Acts of Teaching." *Leadership* 31 (2): 14–17.

Gorman, G. E., and Peter Clayton. 1997. *Qualitative Research for the Information Professional: A Practical Handbook.* London: Library Association Publishing.

McGroarty, Mary E., and Wei Zhu. 1997. "Triangulation in Classroom Research: A Study of Peer Revision." *Language Learning* 47: 1–43.

McNiff, Jean. 1993. *Teaching as Learning: An Action Research Approach.* New York: Routledge.

Rice-Lively, Mary Lynn. 1997. "Analysing Qualitative Data in Information Organizations." In *Qualitative Research for the Information Professional: A Practical Handbook*, 198–221. London: Library Association Publishing.

Twigg, Carol A. 2000. *Who Owns Online Courses and Course Materials? Intellectual Property Policies for a New Learning Environment*. Troy, NY: Pew Learning and Technology Program.

Chapter 10

Avoiding Common Pitfalls in Research

Many research errors and ethical lapses have already been discussed in the specific chapters where they are most relevant, but it is also helpful to have an overview of common problems in the research process. Although research errors and ethical lapses can take different forms because of the unique assumptions and techniques of different research methodologies, most errors and lapses are of common types. Knowledge of these common types helps researchers recognize and avoid potential errors and lapses when using various methodologies—including those not mentioned in this book. This chapter introduces some common errors that have appeared in research projects. These include:

- Not asking the right question or not asking the question in the right way.
- Gathering data at the wrong time or place.
- Using unrepresentative samples or failing to recognize possible response bias among those members of the sample who do respond.
- Failing to control for or consider possible experimenter expectancy effects, which arise when researchers' measurements are shaped to match their own hypotheses or expectations.
- Failing to control for or consider possible Hawthorne or interactional effects, in which the research situation itself, or interactions between components of it, influence research findings.
- Not addressing data's statistical significance or not providing baseline measures for comparison.
- Over-generalizing to conclusions not directly supported by the research data.

Often these errors reflect the intertwined activities of research design and data interpretation. Your research design encompasses how and of whom you ask your research questions in order to gather data. It thus underlies the data you gather, which in turn provides the basis for your conclusions. Especially when problems go unrecognized by the researcher, problems in research design are often compounded in data interpretation.

This chapter also describes standard legal and ethical guidelines for research; provides an overview of institutional review board processes for obtaining approval of research projects; and discusses common legal and ethical lapses in conducting research. This last part is especially important. Focusing on the things that do commonly go wrong, legally and ethically, in research projects shows how difficult it can be to apply abstract guidelines in real world research settings. Legal and ethical lapses are also, like research errors, common pitfalls into which the unwary researcher can stumble. Like research errors, they, too, undermine the researchers' findings by bringing into question the researchers' conduct during the entire research project.

ASKING THE WRONG QUESTIONS

A common adage warns, "Be careful what you ask for; you just might get it." Typically, this caution warns of wishing for something that you may find less than desirable once you have it—like the job at the high-powered law firm that has you working 100 hours a week, with no time or energy to spend the seven-digit salary you earn. This same caution can apply to research. Researchers tend to get data corresponding to exactly what they asked, even if what they asked was neither the "right" question nor what they meant to ask. Your subjects are typically constrained by your understanding, framing, and wording of the research questions—or your sense of what questions should be asked, in what way they should be asked, and in what words they should be asked. If you get the question "wrong" on any of these levels, you are unlikely to get the "right" answers. Your human subjects' answers will be shaped by your questions, while your non-human subjects will be selected based upon your questions.

Your understanding of the research question is shaped by the totality of your prior knowledge and basic assumptions about the topics being researched. Your prior knowledge and basic assumptions help you to determine what questions should be asked of subjects as a way of learning more about the phenomena under study. If you wanted to know why a higher percentage of local residents do not use the public library, you would probably ask them about its hours, its collections, and its service policies. You would do this because you know that the resources and services a library provides to its community help shape community views of the library, and because you believe that a library ought to provide resources and services to its community. Unless you knew or believed staff members' wardrobes—as indicators of their "hipness"—also impacted library use, you would be unlikely to ask your respondents questions about this.

Unfortunately, all too often, findings are skewed by researchers' inadequate knowledge of the phenomena being studied or by their basic assumptions about them. For a number of years, researchers overestimated people's passivity in seeking information from news media. They did not know that people are more active seekers of weather-related information than of other types of information, and so they assumed that no questions about weather-related information were needed to accurately measure people's activity/passivity in information-seeking. When researchers added a category of weather-related information to the list of categories about which subjects were asked how often they "*actively* turn to the media looking for *more* information about something you've *already* heard about" (Gantz, Fitzmaurice and Fink 1991, 633), people seemed to be much more active seekers of at least one type of information.

No researcher can be expected to know everything or make all the "right" assumptions about the topic being studied—if this were the case, there would be little need to conduct research. All researchers should, however, be open to the possibility that they might be missing certain knowledge in their understanding of the research question. Could they be missing some knowledge that would change the questions asked? Are they making the right assumptions about how the phenomena being researched work and what questions should be asked about them?

The framing of a question refers to the broader context within which a question is asked—the question(s) it follows, the question(s) it precedes, its place near the beginning or end of a measurement instrument or interview, or the way in which it is introduced to subjects. A question's framing matters a great deal to human subjects because of context effects; a question's "surroundings" will help to determine subjects' responses to it. We have not yet seen an exploration of the possible effects of question framing, or context effects, in library and information science, but it is probable that such effects do influence findings.

For example, a question about subjects' "worst" experiences with the library's Web site would likely have a very different impact on responses if it were asked first than if it were asked last. When asked first, such a question puts subjects in a negative frame of mind toward the library, so it would not be surprising to find that they consistently rated other library services lower than they would have if researchers had not started with that question. In contrast, if this question were asked last, subjects might be inclined to minimize their "worst" experiences because their responses to prior questions about the library's collections and services had all been positive and they want to be consistent. Studies in other fields have shown that the order of questions actually plays a significant role in subjects' responses. The classic example of this is provided by two different questions asked in different orders of subjects during the Cold War:

Question 1: Do you think the U.S. should allow Soviet reporters to come here and send home whatever reports they wish?

Question 2: Do you think the Soviet Union should allow U.S. reporters to go there and send home whatever reports they wish?

When Question 1 was asked first, only 36 percent of respondents thought the U.S. should let Soviet reporters come here and send home whatever reports they wished. In contrast, when Question 2 was asked first, 73 percent thought the U.S. should let Soviet reporters come here and send home whatever reports they wished. The key difference in the question order was that the 2/1 order put the notion of "our" rights into subjects' minds and their sense of fairness then prompted them to give the same rights to Soviet reporters. The 1/2 order did not have the same effect (Crossen 1994, 25).

Experimenter effects can also become a problem in question framing when, for example, the way in which the researcher introduces the question(s) to the subjects helps to shape their responses. A question introduced with "this may seem like a strange question," or "this may seem like a personal question" is likely to get a very different response than the same question asked without the accompanying phrases.

The question's wording, or how it is asked, influences subjects' answers as much as what question is asked or when a question is asked. It is not uncommon for researchers to get different responses when human subjects answer closed-ended and open-ended questions on the same topic. Closed-ended questions require subjects to select their options from the list given (with perhaps an "Other" category included), while open-ended questions force subjects to come up with their own options, as well as their own terms for expressing these options. Consider what happened when a close-ended survey question asking subjects "what was the most important thing for children to learn to prepare them for life" was changed to an open-ended interview question. Sixty-two percent of survey respondents selected to "think for themselves" from among the list of options given, but only 5 percent came up with such a response on their own (Crossen 1994, 105). Even simple word choices can shape subjects' answers. The people responsible for the Gallup Poll are skilled researchers, but their use of the word "impeachment" confounded their early polling on Richard Nixon and Watergate. When asked initially whether Nixon should be "impeached," most respondents said "no," enabling Nixon to claim that his "silent majority" supported him. However, when later asked whether Nixon should be "brought to trial before the Senate," many of these same people said "yes" (Crossen 1994, 105). While "impeachment" simply means "bringing to trial before the Senate," most people mistakenly think it means "removing an official from office," a confusion that created problems in Gallop's polling. Extensively pre-testing the question can help ensure that people are really answering the question you intend to ask.

Figure 10.1: An "Other" Category?

Particularly when asking close-ended questions of human subjects, who must then select from among the options given to them, researchers often include an option for: "Other. Please list/explain, etc." Here, including an "Other" category might have pointed researchers to the fact that people are active information-seekers when it comes to the weather. If a lot of people had opted for "Other" and added "Weather," researchers could have better understood the importance of weather-related information in accurately measuring people's information-seeking activity. Unfortunately, researchers should *not* count on an "Other; Please list" category to save them from potential problems in their understanding of the question. The very categories given to subjects earlier may persuade them not to include something important to them—but obviously "trivial" in light of the prior categories—under "Other."

GATHERING DATA IN THE WRONG CONTEXT

The time and place in which you ask your research questions will also help to determine answers to them, whether the subjects are humans or non-humans. Human subjects are notoriously sensitive to research settings. Their responses are shaped by the time of day, week, month, and year, as well as by contemporaneous sociocultural events; they respond to different physical environments in different ways; and they react to researchers' presence, sex, race, ethnicity, and occupation in shaping their own responses. Non-human subjects are not as sensitive as human subjects, but one might select samples for bibliometrics or content analysis from the wrong population at the wrong time. For instance, you might have selected newspapers from the first six months after passage of the USA Patriot Act for your content analysis of reactions to it, when it was only in the seventh month and after that criticisms of it came to replace support for it. Or you might have looked at e-prints in solid state physics as a way of tracking authors' acceptance of such publications when it was actually the astrophysicists who were pioneering acceptance of e-prints. Human subjects are especially prone to react to any detectable purposes or agendas underlying research contexts. One classic example is the age distribution data from the 1950 U.S. Census. The 1950 Census revealed more people over the age of 65 than could be accounted for by the 1940 Census numbers plus legal and illegal immigration (Huff 1993, 133–134). Where did all these additional 65-year-olds come from? It turns out that in 1940, people had no positive incentive to give their real higher ages; rather, they often had a positive incentive (feeling younger) to understate their ages. Between 1940 and 1950, however, Social Security benefits for people 65 and over came into being, giving people a definite incentive to report their real higher ages.

Above all else, when it comes to the time and place of your research, avoid mistaking a convenience sample for a representative one. Using a convenience sample puts you in the position of the man looking for his car keys under the street lamp. In this joke, a cop walking a beat at night comes across a man on his knees under a street lamp. The cop asks the man what he is doing. The man replies that he is looking for his car keys. The cop asks where the man lost his keys. The man says, "I don't know." The perplexed cop then asks, "Why are you looking here?" only to be told by the man "Because the light is better under the street lamp."

In other words, the man looks for his keys under the street lamp not because he thinks that the best place to look is under the street lamp. Rather, he looks there because the easiest place to look is where the light is. You should always be open to the possibility that the subjects you happened upon in a convenience sample are not the best indicators of the phenomena under consideration. Library student assistants, who are commonly used in studies by academic librarians, are a type of unrepresentative convenience sample.

USING UNREPRESENTATIVE SAMPLES OR NOT RECOGNIZING RESPONSE BIAS

Asking the right question of the wrong people can lead you astray. Consider two examples of this: one, a classic problem from sociology and another, a recent issue from library and information science. Both examples provide the findings first; see if you can think of who might have been asked (or not asked) to get the answers given.

> *Example 1:* Numerous studies over many years found that heterosexual men reported more sexual partners than heterosexual women, although the number of partners for both men and women should come out equal. Differences persisted despite changes in the methodologies, framing, and wording by which the questions were asked. Men kept reporting up to 74 percent more partners than women. Perplexed researchers thought the studies revealed the subjects were lying; the operation of gender-based attitudes in responses; or some fundamental flaw in the studies' designs (Recer, 2000).

> *Example 2:* A survey found that the "vast majority" of participants (nearly 82 percent) reported familiarity with learning style theories and incorporation of learning style theories into their instructional design. Instruction coordinators found this number implausible based on their reviews of curriculum.

In Example 1, because of how the questions were asked in various studies, one occupational group of women was seriously underrepresented in the samples. That group consisted of prostitutes. With 23 prostitutes for every 100,000 people in America, and with each prostitute averaging 694 male partners a year, much (but not all) of the differences between men's and women's reported number of sex partners disappears (Recer 2000). In Example 2, the survey was distributed by the electronic discussion lists for ACRL's Instruction Section and ALA's Library Instruction Round Table. Both lists are open to anyone but are likely to be used only by those who are seriously interested in instruction. Academic librarians who teach but are not all that interested in instructional issues are simultaneously less likely to subscribe to the IS and LIRT listservs and less likely to be aware of learning styles. As these examples show, watch out for situations when the research population is not synonymous with a larger population it purports to represent.

Also be aware of complications that may potentially arise from the members of your sample who answered your questions. You can ask the right question of exactly and completely the "right" people but be led astray because only some of these people choose to answer your questions. The people who choose to answer your questions may be in some way different from, and unrepresentative of, the people who opt not to answer the questions. Suppose you send a survey on a corporate library's services to all full-time workers at the company. You have probably already realized that the people who are likely to respond are those who have strong opinions (pro or con) about the library and its services. Those with less strong opinions will be less likely to spend the time to answer. The strength of their opinions is not, however, the only thing that could separate respondents from non-respondents here. What if the non-respondents not only had more neutral views about the library but also displayed fundamentally different information-seeking and use behaviors than respondents? Non-respondents might use information more often but find the collections of the corporate library so limited that they rely on a local academic library instead. As this hypothetical example shows, it is often "difficult to know if there is something systematically different about those people who declined to be studied" beyond the fact that they declined to be studied (Case 2002, 173). When examining your findings, consider the possibility that there is something different about them, and that this difference may account for your results.

SEEING WHAT YOU WANT TO SEE

In cases where your findings rely upon patterns you observe in people's behavior or recorded communications, you should be especially careful that what you are seeing is really there, not a figment of your imagination. Many people have a commonsense view that sight is an infallible conduit to "truth": "seeing is believing," or "I'll know it when I see it," we say.

In actuality, though, our senses can play tricks on us—and not just when we are suffering from dehydration in the desert and seeing mirages. Consider two cases from outside library and information science. Library and information science is not a "hard" science, and librarians and information scientists are not specially trained observers. However, even experienced researchers in "hard" sciences, where there are objectively verifiable truths (like gravity), have been fooled by what they want to see. Prosper Blondlot is a good example of this. Blondlot was a well-respected French physicist from the University of Nancy, who in 1903 claimed to have detected N-rays. This was eight years after German physicist Konrad Roentgen discovered X-rays, and two years after Roentgen won the first Nobel prize in physics for his discovery:

> The period was rife with all sorts of discoveries focused on rays, and Blondlot apparently pressured himself to discover some new form of rays. This "discovery" was well received in France, and the French Academy even awarded Blondlot a prize. (Ben-Yahuda 2002, 197)

While Blondlot and his French colleagues were seeing N-rays, American physicist Robert Wood was skeptical. One day, on a visit to Blondlot's lab, Wood secretly removed a critical piece of the experimental apparatus that Blondlot used to detect N-rays. The removal made no difference to what Blondlot saw. Blondlot wanted to see N-rays, so he kept seeing them even though his detection mechanism was inoperative. We now know that there are no N-rays to be seen.

A classic example in the social sciences of "seeing what you want to see" comes from an experiment wherein a person of African descent apparently chased a clown into a meeting room at a conference: "[T]hey stopped in the middle of the room fighting; the clown fell, the [person of African descent] leapt upon him, fired, and then both rushed out of the hall" (Von Gennep 1910, 158–159). Each person in the conference room was then asked to provide a written account of what happened. Out of the 40 accounts submitted, only one was less than 20 percent mistaken as to the principal facts; 14 were 20–40 percent mistaken; 12 were 40–50 percent mistaken; and 13 were more than 50 percent mistaken. A primary reason that people were so mistaken as to what they saw was the fact that they had mental images of how people behave and how situations occur. Actual people and situations were made to conform to these images: if you believe an armed assailant is likely to say "put your hands up," you are likely to hear any indistinct words that assailant says as "put your hands up."

Librarians are neither researching phenomena subject to physical laws (like physicists) nor trained as observers (like psychologists). The difficulties that researchers have had in these other fields with separating what researchers see from what researchers expect or want to see are thus even more important. As Donald Case emphasizes, "People tend to notice things that support their beliefs and ignore things that do not" (Case 2002, 161). For example, if you are observing patrons' use of the library's Web site, you are likely to notice different things—and attribute different meanings to those things—if you think patrons are skilled at searching than if you think they are unskilled. If you think the patron is unskilled, you are more likely to notice all their missteps, all the things they do that take them further from completion of their intended task. Moreover, if you think the patron is unskilled, you are likely to interpret such missteps as "floundering." If you think the patron is skilled, however, you might not notice her missteps, or you might attribute them to her looking for shortcuts or otherwise "exploring" the site. The observer's influence on what is ultimately observed becomes even more pronounced with the operation of halo effects, or the global impact of subjects' likeable personalities or other "desirable" traits that are irrelevant to the research situation but lead to over-inflated and biased judgments of performance. Halo effects mean, for example, that you are more likely to rate attractive or cheerful subjects as more skilled, more knowledgeable, or more highly performing than others. Halo effects become even more pernicious when researchers' cultural prejudices shape their view of subjects—when, for example, a facial expression that gets a Caucasian student rated as "thoughtfully intelligent" leads to a Hispanic student being rated "sluggish and resentful." Given all that can go wrong in the observation process, researchers should always be open to the possibility that their preconceptions may have influenced their perceptions and thus their conclusions.

HEISENBERG'S UNCERTAINTY PRINCIPLE

Heisenberg's Uncertainty Principle is a physics law which holds that the more precisely you determine the position of a subatomic particle, the less precisely its momentum is known. Librarians and information scientists are, obviously, not working with subatomic particles in doing research, but a version of Heisenberg's Uncertainty Principle operates in their work. In bringing one variable under control, you leave other variables to play out their effects in your findings. For example, in grouping research subjects by gender and comparing the mean scores of males and females, you might be leaving differences in socioeconomic backgrounds and reading abilities uncontrolled in ways that skew your findings. Similarly, what you know is always influenced by how you know it. Thus, in a bibliometric study, you know what sources your subjects ultimately cited, but you have no knowledge of why they cited the sources they did. In interviews, in contrast, you know what people say they do, or would do, in certain circumstances; or they give you explanations for why they did what they did. You have no way of knowing, though, whether what they say they would do is what they actually would do, or whether the explanation they gave you for past conduct is the "true" one. Focusing on subjects' past conduct also leaves open the possibility of changes between that and their present or future conduct. For everything that you know, there is something else that you cannot know—simply because of the fact that how you know influences what you know. Researchers should always recognize and respect the limitations of their projects and their knowledge.

PRESENTING NUMBERS WITHOUT ADDRESSING THEIR SIGNIFICANCE

Too often, numbers are presumed to be meaningful without actual consideration of whether they are really meaningful or of what they really mean. Tests of statistical significance should be run on bibliometric, experimental, and other quantitative data before anything is concluded about their meaning. Otherwise you end up making claims like Martin Ebon (1971). Ebon "proves" that ESP works by the following experiment. Try this experiment yourself, if you have a pet, and think about how meaningful it really is! Fill two bowls with food for your pet and put the bowls on your kitchen floor. Picture one bowl in your mind and think really hard about it. Then call your pet to the kitchen to eat. In one out of two cases, or 50 percent of the time, your pet will go to the bowl you had in mind. There! You have proof of ESP, right? Wrong! You have numbers (1 in 2; 50%), but they are not statistically significant. In one out of two cases, your pet would have picked the bowl you were thinking about by chance alone.

Even when your numbers are statistically significant, though, you still need to be cautious in their interpretation. The American Psychological Association (APA) has recently wrestled with this problem in light of studies of differences between men and women. There have been studies that found statistically significant differences between men and women, but although tests of statistical difference include measures of the standard deviation of scores (or the spread of scores around the central tendency) within their calculations, reporting of only mean scores and their statistical significance obscures many similarities between men and women (Barnett and Rivers 2004). As Figure 10-2 shows, mean scores can differ in statistically significant ways, with the scores being distributed so that there is nonetheless more overlap than difference between the groups. Thus, the APA has called for researchers to report the dispersion, range, or standard deviation of scores, as well as their means and statistical significance. The APA's cautionary call is a good reminder for librarians and information scientists researching differences between sociocultural or socioeconomic groups that have been historically marginalized or are sensitive to potentially stereotypical portrayals.

When numbers are not subject to tests of statistical significance, as with frequency counts in content analysis or bibliometrics, you should still ask whether these numbers mean anything and what they mean. Studies of mistaken information on the Web serve as good examples here. McClung, Murray, and Heitlinger found that only 20 percent of the 60 Web pages they examined followed established guidelines for the treatment of childhood diarrhea, while

Figure 10-2: An Overlap in Distribution between Statistically Significant Scores

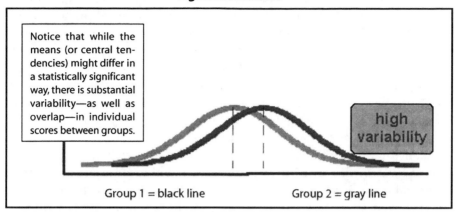

Notice that while the means (or central tendencies) might differ in a statistically significant way, there is substantial variability—as well as overlap—in individual scores between groups.

high variability

Group 1 = black line   Group 2 = gray line

Impicciatore et al. found that just four in 41 Web pages followed established guidelines for managing fever in children at home. These studies are often cited as "proof" that sources on the Web are unreliable, while those in the library are trustworthy. Do they actually prove this, though? Is 20 percent or four in 41 significant? We don't know, because no comparable studies have been done of the accuracy of information sources that people could use instead of the Web. There are no baseline or benchmark measures with which to compare the numbers in these studies.

Also remember that just because all the numbers go in one way does not mean that they are "right," or "eternal truths." As Cynthia Crossen emphasizes in discussing the polling data about whether the public found Anita Hill or Clarence Thomas more credible, "the Anita Hill pollers were certain their results were right because the polls all said the same thing. Less than a year later, they all said the opposite" (Crossen 1994, 112).

JUMPING TO CONCLUSIONS

Our favorite example of researchers who hurt themselves in jumping to conclusions comes from the following study. Researchers surveyed faculty members about the degree to which they used and valued various aspects of librarians' job descriptions (collection development, reference assistance, instruction, and so forth) and concluded that faculty members looked most positively on librarians as "servile." How did the researchers get to that conclusion? Their faculty respondents reported the most interactions with librarians in reference; they also rated these transactions most highly. The researchers assumed that faculty members used and valued reference as service. However, other explanations for faculty members' use and valuing of reference were possible. Faculty members could have viewed reference as expert problem solving, or one-on-one teaching, or some other non-"service" transaction. Because the researchers did not ask their faculty respondents why they valued reference, they were on their own in concluding faculty members valued reference primarily as service. These researchers also assumed that "service" meant "servile" to faculty. Even had faculty agreed that reference was service, it is still not a given that they would have equated service and servile. They might have conceptualized "service" as interaction between professional equals. Here, the researchers managed to get themselves quite agitated about findings that they had never really found. In essence, they hurt themselves in jumping to conclusions.

Another way in which researchers can hurt themselves in jumping to conclusions is by forgetting whether their study measured correlation or causation. Causation results when one thing is the reason for or source of another. Correlation, in contrast, appears when two things occur together. Often, correlations are due to broader trends or causes, not to one thing causing another (Huff 1993, 97). For example, students' taking elective library classes and having higher GPAs than their peers are correlated phenomena. Taking the library class does not cause the higher GPA; rather, both taking the class and higher GPA are due to some other factor (perhaps to the fact that students who take the class are more motivated than their peers).

To avoid jumping to conclusions, researchers should attempt to operate by what science and technology policy professor Marcel LaFollette (1992, 60) has described as the "cardinal rule of cautiousness." LaFollette means that researchers should keep the gap between the data gathered in the study and the conclusions based on this data as small as possible. If your research focused on the database use patterns of elementary school children, you should limit your conclusions to database use and elementary school children rather than speak about all researchers using all types of information sources. It is certainly possible—and permissible—to speculate further than your narrowly based conclusions, but you should always make clear the boundary between your findings-based conclusions and your speculations. (Many researchers do this by distinguishing their "findings" and "conclusions" from their "suggestions for further research.") You should also bring what philosophers call the "principle of charity" into operation in your conclusions. Because philosophers could never finish writing and publish anything if they had to anticipate all possible objections (and the later objections to the replies to earlier objections), philosophers agree that when in doubt about another's arguments or reasoning, you should always credit your opponent with the best possible argument they could make. So, too, in drawing conclusions based upon your research data, or in situating your conclusions in relation to prior findings, you should always attempt to place other responses and ideas in the best possible light. If you consistently interpret your respondents' answers in a negative light, you run the risk of drawing incorrect conclusions (like the researchers

Figure 10-3: Turning Pitfalls into Promising Topics

Asking the Wrong Questions

1. Take a topic that others have investigated and flip the way they frame the question. If many other studies have explored why faculty **do not** use librarian-provided instruction with their classes, you could ask why some faculty **do** use such instruction.

2. Take a topic that other researchers have investigated by using a particular methodology and research it using another methodology. If everyone else has used surveys, use interviews or observations.

Gathering Data in the Wrong Context

3. Take a phenomenon that others have previously investigated and look at a different place. If people have looked at public library use in suburban areas, look at urban or rural areas. If people have looked at information seeking in academe, look at the workplace.

4. Take a topic that other researchers have previously investigated and re-do a prior study to see if the findings still hold true in a different time, or with changed socioeconomic circumstances.

Unrepresentative Samples or Response Bias

5. Take a topic that others have previously investigated and look at a different population. If other researchers have focused upon citations by chemists, for example, look at biologists or geologists.

6. Or, look at a subgroup within a larger population. This strategy is especially effective if you have reason to believe this subgroup is different from the larger population in ways that prior studies have not explored. For example, if studies of public library use have considered all users as a whole, you might focus on parents with preschool-aged children or retirees.

Seeing What You Want to See

7. Try looking for evidence of something different in your observations. If everyone else observing high school students using the online catalog has found evidence that these students are confused, scared, and inept, see if you can construct and spot indicators that students know what they are doing, are confident, and attain success.

   Doing so is not just engaging in sophistry. If you "go looking" for something and cannot find it, the odds are greater that it is not there. However, if you "go looking" for something and can find it, you can inject important notes of caution about the role of experimenter effects in observations about this topic and about the possible need for independent observers.

Heisenberg's Uncertainty Principle

8. Repeat a prior study changing a formerly uncontrolled variable into a controlled one, or introducing new controlled variables. If you think reading ability as well as sex and income could be a predictor of Internet use, test for reading ability as well as sex and income.

Presenting Numbers without Addressing Their Significance

10. Select something which has never yet been counted or measured; then compare your numbers to established baselines for related constructs. If everyone else has focused on how much mistaken information there is on the Internet, look at popular guidebooks, scholarly articles, patient pamphlets, etc., to see to what degree they are correct.

Jumping to Conclusions

11. Write a review article comparing conclusions from multiple studies on the same topic. See to what degree they share similar hypotheses, methodologies, findings, and conclusions. If these studies provide suitable data, you may even be able to conduct a meta-analysis. [See Chapter 11 for more on meta-analyses.]

who said faculty most highly valued librarians as "servile"). Similarly, if you attack or dismiss others' findings when they disagree with yours—rather than seek to understand others' findings within the contexts where they were obtained—you can miss possible insights.

LEGAL AND ETHICAL GUIDELINES FOR RESEARCH

Many introductions to research methodologies or techniques speak of research ethics. Much of what is included under "research ethics" actually describes conduct covered by federal laws. Section 46 of Title 45 of the *Code of Federal Regulations* (45 C.F.R. §46) specifies that "all research involving human subjects conducted, supported, or otherwise subject to regulation by any Federal Department or Agency" must abide by the following rules:

1. Risks to subjects are minimized.
2. Risks to subjects are reasonable in relation to anticipated benefits, if any, to subjects and to the importance of the knowledge that may reasonably be expected to result.
3. Selection of subjects is equitable.
4. Informed consent will be sought from each prospective subject or the subject's legally authorized representative.
5. Informed consent will be appropriately documented.
6. When appropriate, the research plan makes adequate provision for monitoring the data collected to ensure the safety of subjects.
7. When appropriate, there are adequate provisions to protect the privacy of subjects and to maintain the confidentiality of data.

The use of the word "supported" to describe "research" in the *Code of Federal Regulations* helps to explain the broad reach of these rules. They apply to all research in any way underwritten by U.S. government monies. Many institutions have adopted these same rules for non-federally funded research, simply because it is difficult to apply different standards to federally funded and non-federally funded research conducted at the same institution. (Beyond these federal rules, there are usually also local, state, and international laws that apply.)

Informed consent is the most complicated of the concepts included in the guidelines. It is subject to its own detailed rules listed in Figure 10-4. It should also be noted that heightened levels of scrutiny and protection apply to pregnant women (45 C.F.R. §46.201), prisoners (45 C.F.R. §46.301), and children under the legal age of consent (45 C.F.R. §46.401). Researchers working with subjects under the legal age of consent should pay special attention to the requirements in C.F.R. §46.408(a)-(c). These requirements specify under what conditions children are seen as capable of providing consent, as well as who is required to consent to research on minor subjects.

Figure 10-4: Basic Requirements for Informed Consent

(1) A statement that the study involves research, an explanation of the purposes of the research and the expected duration of the subject's participation, a description of the procedures to be followed, and identification of any procedures which are experimental.

(2) A description of any reasonably foreseeable risks or discomforts to the subject.

(3) A description of any benefits to the subject or to others which may reasonably be expected from the research.

(4) Disclosure of appropriate alternative procedures or courses of treatment, if any, that might be advantageous to the subject.

(5) A statement describing the extent, if any, to which confidentiality of records identifying the subject will be maintained.

(6) For research involving more than minimal risk, an explanation as to whether any compensation or any medical treatments are available if injury occurs and, if so, what they consist of, or where further information may be obtained.

(7) An explanation of whom to contact for answers to pertinent questions about the research and research subjects' rights, and whom to contact in the event of a research-related injury to the subject.

(8) A statement that participation is voluntary, that refusal to participate will involve no penalty or loss of benefits to which the subject is otherwise entitled, and that the subject may discontinue participation at any time without penalty or loss of benefits to which the subject is otherwise entitled.

Professional organizations and institutional bodies can also create their own research guidelines that overlay the federal rules and add greater protections for subjects. These guidelines can more properly be described as ethical norms.

Figure 10-5: Who Can Provide Permission for Your Project?

Beyond approval from institutional review boards and informed consent from human subjects, researchers often need additional permissions to conduct their research projects. Suppose, for example, that you wanted to observe children using the libraries of local schools or patrons using public libraries. You would also need the permission of the schools or libraries in which you would be conducting your observations.

Obtaining the proper permissions in such situations can be trickier than you think. Who do you ask in order to conduct observations in a public library?

 • Reference librarian or other staff on duty?
 • Head of reference?
 • Library director?
 • Director of the library system?
 • Library's board of directors?

Typically, you want permission from the highest level of the relevant organizational charts; only these people are really in a position to give consent on behalf of others.

Ethical norms may even overrule the exemptions built into the laws governing research (see Figure 10-6). Take postings to electronic listservs, discussion boards, blogs, and other Internet sites. Such postings arguably fall into the category of "research involving the collection or study of existing data, documents, records . . . if these sources are publicly available"; that is, they are exempt from human subjects' requirements under 45 C.F.R. §46.101(a)(4). This means that

Figure 10-6: Exemptions Built into Section 46 of Title 45 of the *Code of Federal Regulations*

(1) Research conducted in established or commonly accepted educational settings, involving normal educational practices, such as (i) research on regular or special education instructional strategies, or (ii) research on the effectiveness of or the comparison among instructional techniques, curricula, or classroom management methods.

(2) Research involving the use of educational tests (cognitive, diagnostic, aptitude, achievement), survey procedures, interview procedures or observation of public behavior, unless: (i) information obtained is recorded in such a manner that human subjects can be identified, directly or through identifiers linked to the subjects; and (ii) any disclosure of the human subjects' responses outside the research could reasonably place the subjects at risk of criminal or civil liability or be damaging to the subjects' financial standing, employability, or reputation.

(3) Research involving the use of educational tests (cognitive, diagnostic, aptitude, achlevement), survey procedures, interview procedures, or observation of public behavior that is not exempt under paragraph (b)(2) of this section, if: (i) the human subjects are elected or appointed public officials or candidates for public office; or (ii) Federal statute(s) require(s) without exception that the confidentiality of the personally identifiable information will be maintained throughout the research and thereafter.

(4) Research involving the collection or study of existing data, documents, records, pathological specimens, or diagnostic specimens, if these sources are publicly available or if the information is recorded by the investigator in such a manner that subjects cannot be identified, directly or through identifiers linked to the subjects.

(5) Research and demonstration projects which are conducted by or subject to the approval of Department or Agency heads, and which are designed to study, evaluate, or otherwise examine: (i) Public benefit or service programs; (ii) procedures for obtaining benefits or services under those programs; (iii) possible changes in or alternatives to those programs or procedures; or (iv) possible changes in methods or levels of payment for benefits or services under those programs.

(6) Taste and food quality evaluation and consumer acceptance studies, (i) if wholesome foods without additives are consumed or (ii) if a food is consumed that contains a food ingredient at or below the level and for a use found to be safe, or an agricultural chemical or environmental contaminant at or below the level found to be safe, by the Food and Drug Administration or approved by the Environmental Protection Agency or the Food Safety and Inspection Service of the U.S. Department of Agriculture.

researchers could technically use these postings for content analysis or other forms of study without obtaining their posters' consent or permission (so long as copyright laws were followed). However, most researchers hold themselves to higher ethical standards than the requirements of the law here, and will only use such postings with the consent of their authors. Researchers do this in recognition of widespread belief among posters to such sites that their communications are part of "semi-private conversations," as well as "intellectual works in progress" (not necessarily final formulations ready for use) (Kolko 2000, 262–264). Some researchers go further than this, holding that authors of such Internet postings must be asked for their permission prior to citing to, not just conducting research from, their postings. So, in this case, researchers are saying that subjects expect and are entitled to a higher level of protection than prescribed by law.

Applying legal requirements and ethical norms to research situations can be more complex than it sounds, however. For example, informed consent means that subjects are to be provided, among other things, "a statement that the study involves research, an explanation of the purposes of the research, . . . a description of the procedures to be followed, and identification of any procedures which are experimental" (45 C.F.R. §46.116[a][1]). However, simply informing the subjects that they are being researched can cause them to change their behavior because of the Hawthorne effect. People who know they are being watched behave differently than they would if they were not being watched or if they did not know they were being watched. (Would you eat ice cream directly from the container with a spoon, instead of dinner, on nights when you are really tired? If so, would you still do so on a night a dietician was in your home observing your food consumption as part of a study of eating habits?) Every piece of information you give subjects beyond the fact that they are being observed adds further opportunities for them to produce results that do not represent their true behaviors and attitudes. Knowing the purposes of the study leaves subjects prone to response or self-presentation bias, with subjects shaping their responses in order to support certain images of themselves or in order to provide socially accepted answers. Some subjects will choose to "be good" and "align" themselves with the researchers and the purpose of the study, producing false positives. Interview subjects who seldom use their local public library might say they love their public library to "please" a researcher who is a librarian or to give the answer they feel is expected. (They might, in fact, "love" the library but never use it.) Others rebel, exaggerating or making up their positions in opposition to the researchers or to the apparent purpose of the study. To seem "bad" or to shock the researcher, a high school student might overestimate the degree to which she/he cuts and pastes text from the Internet in writing papers.

Knowledge of the research procedures further allows subjects to shape their responses beyond their "true" range, while knowledge of which procedures are experimental opens the door to placebo effects. Placebo effects arise when researchers or their subjects know the existence and type of the experimental treatment. Placebo effects are particularly common among subjects who want the treatments to work, or who want to please the researchers. Researchers can also introduce placebo effects by filtering their observations through the notion that the treatment is "working." A classic study of the placebo effect is a 1983 article by Chalmers, Celano, Sacks, and Smith on bias in clinical trials for heart attacks. Chalmers, et al., found that when subjects were not randomly assigned to treatment and control groups and when they were aware of their treatment status, the treatment was rated effective 58 percent of the time. When subjects were either randomly assigned or blinded as to their treatment status, the treatment was only rated effective 24 percent of the time. If subjects were both randomly assigned and blinded, the treatment was rated effective just 9 percent of the time.

Because informed consent can lead to subjects producing "false" results, "many of the . . . methodologies employed routinely involve at least some level of deception" (Glazier and Powell 1992, 202). For example, instead of telling faculty respondents that you are using the *Learning Organization Practices Profile* to see whether their views on organizational climate correlate with their use of library instruction, you might tell them only that you are interested in their views on organizational climate. Telling them more than this could lead them to filter their views about organizational culture through their experiences with library instruction. Think carefully about how to balance your need for data that "truly" reflect your subjects' behaviors, attitudes, and knowledge, with ethical and legal requirements such as informed consent. When in doubt about how to follow the rules and still get reliable data, talk to your local institutional review board and your fellow researchers.

Similarly, while researchers are required to protect the privacy of subjects and to maintain the confidentiality of data, doing so can block the replication of the study and be legally impossible. Social scientists have recently debated the desirability and impact of obscuring all proper names associated with research studies. (Human subjects are sometimes willing to be identified by name in research projects. Even when they are willing, however, attorneys for most publishers tend to veto subjects' identification by their proper names out of fear that subjects who now consent might subsequently bring lawsuits objecting to their naming [Wolfe 2003]). Alan Wolfe has made the following argument against obscuring all proper names:

> Changing names makes it impossible for others to verify a scholar's findings because, technically speaking, we cannot know for sure what is being observed. . . . Although surely not the intention, the convention of not naming actual places absolves scholars from the process of criticism and revision that is central to advancing knowledge. . . . Protecting the names of individuals, another time-honored scholarly convention, is different from

changing the names of cities, universities, or businesses. Individuals have rights to privacy that institutions, which have public responsibilities, do not. Yet changing the names of individuals raises similar questions. Should a Hispanic person be given an invented Hispanic name? If the researcher does not indicate ethnicity, information is lost. If he or she does, racial or ethnic stereotyping can result. (Wolfe 2003, 13)

As Wolfe emphasizes, the more the contexts of the research—its who, what, when, and where—are concealed, the less adequately that research can be interpreted and the more difficult that research is to replicate.

Moreover, most researchers place too much faith in the inviolability of the privacy of research subjects and the confidentiality of research data. Note that 45 C.F.R. §46.111(a) says only that researchers must take "adequate provisions" to protect privacy and confidentiality. They are not required to provide absolute or total protection, because such protection is legally impossible. Any final reports on their projects produced by researchers for federal funding agencies are public information, and the projects underlying them can be subject to Freedom of Information Act (FOIA) requests. Similarly, research data from any project—federally or non-federally funded—can also be subpoenaed. This means that researchers should take care in the data they gather, as well as the ways in which they track the data. It might not be desirable to ask an interview question about defacement of library materials if you think that the library system whose materials were defaced might be interested in bringing charges against the vandals.

Dealing with Institutional Review Boards

Section 46 of Title 45 of the *Code of Federal Regulations* provides for Institutional Review Boards (IRBs) to review "all research involving human subjects conducted, supported, or otherwise subject to regulation by any Federal Department or Agency" for compliance with the seven criteria listed earlier. Most institutions having IRBs under Title 45 tend to use these same IRBs to review all research projects, federally funded or not. An IRB consists of at least five members selected in accordance with the criteria listed in Figure 10-7 and is responsible for initial, ongoing, and wrap-up evaluation of research projects to ensure their compliance with the seven criteria listed earlier. All institutions of higher education should have IRBs; elementary and secondary school systems, as well as public library systems, may also have them. If you do not know of an IRB for your institution, ask your supervisor for information on any local IRBs or other local procedures for reviewing research projects. The necessary permissions must be obtained before research is undertaken in order to ensure that your study is legally and ethically conducted. Some librarians have recently taken to describing in their publications the processes whereby local IRBs vetted their projects. Other research fields do not do likewise, and we

Figure 10-7: IRB Membership Rules

(a) Each IRB shall have at least five members, with varying backgrounds to promote complete and adequate review of research activities commonly conducted by the institution. The IRB shall be sufficiently qualified through the experience and expertise of its members, and the diversity of the members, including consideration of race, gender, and cultural backgrounds and sensitivity to such issues as community attitudes, to promote respect for its advice and counsel in safeguarding the rights and welfare of human subjects. In addition to possessing the professional competence necessary to review specific research activities, the IRB shall be able to ascertain the acceptability of proposed research in terms of institutional commitments and regulations, applicable law, and standards of professional conduct and practice. The IRB shall, therefore, include persons knowledgeable in these areas. If an IRB regularly reviews research that involves a vulnerable category of subjects, such as children, prisoners, pregnant women, or handicapped or mentally disabled persons, consideration shall be given to the inclusion of one or more individuals who are knowledgeable about and experienced in working with these subjects.

(b) Every nondiscriminatory effort will be made to ensure that no IRB consists entirely of men or entirely of women, including the institution's consideration of qualified persons of both sexes, so long as no selection is made to the IRB on the basis of gender. No IRB may consist entirely of members of one profession.

(c) Each IRB shall include at least one member whose primary concerns are in scientific areas and at least one member whose primary concerns are in nonscientific areas.

(d) Each IRB shall include at least one member who is not otherwise affiliated with the institution and who is not part of the immediate family of a person who is affiliated with the institution.

(e) No IRB may have a member participate in the IRB's initial or continuing review of any project in which the member has a conflicting interest, except to provide information requested by the IRB.

(f) An IRB may, in its discretion, invite individuals with competence in special areas to assist in the review of issues which require expertise beyond or in addition to that available in the IRB. These individuals may not vote with the IRB.

would encourage librarians to emulate these fields. IRB approval should be assumed for any published research project; its presence need not be explicitly stated.

Avoiding Legal and Ethical Problems

A common reaction to legal and ethical problems in research is to deny their existence, or to minimize the frequency with which they occur. Problems are said to be the result of a few "bad apples," or the product of untrained or poorly trained researchers. However, a recent survey of scientists suggests that legal and ethical failures in research are more common than we would wish. A recent survey of 3,247 U.S.-based scientists who had received funding from the National Institutes of Health found the following problems:

- 15.5 percent of respondents reported changing a study under pressure from a funding source.
- 15.3 percent reported dropping data from the analysis based on a "gut feeling."
- 12.5 percent reported overlooking others' use of flawed or questionably interpreted data.
- 10.8 percent reported withholding details of methodology or results.
- 10.0 percent reported inappropriately including their own names or those of others as authors on published research reports.
- 7.6 percent reported circumventing "minor" rules protecting human subjects.
- 6.0 percent reported failing to present data that contradicted their own previous research.
- 1.7 percent reported making unauthorized use of confidential information.
- 1.4 percent reported using others' ideas without permission or credit.
- 1.4 percent reported having "questionable" relationships with students, subjects, or clients.
- 0.3 percent reported not properly disclosing involvement with firms whose products were based on their research.
- 0.3 percent reported ignoring "major" rules protecting human subjects.
- 0.3 percent reported falsifying research data (Weiss 2005).

Let us look more closely at the categories from the poll and consider how and why problems arise.

External Pressure Influencing Research Topics and Findings

The most common problematic behaviors, according the study just mentioned, arise from researchers' responding to pressures from external sources—especially their funders—in selecting research topics and presenting their findings. Sometimes the connection between corporate funding and research findings is merely suggestive: perhaps it is simply coincidence that *Winners, Losers and Microsoft: Competition and Antitrust in High Tech* saw the government's suit against Microsoft as a bad thing and was published by the Independent Institute, over 20 percent of whose budget comes directly from Microsoft (Rampton and Stauber 2002, 9–10). Other indicators of the influence of corporate sponsorship on academic research are more direct. Rampton and Stauber provide a fascinating overview of prior research on the effects of industry funding on academic research. While some 34 percent of biomedical and life sciences researchers had an "identifiable financial interest connected to the research" and another

64 percent had some financial relationship with industry, only 0.5 percent of articles disclosed authors' research-related financial interests. Yet such interests can have a substantial impact on findings: while scientists not funded by the pharmaceutical industry reported findings unfavorable to experimental pharmaceuticals in 60 percent of studies, those funded by industry reported findings favorable to experimental pharmaceuticals in 74 percent of studies (Rampton and Stauber 2002, 204–219). Acting on this awareness that many researchers have corporate sponsors and that these sponsors may seek to conceal unfavorable results, 11 biomedical journals—including the *Journal of the American Medical Association, Lancet,* and the *New England Journal of Medicine*—recently required disclosure of continuing trials, which are often not reported because of negative results, in a public registry as a precondition of publication (Engber 2004). Depending upon contracts or other agreements you may have signed with your research funders, the funder may have legal rights to review any writings based on your research before they are published, or even to block publication of writings to which they object (cf. King 1996).

Library and information science are, to be sure, relatively immune from the temptation to cherry pick topics or spin results because of corporate funding. The level and types of corporate funding available to library and information science are miniscule in comparison to those available to other researchers, especially researchers in biomedical fields. Library and information science are, however, equally prone to other types of external pressures that also help to determine what topics are researched and what findings are reported. "Research agendas" published by professional organizations or journal editors can help shape what topics are researched. Authors seeking to get published often seek topics from such lists in the hope that studies on "hot topics" will be more publishable. Similarly, peer reviewers' and journal editors' preferences for "positive results," or studies whose hypotheses are supported by their data, can tempt researchers to "cook" or "spin" their results as will be discussed below. Internal pressures, or pressures from within individual researchers, are also important. While many people believe in the stereotyped "disinterested researcher," who lets the data speak for itself and pursues the truth whatever its implications, all researchers are personally and professionally invested in their topics. They want to be right; they want to be published; they want to be widely cited and respected. Toward these ends, they may consciously or unconsciously find themselves selecting topics or spinning data so as to maximize their chances of seeming right.

"Cooking" the Data

Virtually all research data is somewhat "dirty." Tape recordings of interviews may have gaps created by battery outages or the unplugging of power cords, code numbers for content analyses can be entered incorrectly, or experimental instruments can be mis-scored. "Cleaning up" your research data thus affords one opportunity for "cooking" the data; you can "correct" supposedly "dirty" data that does not fit your conclusions in order to make it fit better. For example, in reconstructing from your memory an interview whose recording was incomplete, you might over-emphasize (in either duration or importance) a comparatively minor point that struck you as very important during the interview. Even when there is no "dirty" data to clean up, researchers may still engage in practices that nineteenth-century computer science pioneer Charles Babbage described as "trimming" and "cooking" (LaFollette 1992, 47). "Trimmers" smooth out numerical data so that trend lines are neat and percentages total perfectly. Gregor Mendel, the father of genetics, was a notorious trimmer, whose statistics on the inheritance of traits among his pea plants are too perfect to be real. "Cooks," in contrast, include only data that support their final hypotheses in their analyses. Data that are not supportive are dismissed as "atypical" or somehow "flawed." Suppose, for example, you had 100 students take a test as part of an experiment. Most students scored in the 40–50 percent range, but enough students got perfect scores (100 percent) to raise the mean substantially. You decide to throw out the 100 percent scores on the grounds that students must have guessed or cheated; they could not possibly have gotten those scores otherwise. Discounting those scores would be cooking.

Statistics are particularly prone to "cooking." Researchers can calculate significance using inappropriate statistical tests, or they can perform multiple statistical tests, reporting only the ones that showed statistically significant results (Mann accessed 2007). Beyond trimming and cooking comes outright fabrication of data, or manufacturing data from nothing in support of a research project that was never actually conducted or completed. Cancer researcher William Summerlin may provide the most entertaining example of fabricated data: he "used a felt-tip marker to darken skin grafts on two white mice," which had previously received skin grafts from other white mice, in order to make it look as if cross-species skin grafts had worked (LaFollette 1992, 17). Other examples are common in other fields: Stephen E. Breuning's work on hyperactivity, John Darsee's work on cardiology, Jan Henrik Schon's work on single-molecule switches, Robert Slutsky's work on cardiology, Vijay Soman's work on insulin binding in anorexics, and Mark Spector's work on tumor viruses all rested on fabricated data (and were published in some of the most prestigious scientific journals).

Pressures to manipulate data come from various sources. Researchers' personal investments in their own work are one of these sources. After spending two years of your life tracking the digital divide in the production of Web information, it can be difficult—to say the least—to accept the fact that all your data point to the lessening, not the increasing, of this divide. In those two years, you may have publicly stated your belief that country of residence correlates positively with posting of Web information, making it harder to renounce your earlier findings. You will lose face, as well as time, because your data do not support your hypotheses. Another source of pressure for manipulating data comes from the operation of "publication bias." Peer reviewers, journal editors, and authors themselves all like "positive" stories—research projects whose data support their hypotheses, whose data are statistically significant, or whose findings are simply very dramatic (Dickersin 1990). A study by Mahoney (1977) found that identical manuscripts suffered very different fates in the peer review process depending upon the "direction" of the data. Papers reporting negative results, or whose data do not provide statistically significant support for their hypotheses, got *much* lower evaluations than those reporting positive results (or whose data provide statistically significant support for their hypotheses). Gould (1995) has famously likened publication bias to Cordelia's dilemma in *King Lear*. Cordelia keeps silent, rather than compete with her sisters in making extravagant protestations of her love for her father, much as researchers with negative results opt not to publish them given all the attention paid to positive results. Researchers may thus be tempted to cook their data in order to get published. Preventing this kind of misconduct by researchers requires the cooperation of all parties—researchers, peer reviewers, journal editors, and even readers—in overcoming publication bias.

Researchers should also be aware that they may be asked to supply their data at any time and that their inability to do so can be taken as evidence that their data are fraudulent. Wolins conducted a seminal 1962 study, which found that 21 of the 37 authors of papers published in psychology journals responded to a request to see their data by stating that their data were "misplaced, lost, or inadvertently destroyed." Others have replicated Wolins' findings and used these findings as the basis for arguing that researchers' inability to provide their data "should give rise to a presumption that the data do not (or never did) exist" (Mishkin 1988, 136). All researchers are now advised to keep their data for a minimum of three years, although keeping data for as long as possible is recommended (Mann accessed 2007).

In many fields, research using proprietary data—or data that are made available only to one researcher, often with payment of fees to its provider—is considered highly unethical. Allen Weinstein, a professional historian who is currently head of the National Archives, has been roundly criticized for paying for exclusive access to the KGB records underlying his book on Alger Hiss, as well as for repeated failures to make his notes available to those who have requested them (Wiener 2004). Data may, however, be classed as "proprietary," and thus not suitable for widespread sharing, because of contracts or other agreements with research funders.

Figure 10-8:   Penalties for Research Fraud

Researchers who are found to have fabricated data or otherwise lied in federally funded projects face significant penalties. Under 18 U.S. Code § 1001, anyone who "makes any materially false, fictitious, or fraudulent statement or representation" is liable for a fine and/or five years in prison. Such researchers may also be liable under the False Claims Act, which prohibits the submission of false information to the government for the purpose of obtaining money; it provides for penalties of a $10,000 fine, up to ten years in jail, or both.

University of Pittsburgh hyperactivity researcher Stephen J. Breuning pled guilty under the False Claims Act and was sentenced to 60 days in prison and five years probation. He was also forced to repay $11,352 in restitution to the University of Pittsburgh, which itself had to return research funds of $163,000 to the government (LaFollette 1992, 25).

Sins of Omission

Besides omitting non-supporting data from one's analysis and conclusions, researchers can commit three others glaring sins of omission—failure to fully follow or report their methodologies, failure to recognize the existence of studies with contradictory findings, and failure to recognize limitations in prior studies which support their own work. Sloppy research practices, or failures to follow your own research design in gathering data, are significant ethical lapses (LaFollette 1992, 36). By not following your own research design, you keep the controls you had built into this design in order to ensure the integrity of your data from working and thereby compromise the validity of your findings. You also make it impossible for subsequent researchers to replicate your study and obtain similar results; this compromises your study's reliability.

Sloppy research practices can also be due to easily understandable mistakes. Short cuts are often taken because of time pressures; for example, researchers might fail to give subjects the "standard" introduction to the experimental situation because the subjects could only spend a few more minutes at the lab—and the researchers want them to spend this time producing data, not hearing about the experimental situation. Failing to fully report your methodology in your publications is equally ethically problematic; readers who lack the details on how you obtained your results will not be able to replicate them. Yet this is also explicable given the limited number of pages available in most journal articles. Researcher-writers who are pressed for space often sacrifice methodological details in order to discuss more fully their findings and conclusions.

Researchers also behave unethically when they fail to recognize the existence of studies with contradictory findings, or to recognize limitations in prior studies which support their own work. Pretending that work that does not support your own does not exist is ethically problematic for several reasons. It can lead to malformed hypotheses; researchers who "refuse" to recognize work with which they disagree may not have considered all possible explanations for the phenomena under study when crafting their own hypotheses. It also leads you to misrepresent and mischaracterize the literature on the topic by deliberately excluding whole parts of that literature. Researchers relying on your literature review would thus obtain a partial—and inaccurate—picture of the work on that topic. Even more problematic is pretending that there are supporting works that do not, in fact, exist. Law and economics scholar John Lott has been criticized for doing just this (Wiener 2004). Lott is perhaps most famous for his book *More Guns, Less Crime*, wherein he noted that 98 percent of the times that people use guns defensively, they merely have to brandish a weapon to break off an attack. Lott's source for this figure has shifted over time. First it was uncited national surveys. When pressed to specify which surveys, Lott cited polls by the *Los Angeles Times*, Gallup, and Peter Hart Associates, again without naming specific ones. Finally, the source came to be a national survey of 2,424 people that he himself had conducted, but whose data had all been lost in a computer crash. (Lott then went one better by posting defenses of himself on the Internet under the name of "Mary Rosh." Rosh was supposedly a former student of Lott, who—not surprisingly—said, "I have to say that he was the best professor I ever had" [Morin 2003, C1].)

Failure to Respect Human Subjects

Protecting the rights of researchers' human subjects obviously underlies the legal and ethical guidelines created for research projects, so you might think that researchers should have few problems in this area. The responses in the 2005 survey mentioned earlier suggest otherwise: 7.6 percent reported circumventing "minor" rules protecting human subjects, 1.4 percent reported having "questionable" relationships with subjects, and 0.3 percent reported circumventing "major" rules protecting human subjects. "Minor" lapses in protections happen more often, and easily, precisely because they are minor. While the respondents in the survey did not specify what they considered to be "minor," they may have meant lapses such as losing copies of informed consent forms or overstating the benefits subjects are likely to realize from the experiment. "Major" lapses, in contrast, could include using people as subjects without their consent, or knowingly exposing them to harmful substances or procedures. Major lapses are less likely, but still there are incentives toward them, such as the pressure to complete a study or to obtain positive results. Researchers working with human subjects should take great care to ensure that human subjects are aware of what it means to be a human subject. J. Michael Bailey was sued because his book, *The Man Who Would Be Queen: The Science of Gender-Bending and Transexualism*, included the stories of two people who admitted that they had spoken to him but said that he did not obtain their consent as participants before including their stories. Because people may be willing to talk to you and tell you their stories but not want you to re-tell those stories, you should be sure that your subjects understand what being a subject means.

This is especially important for subjects from disadvantaged socioeconomic groups, who may not be familiar with the conventions of academic research.

Many researchers are actually quite concerned about their subjects and will go much further than obtaining their consent to be treated as passive sources of data in others' studies. These researchers will often check their data and their interpretations of their data with their subjects to see if the subjects find their conclusions fair. (It should be noted, though, that researchers retain professional responsibility for grounding their conclusions, and it is not sound scholarship simply to let the subjects' accounts stand as the simple truth on the phenomena studied.)

Problems in Authoring

The pervasiveness of the axiom "publish or perish," which highlights the perils of not publishing, seems to have blinded researchers to some of the perils associated with publishing. While academic researchers have occasionally engaged in the same sort of cut-and-paste plagiarism more commonly seen in undergraduate students, they are less likely to encounter problems with this than with more subtle forms of inappropriate conduct in authorship. Allegations of plagiarism are less clearly proven when they center on the types of questions more likely to plague academic researchers, as LaFollette (1992, 51) makes clear with the following examples:

- Can you "copy" all or most of another bibliography? What if you genuinely used the bibliography to identify sources, which you then read on your own—with the net effect that your writing is based on exactly the same sources as someone else's writing?
- What about reproducing others' data tables, or producing your own tables based on others' data? As facts, data are generally not subject to the same copyright protections as expressions, so to what degree should others' data be reproduced? Does it matter if your use is transformative, creating something out of the data that their original reporters did not?
- What about similar illustrations of so-called "common knowledge" phenomena? What is common knowledge? To what degree must illustrations have things in common to be similar?
- Should descriptions of common experimental procedures or phenomena be credited? Does it matter if the discoverers of these procedures or phenomena had a hard—or an easy—time of discovering these?
- Should chronologically identical descriptions of historical events be credited? What if establishing the precise chronology was incredibly difficult?

There are no easy answers here; all have been the subject of heated debate—and hard feelings—among authors. As a general rule, whenever you wonder whether you should cite a source, you should cite, and when you are proposing a transformative use of others' content, you should inform them of this.

Even more troubling questions about plagiarism and the ethics of authoring arise among co-authors. Can one member of a formerly co-authoring group rework material that group created? This problem—as well as several others— was at stake in the *Weissman v. Freeman* lawsuit (868 F.2d 1313 [2d Cir. 1989]). Nuclear medicine researcher and professor Heidi Weissman sued her former mentor and co-author, Leonard Freeman, in part, over ownership of a syllabus, which in medical terms is "a paper reviewing the recent literature in a field, rather than simply a listing of topics to be covered in a course" (McSherry 2001, 70). Weissman, who had co-authored the original syllabus with Freeman, wanted the court to "affirm her intellectual property rights" to a later version of the syllabus ("which reorganized the original material and added some new illustrations and captions, references to four recent research reports, and some new text"). She alone had created this later version, but Freeman subsequently used it with only his name on it. Part of Freeman's argument for why he should continue to be credited when Weissman did the subsequent work was that he was the principal investigator who involved Weissman in the project and who brought in the funding that made the research possible (McSherry 2001). While problems between co-authors are particularly common, and nasty, such problems can become even nastier when the co-authors have unequal status within their home institutions—when, as in *Weissman v. Freeman*, one is the mentor and the other the protégé. In such situations, the allocation of credit can become very contentious. There have been so many such disputes in the sciences that organizations such as the National Academy of Sciences have endorsed authorship norms such as the following:

- Only people who contributed key ideas, research data, text, or illustrations should be listed as authors. People should not be counted as authors simply because they head the organization where the research was conducted, are the "bosses" of the authors, or earned the funding for the laboratory in which the research was conducted. All who contributed should be listed, but those who did not contribute should not be gratuitously listed.
- The order in which authors' names are listed matters. The conventional view is that, when authors are not listed simply alphabetically, the first author is the person most responsible for the research—unless the co-authors consist of an educator and her/his students. In that case, the students are listed first and the educator last. Researchers do not need to follow these rules, but it is important that all co-authors agree on the ordering of their names, as well as the significance of this ordering.

Ethical authors should also be wary of the "least publishable unit" or the temptation to subdivide a research project into as many smaller publications as possible when a single, longer publication is possible (Mann accessed 2007).

REFERENCES

Barnett, Rosalind C., and Caryl Rivers. 2004. "Men are from Earth, and So Are Women. It's Faulty Research That Sets Them Apart." *Chronicle of Higher Education* 51 (2): B11.

Ben-Yahuda, Nachman. 2002. *Sacrificing Truth: Archaeology and the Myth of Masada.* Amherst, NY: Humanity Books.

Case, Donald O. 2002. *Looking for Information: A Survey of Research on Information Seeking, Needs, and Behavior.* Boston: Academic Press.

Chalmers, T. C., P. Celano, H. S. Sacks, and H. Smith. 1983, Dec. 1. "Bias in Treatment Assignment in Controlled Clinical Trials." *New England Journal of Medicine* 309: 1358–1361.

Crossen, Cynthia. 1994. *Tainted Truth: The Manipulation of Fact in America.* New York: Touchstone Books.

Dickersin, Kay. 1990. "The Existence of Publication Bias and Risk Factors for Its Occurrence." *Journal of the American Medical Association* 263 (10): 1385–1389.

Ebon, Martin. 1971. *Test Your ESP.* New York: Signet Books.

Engber, Daniel. 2004. "Top Medical Journals Make Disclosure of Clinical-Trial Results a Condition of Publication." *Chronicle of Higher Education.* Available: http://chronicle.com/daily/2004/09/2004090901n.htm (accessed May 17, 2007).

Gantz, W., M. Fitzmaurice, and E. Fink. 1991. "Assessing the Active Component of Information-Seeking." *Journalism Quarterly* 68: 630–637.

Glazier, Jack D., and Ronald R. Powell. 1992. *Qualitative Research in Information Management.* Englewood, CO: Libraries Unlimited.

Gould, Stephen Jay. 1995. *Dinosaur in a Haystack: Reflections in Natural History.* New York: Harmony Books.

Huff, Darrell. 1993. *How to Lie with Statistics.* New York: W. W. Norton.

Impicciatore, P., C. Pandolfini, N. Casella, and M. Bonati. 1997. "Reliability of Health Information for the Public on the World Wide Web: A Systematic Survey of Advice on Managing Fever in Children at Home." *British Medical Journal* 314: 1875–1879.

King, R. T. 1996. "Bitter Pill: How a Drug Firm Paid for a University Study, then Undermined It." *Wall Street Journal:* 1, 6.

Kolko, Beth E. 2000. "Intellectual Property in Synchronous and Collaborative Virtual Space." In *Cyberethics: Social and Moral Issues in the Computer Age,* 257–281. Amherst, NY: Prometheus Books.

LaFollette, Marcel C. 1992. *Stealing into Print: Fraud, Plagiarism, and Misconduct in Scientific Publishing.* Berkeley, CA: University of California Press.

Mahoney, Michael J. 1977. "Publication Prejudices: An Experimental Study of Confirmatory Bias in the Peer Review System." *Cognitive Therapy and Research* 1 (2): 161–175.

Mann, Michael D. *The Ethics of Collecting and Processing Data and Publishing the Results of Scientific Research.* Available: http://unmc.edu/ethics/data/data_int.htm (accessed May 19, 2007).

McClung, H. J., R. D. Murray, and L. A. Heitlinger. 1998. "The Internet as a Source for Current Patient Information." *Pediatrics* 101 (6): E5.

McSherry, Corynne. 2001. *Who Owns Academic Work? Battling for Control of Intellectual Property.* Cambridge, MA: Harvard University Press.

Mishkin, B. 1988. "Responding to Scientific Misconduct: Due Process and Prevention." *Journal of the American Medical Association* 260: 132–136.

Morin, Richard. 2003. "Scholar Invents Fan to Answer His Critics." *Washington Post*, Feb. 1. C1.

Rampton, Sheldon, and John Stauber. 2002. *Trust Us, We're Experts: How Industry Manipulates Science and Gambles with Your Future.* New York: Jeremy P. Tarcher.

Recer, Paul. 2000. "Trick Question: Do Women Have Less Sex Than Men?" *San Francisco Chronicle*, Oct. 10. A2.

Von Gennep, A. 1910. *La formation des légendes.* Paris: Ernest Flammarion.

Weiss, Rick. 2005. "Many Scientists Admit to Misconduct." *Washington Post*, June 9. A3.

Wiener, Jon. 2004. *Historians in Trouble: Plagiarism, Fraud, and Politics in the Ivory Tower.* New York: The New Press.

Wolfe, Alan. 2003. "Invented Names, Hidden Distortions in Social Science." *Chronicle of Higher Education*, May 30. 13.

Wolins, Leroy J. 1962. "Responsibility for Raw Data." *American Psychologist* 178: 657–658.

Chapter 11

Synergies in Research

Many librarians and other practitioners balk at the notion of conducting research because they fear that research will simply add to their workload, becoming yet another thing they must do. Such fears are largely misdirected. Research need not be something done in addition to your job; it can be done in conjunction with your job in a way that improves your job performance and simultaneously allows you and the library profession to enjoy the benefits of research as discussed in Chapter 1. This chapter introduces ways to integrate research with your job, as well as two other strategies—conducting meta-analyses and performing secondary research—that allow you to optimize your investment of time in your research activities.

RESEARCHING FROM YOUR JOB

Most of the research projects discussed in this book—and published in the library literature—actually began from a researcher's job. Consider the following examples:

- Reference librarians' concerns about the volume of printing from library computers and their need to devise printing policies led to a survey asking other libraries in the same region about usage of their printing services and printing policies. [Ashmore, Beth and Sara E. Morris. 2002. "From Scraps to Reams: A Survey of Printing Services in Academic Libraries." *College & Research Libraries* 63 (4): 342–352.]
- A subject specialist's need to cancel some serials for budgetary reasons led to a citation analysis of the sources that students in one academic field used in writing their theses. [Thomas, Joy. 2000. "Never Enough: Graduate Student Use of Journals—Citation Analysis of Social Work Theses." *Behavioral & Social Sciences Librarian* 19 (1): 1–16.]
- A library manager's concern about the productivity of the acquisitions budget led to an experimental comparison of the savings realized with

fixed discounts and sliding scales. [Hui-Min, Kuo. 2001. "Comparing Vendor Discounts for Firm Orders: Fixed vs. Sliding." *Technical Services Quarterly* 18 (4): 1–10.]

- A cataloguer's concern about how the number of subject headings impacted circulation of materials led to an experimental study of correlations between the numbers of subject headings for an item and its circulations. [Banks, Julie. 2004. "Does the Number of Subject Headings on a Bibliographic Record Affect Circulation Intensity?" *Technical Services Quarterly* 21 (3): 17–24.]

- An acquisition librarian's concern with the cost effectiveness of operations led to a study of the costs associated with duplicate titles. [Xin, Li. 1999. "Duplicate Copies in Monographs Acquisitions: Examining 1,000 Cases." *Technical Services Quarterly* 17 (2): 37–50.]

- A children's librarian's concern with providing effective public services led to a survey of and unobtrusive observations at ten public libraries as a way of determining what spatial configurations correlated with increased circulation of picture books. [Larkin-Lieffers, Patricia A. 2001. "Informational Picture Books in the Library: Do Young Children Find Them?" *Public Library Quarterly* 20 (3): 3–28.]

- An electronic resources librarian's concern with the usability of online periodicals led to a content analysis of the plug-ins required to access their content. [Kichuk, Diana. 2003. "Electronic Journal Supplementary Content, Browser Plug-ins, and the Transformation of Reading." *Serials Review* 29 (2): 103–116.]

Given that so many studies have originated from researcher's job responsibilities, the question is not whether research can theoretically be integrated into workplace responsibilities but rather how to accomplish such integration in your particular situation.

The key questions in connecting your research to your job actually relate to how broadly you view your job responsibilities and how you think about research. Some people view their job rather narrowly; they think of themselves as, for example, providing in-person and online reference services to users of a branch library in a suburban public library system and doing some collection development for the print reference collection. If such people also think of research as solely involving experimental methodologies, they may find themselves with few viable opportunities for research projects that do not involve significant additions to their job responsibilities. If, however, they take a broader view of research, including such methodologies as action research or classroom research, their research opportunities expand without increasing their workloads. They undoubtedly recognize problems in the provision of reference service or the organization of the print reference collection that could serve as the basis for an action research project, and an action research project would allow them to conduct research without expanding their workload since they would solve workplace problems while conducting research.

Similarly, the more broadly people view their jobs, the more research opportunities become available. If they think of their job as provision of reference services and collection development—regardless of the library setting or the medium—their opportunities for synergistically conducting research also expand. No longer are they limited to the narrow, perhaps parochial, issues that may be raised by the populations they serve or the collections they maintain. Rather, since they see anything impacting reference services and collections as relevant to their job, such topics become research possibilities that complement—rather than compete with—their professional responsibilities.

Since your research opportunities are contingent on your views both of your job responsibilities and of research, it is important to note that neither set of views is static. Your views of both your job responsibilities and of research will shift throughout the course of your professional career, shaping your opportunities for synergistically conducting research as they shift. New librarians often take a narrow view of their job responsibilities. This is not a bad thing: their employers may expect this, requiring them to demonstrate competence in a few responsibilities before branching out to additional responsibilities. New librarians may find it easier to master the field piecemeal, by concentrating on a few items at first and then incorporating additional responsibilities.

**Figure 11-1: Relationship between Research Possibilities
and Views on Jobs and Research**

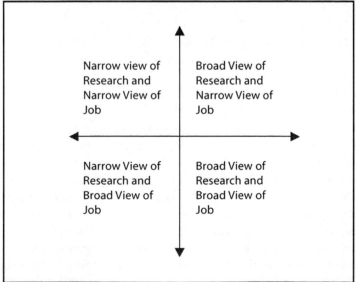

More experienced librarians, in contrast, can often take a broader view of their job responsibilities, especially as they come to appreciate how interconnected various aspects of librarianship are. Similarly, people who trained in an undergraduate or graduate field with a specific research methodology may start off expecting all research to proceed on the strict model of that methodology. Only later, as they learn of new methodologies through reading journals and seeing presentations, will they come to appreciate and employ alternate methodologies.

In other cases, people who start off employing several methodologies—perhaps because of their exposure to them in library school survey classes—may find that they narrow their range of methodologies as time passes because they want to develop expertise in particular methodologies or because they find particular methodologies especially compatible with their personal identities. Just like other aspects of the research process, views of your job and of research are cyclical. Your views should change as you change and grow. If, however, you do find yourself in a rut, where you cannot see additional research options because of your view of your job and/or research, talk to your colleagues, read widely, and attend conferences—especially those of non-library organizations. You may learn more about chemists' information-seeking behaviors from attending one American Chemical Society convention than from attending years' worth of library conferences.

When attempting to integrate your job responsibilities and your research activities, there are a number of things to consider. First, ask yourself which of your job responsibilities will you concentrate upon? Most librarians have jobs with multiple responsibilities (e.g., cataloging and collection development, or reference and instruction). You may be able to find an opportunity to integrate all of your job responsibilities into a single research project (e.g., how the collection development activities of catalogers differ from those of public service librarians, or how librarians teach at the reference desk). Most of the time, though, you must choose a particular aspect of your job responsibilities on which to concentrate. Deciding which aspect to select can be difficult, but there are two broad approaches. Some people pick those aspects of their job with which they are they least comfortable or which they like the least in the hopes of expanding their knowledge and becoming more comfortable. Other people pick those aspects of their job they like most, because they want to spend their time on a topic they like. Yet another approach, which can be a good political move for new librarians, is to consult a supervisor to see which aspects of their job the supervisor would advise them to concentrate upon in their research.

Job responsibilities that lead—or could lead—to the generation of data sources are particularly good choices for creating synergies between workplace duties and research activities. When you are already doing something in your job that produces rich data sets, it makes sense to formalize that activity by making the minimal modifications necessary to transform it into a research project. As the examples in Figure 11-2 show, many job responsibilities furnish the basis for good research projects, in part because they yield a great deal of data. For instance, if you are participating in a program of term paper clinics, you probably already are gathering data about who attends these programs, what classes their papers are for, and what their views of the program are. If you are providing IM reference, you are probably already tracking frequency of use at various time periods, as well as logging patron questions and assessing patron satisfaction. Similarly, if you are authoring print or online subject guides for your library, you are probably already recording usage statistics. If you are offering such programs and are not recording any data about their usage and effectiveness, you need a research program for more than personal reasons. In the current climate of assessment and accountability, no library can afford to offer significant programming or services for which they are not documenting usage and outcomes.

You cannot jump directly from a job responsibility that generates data into a research project, however. Methodologies and ethics dictate that you recast your data gathering from the procedures and norms appropriate for offering programs to the procedures and norms appropriate for conducting research. Suppose your library has been offering chat reference for the past year, and you have access to all of the transcripts. You cannot simply take these transcripts and begin gathering research data from them; interpreting that evidence; and telling

Figure 11-2: Research Projects Based on Job Responsibilities

Cardwell, Catherine, Katherine Furlong, and Julie O'Keeffe. 2001. "My Librarian: Personalized Research Clinics and the Academic Library." *Research Strategies* 18: 97–111.

> *Includes statistical data on research clinics, surveys of users, surveys of librarians.*

Foley, Marianne. 2002. "Instant Messaging Reference in an Academic Library: A Case Study." *College & Research Libraries* 63 (1): 36–45.

> *Uses patron survey, librarian reports, usage statistics. Lots of details on implementation of IM service.*

Norlin, Elaina. 2000. "Reference Evaluation: A Three-Step Approach—Surveys, Unobtrusive Observations, and Focus Groups." *College & Research Libraries* 61 (6): 546–553.

> *Use of surveys, unobtrusive observations, and focus groups.*

Phillips, Lori, and Jamie Kearley. 2003. "TIP: Tutorial for Information Power and Campus-wide Information Literacy". *Reference Services Review* 31 (4): 351–358.

> *Includes usage statistics, student quizzes, student comments.*

Reeb, Brenda, and Susan Gibbons. 2004. "Students, Librarians, and Subject Guides: Improving a Poor Rate of Return." *portal: Libraries and the Academy* 4 (1): 123–130.

> *Use of surveys, usability tests, usage statistics.*

others about what you did and found out. There are, broadly, two reasons for this. The first is methodological. Your possession of data does not short-circuit the need to engage in the second (formulating research questions); third (defining research populations); and fourth (selecting a research design and measurement instrument) steps of the research process. You need research questions to structure your reading of the chat transcripts; otherwise, you would be prone to note only those aspects of the transcripts that happened to catch your eye at the time of your reading. The "Top ten things Lucy Librarian learned from reading chat reference transcripts" might make a fine opinion piece, but it should not be mistaken for a research project. Similarly, your population would be a convenience sample, at best, not one chosen to reflect your target population, and your measurement design would be simply looking for whatever you happened to find in a preexisting set of data.

Moreover, without the controls of a research project, it is quite probable that the data to which you have access were neither gathered nor maintained in ways sufficiently rigorous for a research project. Chat reference hours, for example, might not have been rigorously kept in the early days of the service, or some transcripts might have been accidentally deleted. Ethically, these data cannot be used for a research project, since the participants in these chat reference sessions did not know they would be the subject of a research project and had no opportunity to consent to their participation in the project.

With these caveats stated, some data gathered for particular aspects of your job can form the basis of a research project without too much additional work. You simply need to formalize and systematize your procedures for collecting and storing data. Then you can begin to gather data anew as part of your job using procedures that are part of your research project. (One important caution is in order here. If your research project will involve gathering of data by other library staff as well as yourself, you want to be sure that your proposed changes to the data gathering processes or forms are agreeable to others). It is also important to note that the preexisting data are not useless, even if you typically cannot use them directly in a presentable or publishable research project. Such preexisting data are particularly likely to be helpful in finding a topic and formulating research questions, as your reading of the data can be one source of topical focuses and hypotheses. These can also provide baseline data to which you compare later findings, provided that you do not disseminate the data in more than their most general form.

Having decided which aspects of your job you will concentrate upon in a research project, you need to find ways to integrate this research project into your professional responsibilities as seamlessly as possible. Data gathering for research purposes is more easily incorporated into your job responsibilities, since you would already be recording, for example, attendance at term paper clinics, usage of IM reference services, or usage of subject guides. The more difficult task is making Step 6 (interpreting the evidence) and Step 7 (telling the story) part of your job responsibilities. Too many libraries generate too much data without taking the time to make meaning from them—the numbers may, at best, get shoved into an annual report where they exist without any context to explain their meaning. Encouraging your supervisors to "require" the interpretation and presentation of data is one way to ensure that such activities become part of your job. Making yourself accountable to internal or external constituencies for the production and interpretation of data is another way to incorporate these activities into your job.

CONDUCTING META-ANALYSES

Another way to optimize the investment of time in research activities is to engage in meta-analyses. A meta-analysis is a study that takes several prior studies that address related questions and combines their data. Meta-analysis originated in 1904 as an attempt to overcome the problem of reduced statistical power in studies with small sample sizes—a problem which certainly characterizes many library and information science studies. Medicine, the health sciences, and education have used meta-analyses widely since the 1970s. Librarianship has used meta-analysis less frequently, perhaps because of its statistical underpinnings. However, for researchers with strong math skills but who are less familiar or comfortable with other aspects of the research process (e.g., recruiting a sample, complying with human subjects requirements, or gathering data), meta-analyses can be excellent research projects. Researchers can use the preexisting data directly, concentrating on steps six and seven of the research process by interpreting the data found in other people's studies and compiling new findings. The first five steps of the research process, in contrast, occur in only a minimal fashion. The researcher's work in finding a topic is generally limited to finding topics in the literature where a sufficient number of prior publications provide data on a topic. The questions are formulated by the original studies, whose findings the meta-analysis researcher is aggregating. The populations were similarly defined by the original studies. The research design is provided by the meta-analysis process itself, and data gathering is limited to the extraction of statistical data from prior studies.

A meta-analysis can be conducted on any topic, provided that there is a critical mass of published or otherwise accessible studies that asked similar questions and present their data quantitatively (traditionally in terms of correlation coefficients). Spink, Partridge and Jansen (2006) were able to conduct a meta-analysis of searches for sexual and pornographic content on the Web because there were nine studies of this topic between 1997 and 2005, each of which had similar categories of search topics and presented their data in terms of frequency counts and percentages. Similarly, Thompson (2003) was able to include a brief meta-analysis on student Internet usage as part of a larger research project by drawing on a series of surveys about student Internet use published between 1997 and 2001. Thompson drew on only four studies, but these studies all asked similar questions and presented their results in terms of percentages. We have long thought there is a meta-analytic study waiting to be written in the numerous studies of faculty attitudes toward library instruction. There are more than ten published studies that report on surveys of faculty attitudes toward library instruction; all of these studies ask similar questions; and all present their results in terms of frequency counts and percentages.

Most meta-analyses in other fields, particularly in medicine and health science, are more sophisticated in their treatment of data than Thompson or Spink, Partridge, and Jansen. (See the sources listed in Figure 11-3). They typically work with prior findings expressed in terms of correlation coefficients and present their own results in terms of inferential statistics. However, while such studies remain a model to be striven for, less sophisticated meta-analyses remain viable options for library practitioners—especially since most studies by library practitioners present their data in terms of frequency counts and percentages, not correlation coefficients. Even when performing a meta-analysis using this more "relaxed" model, researchers should be careful to address those concerns that meta-analysis researchers typically address in their projects—especially the comparability of data gathered in different studies by different researchers. Two researchers addressing the same topic might ask largely the same questions in the same ways. This is perhaps most likely if the researchers are working from standardized instruments, or the same published instrument. More likely, however, these researchers will ask questions that differ either slightly or greatly in their substance and phrasing. One researcher might measure printing in terms of pages, while another might measure it in terms of costs to users and yet another might measure it in terms of how long the typical printing job occupies system resources. The meta-analysis researcher has the challenge of deciding

Figure 11-3: Selected Works on Conducting Meta-Analyses

Arthur, Winfred, Winston Bennett, and Allen I. Huffcutt. 2001. *Conducting Meta-Analysis Using SAS*. Mahwah, NJ: Lawrence Erlbaum.

Hunter, John E., and Frank L. Schmidt. 2004. *Methods of Meta-Analysis: Correcting Bias and Error in Research Findings*. Thousand Oaks, CA: Sage.

Lipsey, Mark W., and David B. Wilson. 2000. *Practical Meta-Analysis*. Thousand Oaks, CA: Sage.

Schulze, Ralf. 2004. *Meta-Analysis: A Comparison of Approaches*. Cambridge, MA: Hogrefe & Huber.

Wolf, Frederic M. 1986. *Meta-Analysis: Quantitative Methods for Research Synthesis*. Thousand Oaks, CA: Sage.

how similar is similar enough in terms of finding data that can be aggregated, as well as what differences require treating data as dissimilar. Thus, a meta-analysis researcher needs to pay as much attention to the nuances of the topic as she or he pays to the numbers obtained from prior studies.

PERFORMING SECONDARY RESEARCH

A final way to optimize your research time is to engage in secondary research, or research using preexisting data sets. In secondary research, the researcher performs only highly abridged versions of steps one, three, four, and five of the research process: his or her topic is largely dictated by the choice of available data sets; the population is limited to those within the original study, although the researcher may select a subsection of that population upon which to focus; the research design is limited to choice of methods for extracting and analyzing data from the dataset; and the data has already been gathered by the compilers of the dataset.

Instead, the researchers' attention is concentrated upon steps two, six, and seven of the research process. They must formulate questions or hypotheses to guide the selection and interpretation of data from the dataset; they must interpret the data extracted; and they must present and/or write up the findings of the research. Secondary research is somewhat like meta-analysis, in that it is a good research methodology for researchers who are less familiar or comfortable with other aspects of the research process. Unlike meta-analysis, however, it does not require quite as extensive mathematical skills, since statistical treatments in secondary analyses are as likely to be descriptive as they are to be inferential. For more on secondary analysis, see the sources listed in Figure 11-4.

Figure 11-4: Selected Works on Conducting Secondary Analyses

Bulmer, Martin A. I., Patrick J. Sturgis, and Nick Allum, editors. 2007. *The Secondary Analysis of Survey Data.* Thousand Oaks, CA: Sage.

> *Four-volume encyclopedia.*

Kiecolt, K. Jill, and Laura E. Nathan. 1985. *Secondary Analysis of Survey Data.* Thousand Oaks, CA: Sage.

Sales, Esther, Sara Lichtenwalter, and Antonio Fevola. 2006. "Secondary Analysis in Social Work Research Education: Past, Present, and Future Promise." *Journal of Social Work Education* 42 (3): 543–558.

> *Although specific to another field, this article provides a good overview of secondary research options and issues.*

Thomas, Scott L., Ronald H. Heck, and Karen W. Bauer. 2005. "Weighting and Adjusting for Design Effects in Secondary Data Analyses." *New Directions for Institutional Research* 127: 51–72.

> *Also specific to another field, but a good overview of the issues involved.*

Secondary analysis has been used occasionally within library science, often by library science professors. Whitmire used secondary analysis to examine both (1) the relationship between students' demographic characteristics and their college experiences, including library use (2001), and (2) the relationship between students' library use and their self-reported development of critical thinking capabilities (1998). For the first study, Whitmire took the National Survey of Student Engagement as her dataset, and for the second, she used the College Student Experiences Questionnaire. Bladow et al. (2005) looked at weekly and long-term longevity of search topics on the Yahoo Buzz Index for 45 weeks as a way of tracking trends in popular Web searching. Spink and Gunar (2001) similarly looked at logs of 10,000 Excite queries and 10,000 Ask Jeeves question format queries to determine what percentage of Web searches are business related.

Secondary analysis is also a potential methodology for practicing library and information science researchers at all types of libraries. This is because there are so many datasets, covering so many topics, that almost any researcher can find a dataset or datasets addressing topics of relevance to their job responsibilities that could be productively, and fairly easily, mined. In fact, the potential of datasets for librarians in corporate and public libraries is particularly high since a number of these datasets either track corporate services and productivity or examine demographic characteristics of communities.

The key to getting started with secondary research is becoming familiar with the datasets in existence and thinking creatively about their potential uses. Some datasets will be based, at least in part, upon questions directly relating to libraries. The Association of Research Libraries Statistics: Interactive Edition site, for example, focuses exclusively on library-related data (http://fisher.lib.virginia.edu/arl) (see Saunders 2003), as does the LibQUAL+ study (see Cook, Heath and Thompson 2003). In contrast, the College Student Experiences Questionnaire and the National Survey of Student Engagement include only a few questions relating directly to library use and activities (see Whitmire 1998; Boff and Johnson 2002; Mark and Boruff-Jones 2003). In a few cases, researchers may even need to extrapolate from existing categories to constructs relating to libraries, such as using data about income level and book purchases to examine public libraries' roles in their communities. The Inter-University Consortium for Political and Social Research provides information about a number of datasets on its Web site at www.icpsr.umich.edu/org/index.html (see Figure 11-5). The Statistical Abstracts series (www.census.gov/compendia/statab), the LexisNexis Statistical Universe database, and the Federal Statistics Gateway (www.fedstats.gov) are other potential sources of datasets, as are datasets made available by Internet search engines. In selecting a dataset for use, look beyond its topical focus to its permitted uses to be sure that your proposed activities in researching and publishing are allowed by the usage agreement for the database. The terms of the usage agreement are especially important. In cases where you have clicked "ok" or "I agree" after reading a terms of usage agreement, you could be held legally liable for any damages that could result to the dataset's owner or provider from your use of the dataset because your agreement to these terms created an enforceable contract.

Once an appropriate dataset is located, researchers need to formulate substantial research questions or hypotheses to guide their extraction of data from the dataset. They also need to recognize the strengths as well as the limitations of reliance on preexisting datasets in interpreting their data. On the plus side, you can generally use a dataset knowing that it has been compiled by researchers trained in sampling procedures, that the data were gathered using reliable and valid instruments, and that biasing effects in the data gathering process have been minimized. You can also often be assured that you will have data that represent a broad population and that data have been collected and maintained in appropriate ways.

You should always research your dataset, just to be sure that what is generally true of datasets holds true for the dataset you propose to use. Every dataset has its weaknesses, and most dataset providers explicitly recognize these weaknesses. The U.S. Census Bureau, for example, is aware that it misses more Blacks, American Indians and Alaskan Natives, Asians and Pacific Islanders, and Hispanics than Whites (Census Bureau 2002). Moreover, many datasets

Figure 11-5: Categories of Data Available from the Inter-University Consortium for Political and Social Research

- Census Enumerations
- Community and Urban Studies
- Conflict, Aggression, Violence, Wars
- Economic Behavior and Attitudes
- Education
- Elites and Leadership
- Geography and Environment
- Government Structures, Policies, and Capabilities
- Health Care and Facilities
- Instructional Packages
- International Systems
- Legal Systems
- Legislative and Deliberative Bodies
- Mass Political Behavior and Attitudes
- Organizational Behavior
- Social Indicators
- Social Institutions and Behavior

are periodic compilations (e.g., every year, every two years, every ten years, and so on), allowing researchers to perform longitudinal studies more easily. However, secondary researchers are limited to the questions that the dataset's compilers originally asked and the people of whom they asked these questions.

Research is a very real option for library practitioners, especially if they find ways to transform their jobs into the basis for their research, or if they conduct meta-analyses or secondary analyses. Conducting research also begets more research opportunities. Finding your first research topic, implementing this research project, and presenting or publishing it can seem daunting, even as you are engaged in these activities. However, you will probably also find yourself identifying future research possibilities while you engage in this first project:

- You may think of additional subjects to whom your research question or methodologies could be extended.
- You may find additional themes in interviews or content analyses which are not relevant to your current project, but could form the basis for a future project.
- You will read research and methodological articles and books that trigger ideas. From these you will find things you agree with and would like to develop further, as well as things you disagree with and would like to refute.
- You will identify possible presentation and publication venues, and learn about their preferred topics and styles. Even if you do not work with these in your current project, you will find yourself storing away information about these venues for future reference.
- You will meet, either in-person or virtually, other people researching on the same topic, establishing the basis for future collaboration.

Each subsequent research project will not only help you grow as a researcher, but the act of research will also become "easier"—at least in the sense that research no longer feels like an alien activity. For many experienced researchers, research becomes a way of life and a part of their identity. We hope that research will become an enjoyable part of your life as well.

REFERENCES

Bladow, Nicole et al. 2005. "What's the Buzz About? An Empirical Examination of Search on Yahoo." *First Monday* 10 (1). Available: http://firstmonday.org/issues/ issue10_1/bladow/index.html (accessed May 17, 2007).

Boff, Colleen, and Kristin Johnson. 2002. "The Library and First-Year Experience Courses: A Nationwide Study." *Reference Services Review* 30 (4): 277–287.

Census Bureau. 2002, January 28. *What Is the 1990 Undercount?* Available: http:// census.gov/dmd/www/techdoc1.html (accessed May 17, 2007).

Cook, Colleen, Fred Heath, and Bruce Thompson. 2003. "'Zones of Tolerance' in Perceptions of Library Service Quality: A LibQUAL+ Study." *portal: Libraries and the Academy* 3 (1): 113–123.

Mark, Amy E., and Polly D. Boruff-Jones. 2003. "Information Literacy and Student Engagement: What the National Survey of Student Engagement Reveals about Your Campus." *College & Research Libraries* 64 (6): 480–492.

Saunders, E. Stewart. 2003. "The Effect of Bibliographic Instruction on the Demand for Reference Service." *portal: Libraries and the Academy* 3 (1): 35–39.

Spink, Amanda, Helen Partridge, and Bernard J. Jansen. 2006. "Sexual and Pornographic Web Searching: Trends Analysis." *First Monday* 11 (9). Available: http://firstmonday.org/issues/issue11_9/spink/index.html (accessed May 17, 2007).

Spink, Amanda, and Okan Gunar. 2001. "E-Commerce Web Queries: Excite and Ask Jeeves Study." *First Monday* 6 (7). Available: http://firstmonday.org/issues/issue6_7/spink/index.html#s3 (accessed May 17, 2007).

Thompson, Christen. 2003. "Information Illiterate or Lazy: How College Students Use the Web for Research." *portal: Libraries and the Academy* 3 (2): 259–268.

Whitmire, Ethelene. 2001. "The Relationship Between Undergraduates' Background Characteristics and College Experiences and Their Academic Library Use." *College & Research Libraries* 62 (6): 528–540.

_____. 1998. "Development of Critical Thinking Skills: An Analysis of Academic Library Experiences and Other Measures." *College & Research Libraries* 59 (3): 266–273.

Index

A

academic job analysis, 53

academic librarian, 42

"Academic Library Collection Development and Management Positions: Announcements in *College & Research Libraries News* from 1980 to 1991" (Robinson), 43

"The Academic Library Job Market: A Content Analysis Comparing Public and Technical Services" (Reser & Schuneman), 42

"Academic Subject Specialist Positions in the United States: A Content Analysis of Announcements from 1990 through 1998" (White), 43

"Access and Ownership in the Academic Environment: One Library's Progress Report" (Brin & Cochran), 201

accuracy, of action research data, 211

Ackerson, Linda G.

  content analysis in experimental research, 133

  experimental research study by, 135

  halo effect and, 154

  measurement instrument used by, 148, 150

act phase, of action research, 198, 199

action research

  benefits of, 197–198

  cycle, 198–199

  data analysis, 211

  data gathering, 210–211

  definition of, 195

  drawbacks of, 196–197

  goals of, 195

  methodologies of, 196

  population definition, 202–205

  presentation of findings, 211–213

action research *(cont'd.)*

  questions, formulating, 205–207

  research design, selecting, 207–210

  research focus/researcher characteristics, 17

  research question/data gathering methods, 27

  studies using, 201

  topic, finding, 199–202

  works on, 199

Action Research: A Guide for Library Media Specialists (Howard & Eckhardt), 199

Action Research (Stringer), 199

action science, 196

Adair, John G., 155

Adams, Megan M.

  job analysis study, 42

  population definition by, 47

  research question/hypothesis of, 45

  use of chi-square, 62–63

Adkins, Denice, 44

advancement benefits, of research, 5, 6–7

"Affective Change: Integrating Pre-Sessions in the Students' Classroom Prior to Library Instruction" (Vidmar), 135

Alafiatoayo, Benjamin O., 112

AlltheWeb, 180

Allum, Nick, 275

Alm, Mary, 136

alternate-form reliability, 149

Alvarez, Jaquelina, 76

American Library Association (ALA), 6

American Psychological Association (APA), 246

analysis

  in action research, 211

  of bibliometric evidence, 183–190

  bibliometrics research design, 176–178

  in classroom research, 229–232

About the Authors

Susan E. Beck has over 20 years of professional library experience working in academic libraries in Missouri, Washington, Texas, and New Mexico. She has published on a variety of information literacy topics, among them teaching from the reference desk, evaluating Web information sources, and faculty views of library instruction. Susan earned a Master's degree in Library and Information Science from the University of Illinois, Urbana–Champaign, and another in Linguistics from Ohio University, as well as a Bachelor's degree from The Evergreen State College. Susan is currently Collection Development Coordinator at the New Mexico State University Library.

Kate Manuel is currently attending law school at George Mason University, specializing in technology law. Prior to entering law school, Kate served as Instruction Coordinator at New Mexico State University Library, and before that as Physical Sciences Librarian at California State University–Hayward. She has numerous publications on the topics of teaching Generation Y, e-prints in the physical sciences, evaluating library instruction programs, and teaching online information literacy courses. Kate has a Master's degree in Library and Information Science from Catholic University, another in Classical Studies from Duke University, and a Bachelor's degree in Anthropology and Latin from University of Notre Dame.